NATCHITOCHES
LOUISIANA, 1803–1840

NATCHITOCHES LOUISIANA, 1803–1840

A CREOLE COMMUNITY ON THE AMERICAN FRONTIER

KATHLEEN M. BYRD

LOUISIANA STATE UNIVERSITY PRESS
BATON ROUGE

Published by Louisiana State University Press
lsupress.org

LSU Press Paperback Original

Manufactured in the United States of America
First printing

Designer: Barbara Neely Bourgoyne
Typeface: Minion Pro
Printer and binder: Sheridan Books, Inc.

Cover illustration: Detail of Darby's *Map of Louisiana,* 1816. Map 2207, Map Collection, Cammie G. Henry Research Center, Northwestern State University of Louisiana.

Library of Congress Cataloging-in-Publication Data
Names: Byrd, Kathleen M., 1949– author.
Title: Natchitoches, Louisiana, 1803–1840 : a Creole community on the American frontier / Kathleen M. Byrd.
Description: Baton Rouge : Louisiana State University Press, [2024] | Includes bibliographical references and index.
Identifiers: LCCN 2024001035 (print) | LCCN 2024001036 (ebook) | ISBN 978-0-8071-8219-2 (paperback) | ISBN 978-0-8071-8285-7 (epub) | ISBN 978-0-8071-8286-4 (pdf)
Subjects: LCSH: Creoles—Louisiana—Natchitoches—History—19th century. | Indians of North America—Louisiana—Natchitoches—History—19th century. | Natchitoches (La.)—History—19th century. | Natchitoches (La.)—Ethnic relations—History—19th century.
Classification: LCC F379.N2 B973 2024 (print) | LCC F379.N2 (ebook) | DDC 976.3/6505—dc23/eng/20240327
LC record available at https://lccn.loc.gov/2024001035
LC ebook record available at https://lccn.loc.gov/2024001036

TO DEHAHUIT,

the Great Caddo Chief, who due to his great leadership skills and by working with both the Spanish and the Americans, was able to protect the Caddo and associated tribes from conflicts resulting from the arrival of the Americans to the area.

TO MARIE THÉRÈSE COINCOIN,

an enslaved and then freed woman of African descent, whose children with a French merchant and planter formed the nucleus of the Isle Brevelle community of successful planters and farmers down Cane River.

TO JOHN SIBLEY,

businessman and one-time Indian agent, who through his extensive reports and letters provides a firsthand account, at least from his perspective, of life in Natchitoches during the early nineteenth century.

CONTENTS

ILLUSTRATIONS

Maps

Figures

Tables

ACKNOWLEDGMENTS

My husband and I moved to Natchitoches in 1994 when I was hired as head of the Department of Social Sciences at Northwestern State University. We found that Natchitoches was a quirky town, full of quirky people with quirky historical tales. We grew to relish the unique character of the town and surrounding areas. Over the years, as I learned more about Natchitoches, I found that the history of the area was even more fascinating than the quirky tales. What today is a relatively small, quiet southern town was at one time a frontier settlement with a military fort to protect American interests against Imperial Spain. It was also the site of a government trading post and Indian agency important in dealing with the Native tribes. In time Natchitoches became a bustling jumping-off site for those pioneers heading west into Texas. Some thought it would become a great commercial hub, but the Red River changed its course, leaving Natchitoches behind.

As is often and correctly stated, any work such as this book results from the assistance of many individuals. I would not have attempted it at all without the constant support and encouragement of my husband, Robert W. Neuman, now gone, but whose voice is with me still. I wish to thank the archivists at Hill Memorial Library at Louisiana State University, the Historic New Orleans Collection, and above all the Cammie G. Henry Research Center at Northwestern State University. I particularly want to acknowledge the help provided by the late Mary Linn Wernet, former head archivist at the CGHRC, who arranged access to materials, even dropping information off at my front door during the COVID lockdown. The staff at the Lindenwood University, Independence National Historic Park, Stone Fort Museum at Stephen F. Austin University, Cane River Creole National Historic Park, and Donna Baker, the new head archivist at NSU, assisted me in obtaining illustrations for this book. Barry R. Simmons and Sanders F. Hearne were particularly helpful in gaining access to the portrait of John Sibley. I also wish to recognize the contribution of those writers of letters and keepers of diaries whose firsthand accounts added insights to the sometimes-dry official records and reports.

I was fortunate to have several astute readers such as William Brent and Hiram (Pete) Gregory, both of whom read early versions of this manuscript, and especially Marcy Frantom, who examined multiple drafts of this book and whose helpful suggestions and editorial advice resulted in a much better product. The suggestions of LSU's anonymous reviewer also proved helpful. I also want to thank Rand Dotson and the editorial staff at LSU Press, who guided me through the production of this book and who put up with my limited computer skills during the preparation of this manuscript for publication. Any errors of interpretation are, of course, my own.

NATCHITOCHES
LOUISIANA, 1803–1840

INTRODUCTION

Natchitoches may not be typical of how a rural French Creole community adapted to the influx of Americans after the Louisiana Purchase; its unique position on the frontier and the early heavy American presence set it apart. Nevertheless, we can learn much from how this distinct community reacted to and dealt with the arrival of the Americans and the conflicts that arose, and how it evolved from a predominately French fur-trading, agricultural area into a commercial hub over a period of forty years. This is a story of not only the events that occurred on this portion of the Spanish-American frontier but also the people involved—the less well-known players as well as the leading historical figures. It allows the people to speak for themselves as much as possible, revealing their perspectives and something of their personalities, including their individual foibles—from the terse Captain Turner to the bombastic General Wilkinson and the taciturn Great Caddo Chief Dehahuit.

Louisiana had been settled by the French in the early 1700s, but the colony failed to prosper. In 1762, France convinced the king of Spain to accept Louisiana (viewed by some as something of a white elephant) as payment for losses Spain sustained for supporting France in its war with England. Then in 1800 in a secret treaty, Spain returned Louisiana to France but continued to administer the colony while awaiting the official transfer. American farmers of the Ohio and Tennessee valleys had been shipping their products down the Mississippi River to the Spanish port of New Orleans. Learning of the treaty between France and Spain in May 1801, President Thomas Jefferson feared that, should France take over Louisiana, it would close the New Orleans port to American farmers. He sent envoys to Napoleon Bonaparte, First Consul of the French Republic, with an offer to purchase New Orleans and the surrounding area.

Meanwhile Napoleon, planning to recolonize Louisiana, had amassed colonists and an army on the Caribbean island of St. Domingue and had a military force ready to sail from the Dutch coast. But the continuing slave uprisings and a yellow fever epidemic on the island decimated his army, and winter conditions icebound his fleet on the Dutch coast. These factors derailed his plans. In need of funds for his war with England, Napoleon decided to sell the entire Louisiana colony to the United States for fifteen million dollars. This transaction became known as the Louisiana Purchase. On November 30, 1803, Pierre Clément de Laussat, the French commissioner, formally accepted the Spanish colony in a ceremony in New Orleans.[1]

On December 20, 1803, the two American commissioners, Governor William C. C. Claiborne and General James A. Wilkinson, with their military escort rode into New Orleans to a twenty-one-gun salute to take possession of the new United States territory. Inside the Cabildo the ceremonial transfer of Louisiana to the United States took place. Then in the Place d'Armes, the French flag was lowered, and the Stars and Stripes raised. With the Louisiana Purchase, some 828,000 square miles became part of the United States of America, thereby almost doubling the size of the country.[2]

The United States may have purchased Louisiana, but that didn't make this vast area "American." The French, Spanish, and Creoles, long-term residents of Louisiana, were culturally different from the Americans, with their own laws, beliefs, and traditions. Most did not embrace with any enthusiasm their abrupt transfer to the United States with its strange customs and practices. In fact, the Americans met considerable resistance from the older residents to many of their new initiatives. Many of the "ancient" inhabitants of Louisiana would have been happy to return to French or Spanish rule and were apprehensive about their new status as residents of a territory of the United States.

In Louisiana, many Americans found what in their eyes was a corrupt, despotic government where all authority, both civil and military, had rested with the Spanish governor. The concept of a representative government, such as that of the United States, was unknown. Spanish Louisiana did have an executive council, the Cabildo, in New Orleans, but membership was purchased rather than elected and, not surprisingly, served the interests of the wealthy Creole planters. The only tax had been a small import-export tax of 6 percent, often avoided by smuggling or bribery. The Spanish Crown had borne the cost of the government of Louisiana. The idea of people having to pay a tax to support the government was unfathomable to the Creole population. Spanish civil law, which was based on Roman law, was the law of the land. The language of the courts was French. The American common law system, with its concepts of trial by jury and writ of habeas corpus, was foreign. Roman Catholicism was the official and only religion sanctioned in Spanish Louisiana with the Spanish government supporting the churches financially. The American guarantee of freedom of religion and the idea of a separation of church and state made little sense to Louisiana's long-term residents. There was no currency. The Spanish refused to honor the certificates they had issued, and shipments of silver from Vera Cruz had ceased. Land records were in disarray, with over three-quarters of the land claims lacking clear and complete titles; the Spanish administrators had taken many of the land records with them when they left. The inheritance laws of Louisiana complicated the land-title system even further. Schools were virtually nonexistent for most Louisianans. At least half the white population was illiterate. Even the exact borders of the Louisiana Purchase were not fully known. Thomas Jefferson believed, or said he believed, that the purchase extended west to the Rio Grande and included West Florida, the area north of Lake Pontchartrain and south of the Thirty-First Parallel, east to the Perdido River, near present-day Pensacola. The Spanish claimed that the Louisiana Purchase included neither Texas nor West Florida.[3]

For now, the United States needed to take physical possession of Louisiana and protect it from invasion by its neighbor to the west, Imperial Spain. This included establishing a presence on the international border. The U.S. government identified the settlement of Natchitoches, the oldest town in the Louisiana Purchase, as the site for this effort. When the American military arrived in the spring of 1804, Natchitoches had a population of a little over 1,630 and had already existed for ninety years.

The French had built their first two buildings at the location of the old Natchitoches Indian village in 1713. At the time, it was the head of navigation on the Red River. Above the new French trading post a tangled mass of logs, brush, and limbs, known as the Great Raft, clogged the Red River channel, making it difficult to navigate above this point. In 1716, the Spanish established a fort and settlement known as Los Adaes just twelve miles to the west of the French outpost to protect its interests on the frontier. Over time, commerce developed between French Natchitoches and Spanish Los Adaes and, after the closure of Los Adaes, with the Spanish settlement of Nacogdoches. The Spanish found it much easier to supply the settlements in East Texas through Natchitoches than overland from the coast or from other Spanish settlements to the southwest. At its peak in the early 1800s, one trading firm shipped goods from Natchitoches 130 miles overland on the Camino Real, or King's Highway, to Nacogdoches once or twice a month and from there to San Antonio. This road and Natchitoches' location on the Red River with its water access to points south made it the logical choice for the United States to locate three U.S. governmental institutions to protect its territory from Spain—a military fort, a government trading post, and an Indian agency.

Not all Natchitoches residents were enthusiastic about the "invasion" of Americans and their establishment of institutions in the French Creole settlement. These institutions, their looming presence, and the threat of war with Spain would have a pronounced impact and change the character of the town over the next fifteen years. Even after the removal of these institutions in the early 1820s, Anglo-Americans continued to arrive, and Natchitoches evolved into the staging ground for filibuster invasions into Mexico and a major jumping-off point for immigrants heading west. It seemed that Natchitoches was slated to become a great commercial center on the Red River, but this was not to be. The changing course of the Red River from its Cane River channel, which flowed directly in front of the town of Natchitoches, to the Bon Dieu channel to the east beginning in about 1828 left the town without river access for part of the year. The removal of the Great Raft above the town, commencing in 1833, allowed the settlement of Shreveport on the Red River to grow and eventually surpass Natchitoches in size and importance. These events brought Natchitoches' role as a potential great economic hub to a close, but Natchitoches would remain a commercial and cultural center for the many wealthy cotton planters in the area.

This study concerns a small part of the Louisiana Purchase. Chapter 1 describes the area in and around the old French settlement of Natchitoches—its rich river bottoms, the less fertile upland areas, and the rivers and streams that provided major transportation corridors for the area. When Americans arrived to take over Louisiana, they encountered people that were predominately of

French and/or African descent. Even after forty years of Spanish rule, most people, white and Black, spoke the French language and followed French cultural practices. In addition, there were various Indian tribes in the area—some long-term inhabitants, others more recent immigrants who had been pushed off their lands to the east and resettled in Louisiana. The Americans needed to convert all these peoples to the American way of life. It would prove a formidable task to incorporate the white population, who were of largely French and to a lesser extent Spanish descent, into the United States and acculturate them to American customs and social norms. It would be years before all the conflicts and confusion would be resolved.

The people of Natchitoches experienced virtually overnight the transformation of their sleepy agricultural and fur-trading community into the hegemony of the United States. Within months of the purchase, the U.S. military arrived to establish a fort in the town, followed in close order by a government factory or Indian trading house, and an Indian agency. These three bastions of American rule would dominate the landscape of the settlement of Natchitoches for most of the next twenty years. Chapter 2 examines Fort Claiborne, the fort at Natchitoches, and the events that surrounded it in the military confrontations between the Spanish and the Americans on the international frontier in 1806, which almost led to war and resulted in the Neutral Ground Agreement, creating additional problems for the residents of the area. It also looks at the day-by-day activities—the less glamorous and more mundane experiences of soldiers at Fort Claiborne—during the fort's existence in the town of Natchitoches. Chapter 3 focuses on the United States and its dealings with the Native tribes. The French had treated the Native people as trading partners, and several of the early French had chosen Native women as spouses. The concerns of the Americans were more political. The U.S. government recognized that the loyalty or at least neutrality of the Indians was vital to its success on the frontier. The government trading post in Natchitoches attempted to buy the loyalties of the Native population to the American cause by offering trade goods at a low cost. This was detrimental to the local French Creole merchants, who had supplied the Indians with goods in the past. The establishment of the Indian agency provided a governmental representative to negotiate treaties and resolve conflicts between whites and Indians and among the various Indian groups of the area, thereby maintaining peace on the frontier. It also resulted in an influx of sometimes large numbers of Indians from different tribes into the town, who came to deal with the Indian agent. These activities were not welcomed by many of the town's long-term residents. This chapter both explores the trade with the Indians at the trading house and provides a sample of the day-to-day activities engaged in by the Indian agent in the year 1807. The description of the Grand Council, held in 1807, highlights practical concerns of the Indian tribes as they too adapted to the arrival of the Americans.

Chapter 4 describes Natchitoches' commercial ties with Spanish Texas, problems associated with the Neutral Ground Agreement and its outlaw element, and the armed invasion of Spanish Texas by filibusters who used the Neutral Ground as a staging area for their efforts. Natchitoches in 1810 had grown, due in no small part to the migration of Americans into the area. The older French residents were slowly adapting, not necessarily willingly, to the American presence, while continuing their own cultural practices. To the west in Texas, Mexico was fighting for its independence, and in 1812 hundreds of Americans were moving through Natchitoches to participate in this effort with the hope of acquiring land in Texas. The revolt failed, and soon not only the filibusters, but also rebels and their families and several Indian tribes that had sided with the revolutionaries came streaming across the border into Louisiana. The negotiation of the Adams-Onís Treaty brought an end to the uncertainty associated with the Neutral Ground, although not to all the crime. The treaty did result in the government moving the fort closer to the new frontier. After years of efforts and complaints, the townspeople finally saw the relocation of not only the fort but also the trading house and Indian agency outside the environs of the town. This occurred not necessarily due to the efforts of the local people, although they were vocal, but more because of the changing nature of the frontier.

The last chapter looks at the town and parish of Natchitoches as it developed into a regional commercial center and a jumping-off place for immigrants heading west into Texas. The population had increased, largely because of the arrival of Americans but also Europeans, some from France, but the old French Creoles continued to maintain a notable presence. The town had grown but, in 1823, a fire broke out in the Catholic church and, before it could be extinguished, destroyed a large portion of the downtown buildings. The residents rebuilt. In the late 1820s the town had a courthouse, a new Catholic church replacing the one destroyed by fire, and a newspaper that published articles in both French and English. Its merchants sold a variety of goods, and the town had doctors, lawyers, and druggists. The Rio Hondo District, the old Neutral Ground, was being rapidly settled. Fort Jesup, a new American fort, had been erected halfway between Natchitoches and the Sabine to protect American interests from those of Mexico, which had won its independence from Spain. This was primarily an upland area of farmers and herders, although cotton was raised. The river districts, Natchitoches Proper and the River aux Cannes, were the primary cotton-growing areas, where many of the wealthy long-established French and Creole planters and their slaves lived along with the recently relocated American planters. In the uplands to the east, small-scale farmers and herders settled. The Red River still served as the main transportation route. In the early years up through the 1820s keelboats provided most of the river transport. By the early 1820s steamboats had begun to replace the keelboats and new forms of entertainment had reached the area, including touring thespian performers, showboats, and early circuses. Meanwhile, a sandbar was forming at the upper end of the Cane River channel and the federal government was attempting to remove the Great Raft blocking the river above Natchitoches. These events resulted in more and more of the flow of the Red River down the Bon Dieu channel rather than the Cane River. As a result, the town of Natchitoches lost its primacy as a river town. For the Caddo Indians, the removal of the raft had a worse outcome. Eventually, the Caddo were forced to sell their land to the United States for a fraction of what it was worth. The early 1830s saw a cotton boom, with cotton selling at 21 cents a pound. However, monetary practices at home and financial concerns in Europe brought on the Panic of 1837, which had a devastating effect on Natchitoches and the entire country, from which it would take years to recover.

1

WHAT THE AMERICANS FOUND

> I have the honor to inform you that I took possession of this Post on the 26th Inst—The French Flag superseded the Spanish at eleven, and the American the French at 12 o Clock—to the seeming satisfaction of every one—though I have understood some are not altogether pleased.
>
> —CAPTAIN EDWARD D. TURNER to Governor Claiborne, May 1, 1804

Captain Edward D. Turner with forty-four soldiers of the Second Infantry Regiment and ten artillerists had arrived in Natchitoches in April to officially take possession of this frontier post for the United States. The insignificant Spanish force of seven or eight men readily yielded the town to the Americans. The official transfer ceremony occurred on April 26. At 11:00 in the morning, Captain José Joaquin de Ugarte, the commandant at Nacogdoches, Texas, and the Spanish representative at the transfer, officially turned the settlement over to the French designee Felix Trudeau, and the Spanish flag was lowered and the French flag raised. Then at noon, Captain Turner accepted the outpost from Trudeau and the American flag flew over what was now the farthest western outpost of the United States.[1]

The Spanish, who had been suffering for years from inroads into Texas by first the French and more recently the Americans, wanted the frontier closed. José Joaquin de Ugarte was heard to utter, "It is now finished, and the door is shut forever."[2] This was wishful thinking on the part of the commandant. The frontier settlement of Natchitoches was to become the American gateway to Texas and Spain's Interior Provinces. In the early 1800s Natchitoches' strategic location made it third in importance only after New Orleans and St. Louis, and activities in the Natchitoches area and along the Red River would bring Imperial Spain and the brash, young United States of America to the brink of war.[3]

The Land and Settlements

No population census had been taken in Louisiana since 1788, but in 1803 the consul of the United States in New Orleans attempted to arrive at an approximation based on available documents, which resulted in an estimate of 49,473 people, not including the Indian populations living in the area of the Louisiana Purchase. Of these, 7,610 lived in Arkansas and in the vicinity of St. Louis, Mobile, and Pensacola. The rest, 41,863, dwelled in what became the Territory of Orleans, and three-quarters of these lived south of Pointe Coupee. This same area contained seven-eighths of the wealth of the territory. In addition, there were three settlements along the Red River: Avoyelles, Rapides, and Natchitoches. Of these, Natchitoches was the largest with over 785 whites and 846 slaves. Most of the residents of Natchitoches were of French origin and engaged in agriculture and the Indian trade.[4]

The village of Natchitoches in 1803 was anything but imposing—at least to northern eyes. John Sibley, a New Englander and a recent arrival to the area, describes the town as a "small, irregular and meanly built village, half a dozen houses excepted," of "about forty families of which twelve or fifteen are merchants, or traders, nearly all French." Forty years earlier the village of Natchitoches had been much larger, but the decrease in the Indian trade and the increase in the importance of agriculture resulted in many of the families moving from the town to outlying plantations. The area "downriver" from the village had become thickly settled with "a number of wealthy inhabitants"[5] who grew cotton, corn, and tobacco. In 1802 the Natchitoches planters had shipped almost three thousand bales of cotton and a large amount of high-quality tobacco to New Orleans.[6] But as Sibley noted there was not a single water-driven mill in the area. Horses powered the cotton gins, and it had only been in the last twelve or fifteen years that an Irishman from Pennsylvania had introduced a ferry to cross the river and the plow for agriculture. Sibley also observed that there was not a "single mechanic, in the district, who is a native to it, one tailor excepted; every thing of the kind is done by strangers, and mostly Americans."[7]

The village sat on the west or right descending bank of the Red River on a narrow strip of alluvial land. Pine woods began on hills about three hundred yards back from the riverbank. The earlier French settlement had been located about a half-mile south of the current town center where, in the early 1800s, the remains of the old French-Spanish fort and gardens could still be seen. Natchitoches had served for years as a trading center for both the Spanish in East Texas and the various Indian tribes of the area.[8]

The rusty, brackish-tasting water of the Red River flowed in a southeasterly direction past Natchitoches on its way to the Gulf of Mexico. At its mouth the Red River was about a half-mile wide but contracted to about a quarter-mile a short distance upstream and then to about 120 yards. Much of the land from its mouth to about 100 miles upstream flooded during the wet season. River willows and cottonwoods predominated on the low ground, but on higher land oaks, hickory, and ash could be found.[9]

About 120 miles from the river's mouth, a series of siltstone ledges extended across the riverbed, forming rapids. Here the river was about 300 yards wide. During high water, boats could easily float over the ledges, but during low water, generally August through December, the ledges were exposed, creating two sets of cascades about three-quarters of a mile apart. During the dry season the current could be very swift with a ten-foot fall within fifty feet at the lower falls. At low water the boats had to be unloaded, the cargo carried to above the rapids, and the boats pulled over the ledges. During extreme low water even this was impossible. Just below the rapids on the south bank of the river sat the settlement of Alexandria. By the early 1800s about 640 whites, mostly Americans, and 200 slaves lived in the surrounding area. One of the residents operated a water-powered sawmill.[10]

Above the rapids the river meandered from one side of the valley to the other, dividing, reforming, and creating large and small islands in the flat alluvial plain (map 1). One of these islands, Isle Brevelle, was 4 miles wide and 32 miles long. On another island, Isle de Natchitoches, the French in 1713 had built their first two huts to use as a trading post. Floods overflowed the riverbanks in the flat valley, depositing rich alluvial soils on the bank crests, producing natural levees. These levees formed a narrow band of higher land of 300 to 400 yards wide paralleling both sides of the river. It was along these narrow but very fertile natural levees that farmers grew productive fields of cotton, tobacco, and corn. One

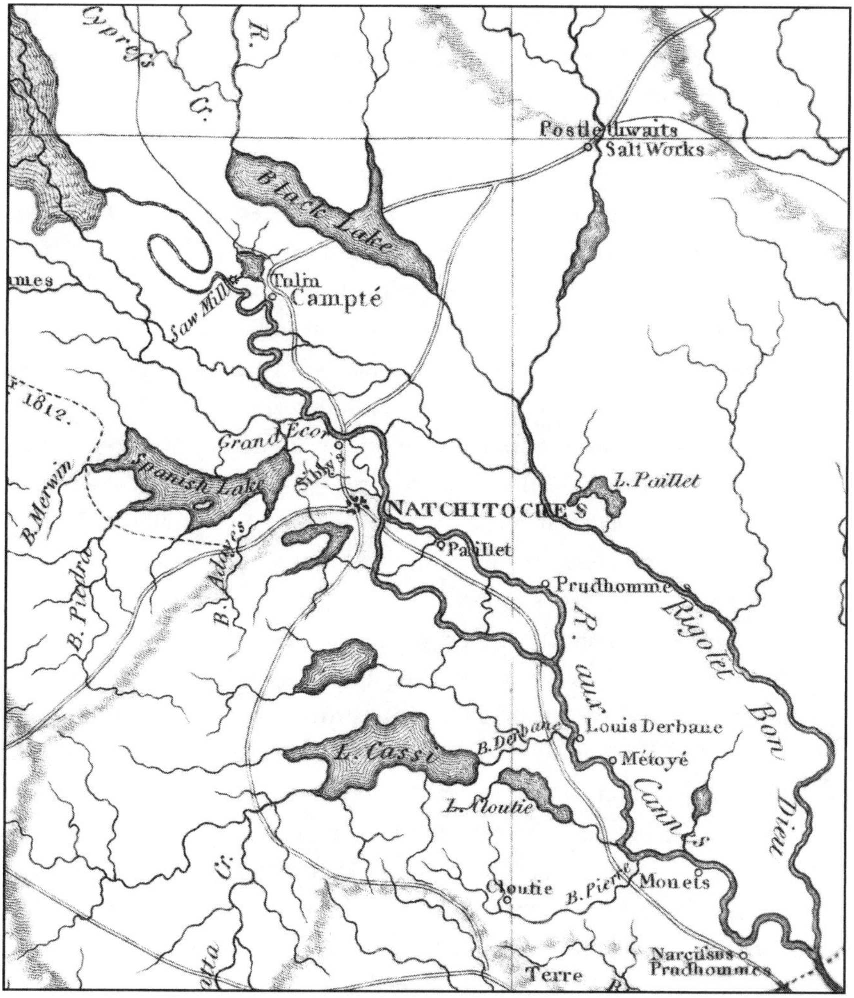

Map 1. Natchitoches and surrounding areas, 1816. Great Raft with impounded water, *upper left corner.* Detail of Darby's *Map of Louisiana,* 1816.

observer wrote, "Perhaps cotton and tobacco are raised on Red river in greater perfection than in any other quarter of the union; certain it is, that they command the highest prices in the market." On the higher ground, ash and elm trees occurred in abundance, but pecans and cottonwood were also plentiful. Some of these trees grew large, with one pecan measuring nineteen feet in circumference at five feet off the ground. Back from the levees, swamps and lakes occupied the wet and waterlogged soils. In the swamps and along the margins of the lakes could be found stately stands of cypress and tupelo gum.[11]

Near Natchitoches there were several large lakes. These would fill as the river rose with the late winter rains and spring floods. Then they would gradually drain as the river fell in the late summer and autumn, exposing great expanses of luxurious meadows where the people grazed their livestock. Among the cypress swamps, flocks of bright-green, yellow-head, orange-cheeked Carolina parakeets were found in abundance. In the autumn and winter the lakes teemed with ducks, geese, swans, and cranes; huge flocks of passenger pigeons arrived in October to winter over in the area. It was not uncommon "for a single man to kill from two to four hundred fowl in one evening; they fly between sundown and dark; the air is filled with them; they load and fire, as fast as they can, without taking any particular aim." Fish were equally abundant, and the Indians, sometimes using bows and arrows, could kill them with great speed. Some of the fish weighed up to forty pounds.[12]

In 1713 the old Natchitoches Indian village was the head of navigation on the Red River. Above the village a series of logjams choked the channel, impeding navigation. Known as the Great Raft, these obstructions extended intermittently for one hundred miles upriver. The meandering course of the river, its shallow bottom, seasonal flooding, and the easily eroded soils on its banks resulted in large and small trees tumbling into the river, where they floated downstream until they came to rest on the shallow point bars. Here they accumulated, forming a thick tangle of logs, tree trunks, and brush. In time this wooden mass extended across the channel, damming the Red River and also streams and bayous that flowed into it. On occasion these dams created large lakes, known as raft lakes, such as Lake Bistineau. In 1713 the raft started just above the Natchitoches trading post. Over the next ninety years the raft snaked its way northward with the logs and tree trunks slowly rotting at the foot of the raft while at the upper end the river deposited about four-fifths of a mile of additional material each year. By 1806 the lower end of the raft was about thirty miles upstream from Natchitoches, a short distance above the French settlement of Campti. The French found navigating the Red River through the raft especially difficult during low water. Generally, they chose Bayou Pierre, which hugged the west side of the valley, to provide a water route around most of the raft at least during part of the year. But many of the hunters and traders journeying north avoided the raft altogether by taking pack animals overland through the uplands.[13]

On both sides of the ten- to fifteen-mile-wide Red River Valley, a series of ridges and narrow valleys, known to geologists as the Nacogdoches Wold, extends in a southwest-to-northeast direction across the area. At Grand Ecore Bluff, about four miles north of Natchitoches, the geologically younger Red River had cut through the soft white rock and gravel loam of the wold deposits, revealing the sixty-five million years of the sedimentary history of this feature. West of Natchitoches toward the Sabine River the land is hilly with pine, black oak, sweet gum, and various types of hickory abundant, with pine becoming more dominant about ten miles west of Natchitoches. As one traveler noted, "The country is extremely broken, and often stony. The hills are not very elevated, but steep. The bottoms are often fertile, though not very extensive."[14] The highly weathered sandy and acidic soils of the uplands contain low amounts of organic matter. These did not prove as fertile for agriculture as the soils of the Red River Valley, but the extensive prairies and the herbaceous ground cover under the towering canopy of climax hickory, oak, gum, beech and particularly under the parklike stands of long-leaf pine afforded forage for livestock.

During colonial times the people used these rolling uplands for *vacheries* or ranches, and large herds of cows, horse, and hogs could be found in these areas. In fact, the Bayou Pierre settlement, a string of small farms and ranches beginning about twenty miles northwest of Natchitoches and extending for fifty miles or so north, was known for its cattle operation with several *vacheries*. Here the uplands were interspersed with prairies, providing good grazing for the livestock. The Bayou Pierre settlement produced butter, cheese, and "bacon hams" for the Natchitoches residents and undoubtedly shipped cured meats south to New Orleans and other southern markets. The people preserved their hams with salt obtained from a nearby saline. The inhabitants of the Bayou Pierre area were primarily of French and Spanish descent although, in the early 1800s, Americans and Italians began to settle in the area. Many of the early inhabitants had been involved in hunting, smuggling, and in the Indian trade, but by the early 1800s farms produced corn, cotton, and tobacco in the narrow valleys and upland areas. During colonial times this area had been under the jurisdiction of the Spanish—first at Los Adaes and then at Nacogdoches. But the people had more economic and familial ties with Natchitoches than with Nacogdoches. In 1805 the Spanish still had a small detachment of eight soldiers under the command of a noncommissioned officer in the area and claimed the area for Spain. Farther west toward the Sabine River the land wasn't as fertile, and the area was covered with oak and pines with only small areas of cropland.[15]

By the early 1800s a public ferry connected Grand Ecore and the settlements on the west side of the Red River with those to the northeast. The rolling uplands east of the Red River Valley were viewed as "greatly superior to the land on the west side. The creek bottoms were more extensive, the soil more fertile, and the hills although higher had a more gradual slope."[16] When French Louisiana was transferred to Spain in the 1760s, the former French soldiers and settlers from the old La Harpe's trading post, located not far from present-day Texarkana, Arkansas, had purchased land from the Indians and settled on the east side of Red River, forming the nucleus of the Campti settlement. By the 1800s people had established plantations and farms in the area where they grew cotton, corn, and tobacco. The northernmost habitation was located just south of the foot of the Great Raft. Ranching operations also occurred in this area and to the northeast near Black Lake.[17] About twelve miles east of the Campti settlements along Saline Bayou and its tributaries were salt flats. Native peoples had worked these salines since prehistoric times to extract salt. The French at Natchitoches acquired most of their salt from these areas as well. In 1805 "two old crippled men" using ten or twelve old pots and kettles could make about six bushels of salt a day and in twelve months produced enough salt for the whole district. Dr. John Sibley noted that the "salt is good; I never have better bacon than I make with it."[18]

The People

When the Americans arrived to take over Louisiana, the people they found were predominately French. Even after forty years of Spanish rule, most people, whites and Blacks, spoke the French language and followed French cultural practices. To many of the newly arrived Anglo-Americans, the French Creoles' habits and customs seemed strange. Major Amos Stoddard, a New Englander, who served five years in the lower Mississippi Valley, including six months at Fort Claiborne in Natchitoches, left a description of Louisiana in the first decade of the nineteenth century. He provides a window into the lives of the French Creole population during this period. He also reveals the biases of the newly arrived Anglo-Americans, explaining some of the cultural clashes that occurred.[19]

Stoddard describes the Creole French as appearing small and slender with "a keen piercing eye," the men having a rather sallow complexion resulting perhaps from their heavy smoking. He found the men proud and vain but noted that these traits inspired them "with a high sense of honor, to render them honest in their dealings, and to stimulate them to be as punctual in the payment of their debts as their abilities will admit." He noted that the men had a "peculiar cast to their manners" which Stoddard attributed to the fact that, except in the Delta area, the men were involved to some degree in the Indian trade." Stoddard claimed that it was "not uncommon to see thirty or forty charming females in a ball-room, dressed with taste and even elegance, suited to the most fashionable society, when perhaps the males of their own families appear in their blanket coats and moccasons [*sic*]." He added that it was "rare to see in such an assembly more than four or five young men, whose appearance is even tolerable. This strange diversity is prevalent in the detached settlements of the country, and it even appears in some of the villages."[20]

Stoddard found the women much fairer and "usually handsome when young, but when arrived to the age of thirty-five or forty, their bloom mostly forsakes them, and they become wrinkled and withered." He noted that the women were "less guarded in their manners and conversation" than was common in the United States, which could lead some to think, incorrectly, that there was "a laxity in their morals." To Stoddard the women seemed to have "more influence over their husbands than is common in most other countries." This might have been because women often retained rights to property as listed in contracts which were signed prior to their marriages. It was not uncommon for a woman in colonial Louisiana to assume the management of property upon the death of her husband.[21] Stoddard describes the women as "extremely fond of dress . . . remarkedly loquacious, and their manners . . . more polished than those of the men." But he identified one fault that was "not easily extenuated; they are habitually cruel to their slaves."[22]

There was widespread illiteracy in the old French-Spanish colony. Even the wealthy planters Stoddard found to be "at least a century behind other civilized nations in the arts and sciences, if not in the amenities of life. Many of the most opulent planters along the Delta and Red River cannot either read or write." This backwardness and lack of education was probably the results of the traditional poverty of the colony, but Stoddard suggested that it might have been Spanish policy to keep the people uneducated. He believed that "the prevalence of knowledge had a tendency to expose the absurdity of some of their [Roman Catholic] religious creeds; and to weaken the ties, which connected them with the established church." He held that the "human mind, when once liberated from the fetters of religious servitude, reflects with pleasure on the emancipation of itself, and views with a mixture of horror and satisfaction the prison from which it has escaped." Stoddard proudly states that the United States had "restored the professors of all religions to liberty."[23] Nevertheless, Stoddard found that many of the wealthy planters, who could neither read nor write, could "converse fluently, and with much seeming confidence, on a variety of subjects, where mathematical learning is necessary to a solution. They will debate on complicated machines, the utility or defects of which cannot be determined without a knowledge of mechanics, and propose substitutes and experiments with as much apparent judgment as if they were complete masters of the principles of the art." As Stoddard noted, "This want of information cannot be imputed to all; for some of the Creoles possess real intelligence, and are well instructed in several branches of useful learning, though their number is too limited to afford, in this respect, a very favourable reputations to the country."[24]

The Creole work ethic baffled Stoddard. He describes the people as indolent and lazy, noting that "while the English Americans are hard at labor, and sweat under the burning rays of a meridian sun, they [the French Creoles] will be seated in their houses, or under some cooling shade, amusing themselves with their pipes and tobacco, in drinking coffee, and in repeating the incidents of their several perambulations over distant lakes and mountains." The French Creoles had clearly adapted to the sweltering heat and energy-sapping humidity of midday, something that the Anglo-Americans had yet to learn. Stoddard did note that, when necessary, the French Creoles were "not deficient in exertion. Many of them follow boating and the Indian trade; and these require much labor, activity, and circumspection." Stoddard found that the French Creoles were "honest in their dealings, and punctual in the performance of contracts." "They usually live within their incomes, and are never so uneasy as when in debt." But Stoddard noted that they didn't seem driven to acquire more and better things.

"They obtain but little, and little satisfies their desires." "They enjoy what they have, and are perfectly contented with it." This clearly puzzled the American.[25]

The French Creoles were generally temperate in their normal eating habits, relying heavily on vegetables, soups, and coffee. Stoddard attributed the generally healthy condition and the near absence of disease such as "gout, consumption, gravel and stone in the bladder, and in general to all chronic complaints" to their moderate eating and drinking habits. When entertaining friends or distinguish visitors, however, the French Creoles provided "sumptuous" meals with their tables "covered with a great variety of dishes; almost every sort of food dressed in all manner of ways." On these occasions they served the best wine and a variety of desserts. "The master of the house, out of respect to his guests, frequently waits on them himself." The well-to-do seldom consumed hard liquors, preferring instead red wines, such as Claret, which they drank in quantity. The laboring class, however, drank hard liquor, arguing that it would drive away the gout, warm the body during cold weather and cool it during hot weather, calm the mind, purify the water, and steady the nerves.[26]

The French Creoles were a vivacious and sociable people with a passion for dancing. They were particularly fond of balls. As Stoddard noted, "Neither the severity of the cold, nor the oppression of the heat, ever restrains them from this amusement, which usually commences early in the evening, and is seldom suspended till late the next morning." The Creoles were also fond of a variety of games, particularly hazard but also other card games, as well as billiards and dice. Their socializing extended into Sundays. The French Creoles attended morning mass with devotion and strictly observed the religious holidays and feasts of their favorite saints. However, after Sunday mass they would "collect in parties, and pass away their time in social and merry intercourse. They play at billiards and other games; and to balls and assemblies the Sundays are particularly devoted." To the more straitlaced and puritanical Anglo-Americans, these practices on a Sunday appeared impious, inappropriate, or even sinful. But the French Creoles believed that there was "true and undefiled religion in their amusements." When Stoddard questioned them on their activities on the Sabbath, they answered "that men were made for happiness, and that the more they are able to enjoy themselves, the more acceptable they are to their Creator." They believed that "a sullen countenance, an attention to gloomy subjects, a set form of speech, and a stiff behaviour, are much more indicative of hypocrisy than of religion; and they have often remarked, that those who practice these singularities on Sundays will most assuredly cheat and defraud their neighbors during the rest of the week."[27]

Although the French Creoles had ruled, the largest number of people in Lower Louisiana was of African descent. In 1800 an estimated 24,264 enslaved people made up 55 percent of the total population. The French had imported slaves from Africa, the first slave ship arriving in 1719. Eventually somewhere between 5,800 and 6,000 Africans reached French Louisiana. Two-thirds of these came from the Senegambia region of West Africa. This was a rich agricultural area where the people grew millet, corn, rice, peas, melons, and other vegetables as well as tobacco, indigo, and cotton. The area was known for its highly skilled metalworkers, and the literacy rate of some groups was high. Warfare was prevalent in West Africa at the time, and many of the slaves who were transported to the New World were captives from these wars. These captives were sold by African middlemen to the European slavers. At first the newly arrived slaves grew foodstuffs such as rice and worked in the Louisiana swamps and forests, cutting timber for buildings and for the masts and planking of ships. But quickly they became involved in tobacco and indigo production, which were major exports for the French colony.[28]

In 1724 the French promulgated the *Code Noir* or Black Code, which regulated the slaves and placed restrictions on how owners could treat their slaves. Slaves could not congregate with slaves of different masters and could "never be a party in a civil suit or a complainant in a criminal suit." Running away was severely punished. If away for more than a month, the slave's ears were cut off and his shoulder branded with a fleur-de-lis; for a second offense he was hamstrung and his other shoulder branded; for a third offense he was put to death. In theory the code did provide some protection for the slave. Owners had to furnish adequate subsistence and clothing, were to support the slaves in their old age or if they became disabled, and were forbidden from mutilating any one of the limbs or part of a slave's body. Punishment allowed included putting the slave in irons and/or whipping with rods or ropes. Criminal charges could be brought against a master or overseer who killed or mutilated a slave. Here, the government was probably more concerned about protecting its investment in labor than any real concern for the slave. The code required that owners provide religious instructions in the Roman Catholic faith for their slaves. Slaves were to be baptized in the church, could marry in the church, and must be buried in consecrated ground. Sundays and religious holidays were to be strictly observed. Under the code the slave family, the husband, wife, and children under fourteen years of age were to be sold as a unit. Owners were not to sexually exploit slave women. The code strictly forbade marriage between a white and a Black even if the Black was manumitted or freeborn or living in a state of concubinage. Noncompliance to this rule could result in a fine for the white person, the confiscation of the slave and any children, and the slave could never be freed. Masters could manumit their slaves but only with the permission of the Superior Council. The Code Noir prohibited slaves from selling anything without the permission of their owners, but many owners did allow their slaves to work for pay on their own time. As a French officer recorded, many of the slaves cleared land and grew "cotton, tobacco, and other products which they sell." Some of the French gave their slaves Saturday and Sunday off. During this time the slaves could hire themselves out to settlers. As he noted, "some of the Negroes do so well that they have earned the wherewithal to buy their liberty, and have built their habitations in this province in imitation of the French." Slaves could be given their freedom under French rule. Once freed, the former slave was to have the same rights and privileges as other free people. The actual treatment of slaves varied. Owners tended to adhere to practices that resulted in effective management of the slaves and ignored those that they found too restrictive. During the French reign the slave population grew and, after 1727, it outnumbered the free population sometimes as much as three to one.[29]

With the Treaty of Fontainebleau in 1762, Spain obtained control of Louisiana. The planters clamored for labor to work the tobacco and indigo fields and, in an effort to make the colony more profitable, Spanish officials reinstituted the slave trade. Soon British, Scottish, and American slavers were arriving in Spanish Louisiana. To the second- and sometimes third-generation French-speaking Creole slave population was added new arrivals from not only West but also Central Africa. During the Spanish period both the overall number of slaves grew as well as the number of slaves held by any one family. On the older plantations, the slave population often included a proportionally large number of Creole slaves with a balanced ratio of men to women and strong slave families. But on many of the newer, larger, commercial plantations, those heavily involved in growing indigo and tobacco, the slave populations often had a disproportionally larger number of men, many of these recent arrivals from Africa. Some plantations had significant numbers of slaves from one or two ethnic groups. Many of these associated with other members of their tribe.[30]

In some ways, the slaves fared better under the Spanish than the French. Spanish law allowed a master to manumit his slave without obtaining prior government approval. This is what the Frenchman Claude Thomas Pierre Metoyer, a resident at the Natchitoches Post, did when he freed Marie Thérèse Coincoin and several of their children. If slaves believed they were being treated cruelly, they could petition the government to be sold to a different master. A case in point was Jeanne, a fifty-year-old woman in 1782 owned by Pierre Derbanne of the Natchitoches Post. In 1782 Jeanne and several other slaves complained to the post commandant, accusing Derbanne of punishing them for no reason, of not providing the required rations, of forcing the slaves to work on Sunday and other religious holidays, as well as other offences. The commandant met with Derbanne and admonished him to treat the slaves as required by law and told the slaves to return to their master. Eventually Jeanne fled to the commandant and demanded that she be sold to another master. Slaves could own property and buy their own freedom, and a system existed to ascertain the fair market value of the slave. If the owner didn't want to sell the slave, the slave or someone working on the slave's behalf could bring the matter before the local officials. Once the officials had established the value of the slave and the price had been paid, the slave was freed. At the Natchitoches post, Françoise, a slave belonging to Marie Poissot, was able to attain her freedom in 1784 through this method. By the 1790s there was a small but growing number of free people of color in Louisiana. In urban areas many of the freemen of color worked as artisans, and in rural areas some managed to obtain property, engage in agriculture, and in time buy slaves of their own.[31]

The 1790s were a turbulent time for the Louisiana colony. In the 1780s many larger planters had purchased slaves on credit, expecting to pay off their debts with future indigo and tobacco crops. But in 1789 the tobacco market became glutted and, in 1790, Spain greatly restricted the amount of tobacco it would accept. Louisiana planters marketed their indigo to France through the French West Indies. The outbreak of the French Revolution in 1789 and the war between France and Spain beginning in 1793 had a crippling effect on Louisiana's indigo exports. With no market for their crops, the planters could not pay their debts. Many planters faced financial ruin.[32]

At the same time, a larger multiracial abolitionist movement swept across the Caribbean in part as an outcome of the French Revolution. Slaves in St. Domingue revolted in August 1791, resulting in the eventual abolition of slavery in Haiti. News of this successful upraising undoubtedly reached Louisiana's slave population along with knowledge that France had abolished slavery in its colonies and had given full citizenship to those of African descent. Many whites and Blacks carefully watched the developing war between France and Spain. If France won and took back her former Louisiana colony, the slaves would be free, and the slave owners would lose the greatest portion of their wealth. Rumors flew through the quarters that the slaves in Louisiana had already been freed and that the masters were refusing to acknowledge this fact.[33]

The planters always feared slave uprisings. There had been unsuccessful attempts in the past. In April 1795, the Spanish learned of a major plot by slaves from several plantations along with several whites in Pointe Coupee (west of Baton Rouge) to kill the planters on the plantations in an attempt to overthrow slavery. The conspirators planned to set fire to one of the buildings on the plantation of Julien Poydras and, when the planters from the neighboring estates came to help put out the blaze, they would be killed. The slaves would seize the guns and ammunition from the plantation storehouse and systematically slaughter the remaining planters and any Creole slaves who refused to participate in the revolt. In the end the Pointe Coupee revolt failed. Several Tunica Indian women who lived on the Poydras plantation alerted the whites to the plot and the conspirators were arrested. The whites hanged twenty-three of the slaves and, in a hope of deterring other slaves, cut off the heads of the slaves and nailed the severed heads to posts displayed at several places along the Mississippi River. They flogged another thirty-one slaves and sentenced them to hard labor outside of Louisiana and deported three white men, with two of them sentenced to six years of hard labor in Havana. Although unsuccessful, the conspiracy sent waves of terror throughout Louisiana. As one Spanish official noted, if the conspiracy had gone undiscovered, "the fire would have gone from plantation to plantation throughout the length of the Province, and the settlers would not have had the time to assemble for their respective defense because all the plantations are spread out and distant from each other." The few whites at a plantation would have been unable to defend themselves against twenty, fifty or a hundred slaves.[34]

The conspiracy had long-term effects on both the white and the Black populations in Louisiana. Where before there had been a certain openness and the Black and white populations lived in semi-egalitarian status on the insecure frontier, after the conspiracy the white populations became increasingly fearful. The white planters believed that slaves were only waiting for an opportunity to slaughter all the whites except for the young white women, whom they would use in other ways. As one historian has noted, this fear "became the cornerstone of ideology justifying racist violence and oppression of Afro-Louisianans and of whites who opposed slavery and racism. . . . it was only fear instilled by racist terror that ensured the survival of the white race and protected white womanhood from a fate worse than death."[35]

By the time of the Louisiana Purchase, the Louisiana slave population consisted of French-speaking Creole slaves who had been born in the Louisiana colony, many of whom had been baptized in the Catholic Church and a number of whom were of mixed African, French, Spanish and/or Native American ancestry. To these the Spanish had added more recently arrived slaves from different African tribes and nations who still spoke their Native languages, continued a number of their own cultural practices, and congregated with members of their own groups. With the Americans came English-speaking slaves from the Eastern Seaboard of the United States.

Whites, slaves, and free people of color were not the only residents in Louisiana. For over twelve thousand years various Native American groups had called Louisiana, including the Red River Valley and the surrounding uplands, home. In the 1500s large Caddo Indian villages and civic and ceremonial centers clustered in the valleys of the Red, Arkansas, Ouachita, and Little rivers with smaller settlements scattered along rivers in East Texas, western Arkansas, southeastern Oklahoma, and northwestern Louisiana. Some estimates place the total population of this cultural group, the ancestors of what became known as the Caddo Nation, as high as 250,000.[36]

By the 1600s the Caddo were experiencing dramatic population decline. Smallpox, measles, plague, diphtheria, whooping cough, and influenza, diseases brought to the New World by the Europeans and to which the Native populations had no natural immunities, had swept across the entire continent. Only between 8,000 and 40,000 Caddoan people remained. With the catastrophic population decline came a corresponding collapse of century-old cultural tradition such as the building of elaborate ceremonial centers.[37]

When the French arrived at the beginning of the eighteenth century, the Caddo were organized into three loose confederacies. The smallest was the Natchitoches Confederacy, made up of three or more tribes including the Natchitoches and later the Yatasi. They lived near the settlement of Natchitoches and extended up the Red River to the vicinity of present-day Shreveport and numbered fewer than 2,000. The Kadohadacho Confederacy, which numbered about 2,500, included the Kadohadacho and several other tribes. In the early to mid-1700s they were settled along the big bend of the Red River in present-day Arkansas and Texas. The Hasinai, third and largest confederacy, numbering between 4,000 and 5,000, including among others the Hainai, Nacogdoche, Nabedache, and Anadarko tribes, was centered along the Neches and Angelina drainages in East Texas. Two smaller groups, the Ais and the Adai, lived in the area between the Natchitoches and Hasinai confederacies.[38]

The Caddo, primarily agriculturalists, grew corn, beans, and squash in fields around their farmsteads, which stretched intermittently along the rivers and streams. The men hunted deer and other game and, in the winters, traveled out onto the plains in pursuit of buffalo. The Caddo were also traders. Some of the groups held annual trade fairs where peoples from the Great Plains would exchange goods that they acquired from the pueblos to the southwest for products of the southeast such as corn and beans and bois d'arc, a wood prized for the making of bows. Soon they would be exchanging deerskins, bear oil, buffalo robes, and other products of the forest and plains with Europeans for guns, metalware, blankets, cloth, and other goods.[39]

The French visited the Red River and the Caddo in 1700 and established a trading post among the Natchitoches Indians in 1713. When the Spanish learned of the French presence on the Red River, they quickly built a string of missions in East Texas and two forts, one along the Neches River and the other fort along with a mission, which became known as Los Adaes, just twelve miles west of the new French settlement in Natchitoches. Thus the Caddo tribes found themselves on the border between two superpowers. Both the Spanish and the French actively courted the allegiance of the Caddoan tribes through gift-giving and trade. For years the Caddo played one side off against the other to the Caddo's advantage.[40]

When France transferred Louisiana to Spain, the fate of the Caddo changed. The Spanish were not as forthcoming with trade goods, items on which the Caddo had come to rely. No longer sitting on an international border, the Caddo's importance to Spain declined. Also, the Osage pushed southward and preyed on the Caddo villages with raiding parties stealing deerskins and horses to sell in St. Louis. The Kadohadacho led punitive attacks against the Osage and asked the Spanish government for help. But the Spanish seemed unwilling or unable to stem these attacks. In 1788 the Kadohadacho abandoned their villages and moved down the Red River to be closer to other Caddo tribes. Repeated waves of smallpox and other diseases, the depredation afflicted by the Osage, and the lack of support from the Spanish radically and tragically affected the tribe.

By 1805, the Kadohadacho, called the Caddo by the Americans, had a village, made up of about 100 warriors and maybe 500 to 600 people, located about 120 miles north of Natchitoches on Sodo Creek about thirty-five miles west of the Red River on the Louisiana-Texas border. Here the people grew corn, beans, pumpkins, and raised horses. John Sibley, the first Indian agent in the area, noted that the Caddo warriors were "looked upon somewhat like Knights of Malta, or some distinguished military order. They are brave, despise danger or death, and boast that they have never shed white men's blood."[41]

The Yatasi, another Caddoan tribe, lived about fifty miles above Natchitoches, about halfway to the Caddo. The French established a trading post among the Yatasi, and over the years French families settled in the surrounding area (the Bayou Pierre settlement). The Yatasi cultivated corn, beans, pumpkins, and tobacco on a large prairie and raised horses, cattle, hogs, and poultry. By 1805 disease had greatly reduced their number to only 8 men and about 25 women, but people from other tribes had settled in the area and intermarried with the Yatasi and the community had about 40 men with a total population of about 160.[42]

Below the Yatasi on Lac Macdon lived the Adai. Traditionally the Adai roamed all the way to the Sabine. During the first three-quarters of the eighteenth century the Spanish maintained a mission for the Adai, and the priests made a concerted but largely unsuccessful effort to convert them to the Roman Catholic faith. The Spanish located this mission and an associated Spanish fort just twelve miles west of Natchitoches, and for over forty-five years it served as the capital of the Spanish Province of Texas, known as Los Adaes. The Adai spoke a distinctive language but could also converse in Caddo and most of them in French. In 1805 the tribe had about 20 men but more women.[43]

When the French first established their trading post at Natchitoches in 1713, they chose the location of the old Natchitoches Indian village. Over time the Natchitoches moved their village and, by 1805, they were living about twenty-five miles above the old French post. As Sibley noted, "The French inhabitants have great respect for this nation, and a number of very decent families have a mixture of their blood in them," but the Natchitoches were "gradually wasting away; the small pox has been their great destroyer; they still preserve their Indian dress and habits." The area experienced a smallpox epidemic in 1800, followed by a measles epidemic in 1803 which effected the Louisiana tribes as well as those in East Texas.[44]

Remnants of the once large and powerful Hasinai Confederacy of the Caddo Nation, still recognizable in 1805, were located west of Natchitoches in Texas. The Nadaco lived on the Sabine River, west of the Caddo. They had recently experienced the smallpox epidemic, and their village contained about 200, including 30 to 40 warriors. The Hainai, Nabedaches, and Nacogdoches still maintained villages along the Angelina and Neches rivers in East Texas. All three tribes had about 150 members each. The Hainai and the Nabedaches had between 50 and 75 warriors total, with the Nacogdoches having about 40.[45]

Not all the tribes in Louisiana in the early nineteenth century had been long-term residents. The Biloxi, Apalachee, Pascagoula, and Chacato moved to the area in the mid-1760s. The Apalachee and Chacato originally lived in northern Florida and in the seventeenth century became early converts to Christianity due to the effort of Spanish friars. After the War of Spanish Succession (French and Indian War), these tribes left what had become British territory to resettle in the French colony near Mobile. When the British obtained control of Mobile in 1763, following the end of the Seven Years' War, the Spanish invited these tribes as well as the Biloxi and Pascagoula from the coastal areas of present-day Mississippi to move to what had become Spanish Louisiana. The Spanish hoped these groups would form part of a barrier to protect the Spanish colony from the aggressively westward-spreading English. By the time of the Louisiana Purchase, all four tribes had villages along the lower Red River. The Biloxi first settled near the Avoyelles prairie, downriver from the rapids at present-day Alexandria, but by 1806 had a village near Rapides Bayou. The Chacato lived along Red River near

Bayou Boeuf, about ten miles below the rapids. Men from both of these tribes often worked as boatmen. The Apalachee had their village about twenty-three miles above the rapids and the Pascagoula upriver from them near present-day Colfax. By 1806 some of the Pascagoula and Natchitoches had a village on the east side of the Red River north of Natchitoches. Members of these tribes spoke French and/or Spanish as well as their own languages, and several spoke Mobilian, the *lingua franca* or trade language of the tribes east of the Mississippi. All four tribes were primarily farmers, having adopted to some extent European agricultural practices, and were growing corn and vegetables in the rich alluvial soils along the Red River and raising cattle, horses, and poultry. Sibley described the Biloxi as an "honest, harmless, and friendly people" and noted that the Apalachee were "highly esteemed by the French inhabitants."[46]

The Spanish also encouraged other tribes to relocate in Louisiana, including the Alabama, Coushatta, and Pacana, all tribes of the Upper Creek, one of the large divisions of the Creek Confederacy, which by the eighteenth century covered large portions of Alabama and Georgia. All three tribes had been located in the Upper Creek area of northeast and central Alabama. When the British gained control of the area around their towns in 1763, the Alabama began to migrate out of the area. The Spanish invited them to resettle along the east bank of the Mississippi between Baton Rouge and New Orleans, again to protect Louisiana from the inroads of the English. Eventually the English pushed all the tribes across the Mississippi and the Alabama resettled in the Opelousas District and above Bayou Rapides on the Red River. The Coushatta remained in their ancestral homes on the Alabama River until they too resettled above Bayou Rapides in 1793. By 1800 a number of the Coushatta under the leadership of Red Shoe had moved their village to the Sabine River about eighty miles southwest of Natchitoches. Pia Mingo, leading a party of 450 Coushatta from the Mississippi Territory, established a village near Red Shoe in 1804. Other Coushatta moved into Texas and lived along the Trinity and Neches rivers. A group of Alabama and Coushatta asked the Caddo for permission to locate a village on Caddo lands and, in 1804, the Coushatta chief Echean settled his people about twenty miles above the Great Raft on the east bank of Red River. The third Creek group, the Pacanas, occupied an area along the Calcasieu River. All three groups spoke Creek and Mobilian, and some of the Alabama also spoke French as well, and some of the Coushatta could converse in English. The Coushatta-Alabama numbered about 600, with about 150 of them warriors.[47]

The Spanish also urged the Choctaw from Mississippi to cross the Mississippi River to occupy the vacant lands in what is now northern and central Louisiana. In this case the aim was two-fold: again to provide a barrier against the English and to split the Choctaw Nation into smaller units, thereby diminishing the power and size of the tribe as an outpost of British influence. Parties of Choctaws began to routinely cross the Mississippi for their winter hunts, killing deer and other game for the fur trade. Here they impinged on the traditional hunting grounds of the Caddo, creating considerable frictions between the two groups and problems for the Spanish commandants. Eventually a number of these bands settled in Louisiana and, by 1803, at least 1,500 Choctaw had made Louisiana their permanent home, with two villages near Fort Miro (present-day Monroe) and two other villages south of the Red River, with a total of about 80 warriors between them. Other Choctaws continued to come in the winter to hunt.[48]

As the white settlers encroached on tribal lands east of the Mississippi, clashes between settlers and Indians increased. With the purchase of Louisiana by the United States, President Jefferson saw the expanse of "vacant" land of Louisiana as a place to remove all the tribes east of the Mississippi to the west side of the river. The U.S. government immediately began targeting the Cherokee, Creek, Chickasaw, and Choctaw, all tribes in what was now the southeastern United States, to exchange their lands and move west. The Indian nations, not always willing to abandon their ancestral homes, successfully blocked the government's efforts to remove them, at least for a time. Governmental programs, however, and increasing pressure from white settlers forced many small bands to relocate, and increasing numbers of Shawnee, Delaware, Cherokee, and Chickasaw began to arrive in Louisiana.[49] Many of these groups would come to Natchitoches to trade.

In 1804, it is estimated that as many as 5,000 Indians lived in the Orleans territory. Although relatively small in number, the tribes had considerable importance on the Louisiana-Texas frontier. The Americans needed the support or at least the neutrality of these Native peoples during their boundary dispute with Spain. Both Spain and the United States went to great lengths to forge alliances with the tribes. Most of the tribes would choose neutrality, accepting gifts and traders from both sides.[50]

2

FORT CLAIBORNE AND THE MILITARY ON THE FRONTIER

> Citizens of Natchitoches, henceforth you are under the jurisdiction of the United States. Its flag this day waves in your district and affords a shield for the protection of your persons and property and, while it secures your rights, it demands of you respect and fidelity. . . . his excellency, the governor-general has been pleased to appoint me civil commandant, with full authority to exercise the functions of that office over the district, and as I shall in all my proceedings be invariably guided by justice. I flatter myself my conduct will meet your unanimous approbation.
>
> —CAPTAIN EDWARD D. TURNER, address to the residents of Natchitoches upon its transfer to American control, April 26, 1804

Toward the end of April 1804, Captain Edward D. Turner with soldiers of the Second Infantry Regiment and artillerists arrived in Natchitoches. Undoubtedly, the arrival of the American force created quite a stir. The flotilla of boats had passed numerous farms and plantations, and news of the Americans' pending appearance undoubtedly spread rapidly. Unquestionably, the Spanish post commandant Felix Trudeau would have been there to meet the Americans upon their landing. It is easy to imagine the merchants and traders with their families, town slaves, and visiting Indians lining the riverbank to watch the soldiers disembark and then set up camp. The insignificant Spanish force of seven or eight men readily yielded the area to the Americans. How welcoming the local French and Spanish people were is uncertain, but it is likely that Americans living in the area were pleased to see the United States' troops. The American military force was to have a commanding presence in the area for the next fifteen years.

Fort Claiborne

As soon as Captain Turner reached Natchitoches, he began scouting for an appropriate site for a fort. At first, he evaluated the Grand Ecore area. A fort on the bluff overlooking the Red River would furnish a strong defensive position and a good place for depositing supplies. But there were three main roads in the area (see map 1). The Grand Ecore road crossed the Red River at a break in the bluffs and led south to Natchitoches. The second road, the old Camino Real, intersected the Grand Ecore Road about a half-mile north of Natchitoches (in the area of current-day Texas Street) and led north of Lac Terre Noire (part of which is the current Sibley Lake), crossed the Arroyo Hondo, and continued in a southwesterly direction toward the site of the old abandoned Spanish presidio at Los Adaes and eventually to the Spanish settlement at Nacogdoches and beyond. The third major road, the St. Maurice Road, started on the left or east bank of the Red River (current Cane River Lake) across from Natchitoches and went east a short distance before bending southward to run parallel to the river as far south as Alexis Cloutier's plantation (south of present-day Cloutierville). Turner reasoned that any attack by the Spanish would probably come from the west via the Camino Real; therefore, the fort needed to be between that road and the town of Natchitoches.[1]

After reconnoitering the area, Turner selected a small knoll about three hundred yards west of the river on the northwest side of the village of Natchitoches and adjacent to the road leading north through the woods toward the Camino Real and Grand Ecore. With cannon mounted on a platform at the northern end of the hill, Turner could cover the approaches to the fort from the north along the Grand Ecore Road, from the west from the Camino Real, and the river crossing from the St. Maurice Road. This would be the site of Fort Claiborne, named after the territorial governor William C. C. Claiborne.[2]

Turner had assumed that this hill on which he chose to build the fort was public land, but on July 6, 1804, Pierre Joseph Maes informed Turner that he was building the fort on land that the Maes family had owned for over thirty years. Maes presented a bill of sale for the land as proof of his ownership. Since Maes did not have a deed that was recognized by U.S. governmental authorities, Turner did not accept this as adequate proof. Turner believed that it was public land and as such available for the construction of the fort. Unable to settle his claim with the government, Maes sold the rights to some of his land to John Nancarrow, a recently arrived American. Nancarrow attempted to charge the government rent for the use of this property.[3]

This was not the only evidence of friction between the newly arrived American commander and the French Creole residents. Turner seemed to have little respect for the French Creole population. In a letter to Governor Claiborne several months after his arrival in Natchitoches, Turner described the residents as "ignorant almost to Stupidity, and never having known any other government than that by which the Spaniards governed them, they look upon a different one, as a sort of Hocus-Pocus, tending to worst their condition." He went on to say that once the inhabitants came to understand the new government that they would be "better pleased than they have formerly been," but Turner believed this would take a very long time.[4] Nine months later, Turner reported to Claiborne: "At present every thing is tranquil here, and in fact I flatter myself that except by a few people of wealth who are here, there never has been any demonstration shown, but these gentlemen I believe sincerely wish the American Government to the Devil."[5] He, however, was suspicious. In May 1805 he expressed his concerns to the governor about one of the Prudhommes, a member of an old and prominent Creole family (fig. 1).

> Mr. Prudhomme's party I suspect are secretly working to injure the government. They have lately had a meeting glossed with the pretense that it was to devise means to induce the Cure to continue with them who on Easter Sunday gave out to the astonishment of his congregation that he was about to leave the parish, but who I believe in truth, had no such ideas and was only scheming to get the people together—at the meeting I am informed he kept the ostensible in sight, but deviated much in substance after reading an exordium which accused the people of being led away by the Americans, they professed to discountenance all persons settling within the district, but true Romans [Catholics].[6]

The curé in question was Father Pierre Pavie, who had served Natchitoches since his arrival in 1795. He would leave Natchitoches in 1806.[7] C. C. Robin, a Frenchman who traveled through Louisiana in 1803–5, had a negative opinion of many of the American commandants appointed to various posts in Louisiana. "These American commandants: young, ignorant drunkards; not knowing

Fig. 1. Emanuel Prudhomme, a prominent Creole planter and member of the extended Prudhomme family, 1819. Courtesy of National Park Service, Cane River Creole National Historic Park, CARA 22695.

a word of French, or having the least notion of the customs of the people they were governing; often had resident in their districts, venerable heads of families who were former French and Spanish military officers. The haughtiest conqueror never treated the vanquished with less consideration."[8]

Captain Turner had set his soldiers to work clearing the hill of pine trees for the fort. Turner's men first constructed a redoubt for the artillery on the hill and then cut and trimmed timbers and began digging foundations for the buildings and the fort walls. By the second week of June, some of the interior buildings and at least one warehouse had been completed and work had begun on the fifteen-foot palisade that was to enclose the fort.[9]

The army modified the buildings at Fort Claiborne over time, but the basic palisaded area covered about one acre, with additional buildings outside the

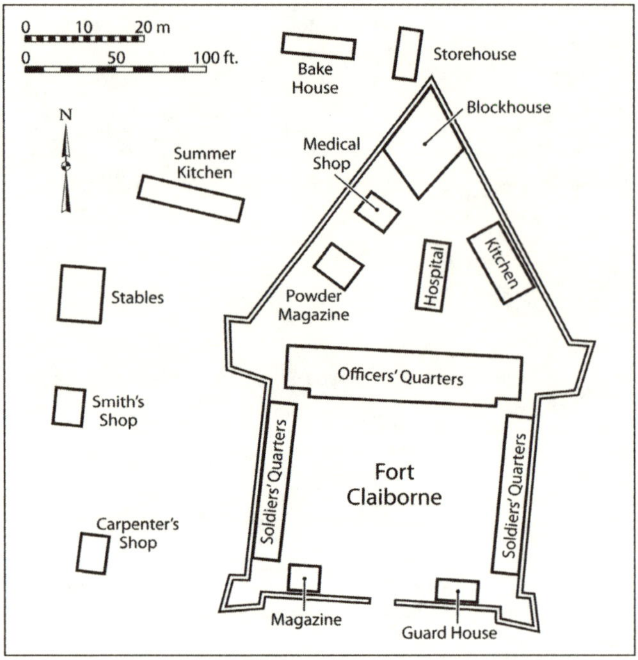

Map 2. Fort Claiborne. Based on Smith, ed., *Military Heritage,* 90.

stockade to the west and north. Turner reported to General James A. Wilkinson, commander in chief of the U.S. Army in the Mississippi Valley, that he took more care in the building of the fort than he generally would, because he believed that the buildings could be converted into warehouses when the garrison moved westward with the frontier. The main block of the fort was rectangular, with a triangular service area extending to the north behind the officers' quarters.[10] The main gate of the fort faced south. Originally, an additional gate existed on the west side of the fort's palisade, but by 1814 barracks extended the length of the west wall. On each side of the center parade grounds were the barracks for the enlisted men with the officers' quarters to the north facing the south gate (map 2). The enlisted men's barracks placed up against the palisade wall measured 18 by 92 feet and consisted of five rooms. The officers' quarters measured 36 by 116 feet with three rooms on each side of a hall and both a front and a back gallery. A 14-by-14-foot magazine stood on the west side of the main gate with the 14-by-20-foot guardhouse on the east side. In the service area behind the officers' quarters stood the powder magazine, medical shop or dispensary, hospital, and kitchen (see table 1 for a list of the ordnances at the fort). At the northernmost tip of the triangle stood a two-story blockhouse. In addition to the blockhouse, bastions existed on both ends of the south wall and on each side of the palisade walls by the officers' quarters. Outside the palisaded area at various times were storehouses, a bakehouse, summer kitchen, stables, corncrib, a harness and blacksmith's shop, and a carpenter's shop. The fort had a garden for fresh vegetables north of the fort and pens for cattle and corrals for horses outside the palisade. After September 22, 1804, the fort had a cemetery.[11]

Table 1. Ordnances at Fort Claiborne

Brass cannons		*Small arms and accoutrements*	
4 pounders	2	Muskets, complete	138
3 pounders	2	Muskets, damaged but repairable	15
		Cartouch boxes	100
Howitzers		Cartouch boxes & belts	100
24 pounder	1		
Carriage	1	*Munitions*	
		Cannon balls for 4 pounder	921
Equipment		Shells for 24 pounder	192
Rammers and sponges	4	Strapped shot for 3 pounder	202
Worms and ladles	2	Case shot for 3 pounder	169
Portfire stocks	12	Musket flints	6,850
Linstocks	3	Pounds of cannon powder	1,238
Gunners' belts	1	Pounds of musket powder	800
Gunners' haversacks	4	Musket cartridges	52,700
Powder horns	2	Pounds pig lead	650
Budge barrels	3		
Bricules	14		
Drag ropes	14		
Sets of harness for 2 horses	4		

Note: Statement of the number of cannon, arms, equipment, and munitions from the latest returns on file with the Department of War for the period January 1, 1816 to December 31, 1824 (*American State Papers, Military Affairs* 2: 487–94).

Gathering Storm

Almost from the day of transfer, the United States and Spain jockeyed for position on the frontier. The French by the Louisiana Purchase Treaty had sold Louisiana "with all its rights and appurtenances as fully and in the same manner as they have been acquired by the French Republic in virtue of the treaty of San Ildefonso."[12] The problem was that neither the San Ildefonso Treaty nor the Louisiana Purchase Treaty actually identified the boundaries of the land that made up the Louisiana Purchase. When the French government sold Louisiana to the Americans, it made no attempt to clarify the limits. In fact, some believed that the French kept the boundaries purposely vague in the hope of creating tension between the United States and Spain. If this was their intent, they succeeded.

Some, such as Thomas Jefferson, believed, or claimed to believe, that the Rio Grande was the rightful western boundary of the purchase, while others thought it was the Sabine River. The Louisiana-Texas border question was part of a larger issue that included the boundary between the United States and Spanish Florida. There were few maps of the Louisiana-Texas border area at the time, and knowledge of the area was almost unavailable to people in Washington. The Spanish were somewhat better informed. The French and Spanish on the frontier had recognized the Arroyo Hondo (also known as the Bayou de Lauriers or Bayou del Laurel and today appears as an insignificant creek call Rio Hondo) as the border between the two nations. During French colonial times the settlement at Bayou Pierre, which appeared in the Spanish records as Bayupier, was also recognized as under the jurisdiction of Spain. The Spanish argued that the Arroyo Hondo, about five miles west of Natchitoches, was the border of the Louisiana Purchase, but the United States was intent on acquiring as much territory as possible. While American and Spanish officials negotiated to settle the boundary question, those on the frontier attempted to deal with the problems associated with the ill-defined border and conflicting claims.[13]

From the start, the Americans thought the Spanish were spreading rumors and discontent among the residents to create friction between the newly arrived Americans and the long-term inhabitants of the Natchitoches area. This might have been true but, less than a year earlier, the inhabitants of Natchitoches were Spanish subjects and had been for over forty years. Captain Turner, the first American civil and military commandant at Natchitoches, reported to his superiors that the Spanish referred to the Americans as "mere Hogs" who "do not live like Christians" and who planned to keep the Louisiana planters poor by instituting "immense Taxes."[14] Turner also thought the Spanish were spying on the Americans. In this he was probably correct. Some Spanish dragoons had visited Natchitoches allegedly seeking medical treatment, and a Spanish officer had arrived in town to buy supplies. In both cases, the Spaniards left without accomplishing their tasks. Turner suspected the Spanish had come to assess the strength of the American force and evaluate the terrain around the post for a possible attack. Rumors circulated in the community that two hundred Spanish reinforcements had reached Nacogdoches and that the Spanish planned to send between two hundred and five hundred men to the area of the long-abandoned Spanish fort at Los Adaes, about twelve miles west of Natchitoches. This could be a jumping-off point for an invasion.[15]

And, indeed, the Spanish did attempt to make things difficult for both the Americans and those Louisianans who had business dealings in East Texas, especially Nacogdoches. Within days of the arrival of the American military, Captain José Joaquin de Ugarte, the commandant at Nacogdoches, met with Turner concerning travel across the frontier. Ugarte explained that rumors of a group of Americans, who had recently entered Spanish territory, resulted in 150 soldiers being sent to try to locate them. Searching for this group caused the Spanish great expense. Ugarte proposed that no individual should cross the frontier without written permission. At first Turner replied that "Americans were always free to go where they pleased . . . and that free ingress and regress was allowed to all Foreigners who thought proper to visit" the United States.[16] After consulting with Governor Claiborne, however, Turner agreed to the passports. In time Ugarte restricted travel to only those with "debts to discharge." Turner reported that the Spanish searched all those going to Nacogdoches, and all letters found were opened and "perused with an expectation of finding them big with treason, stratagems, and crimes."[17] The Spanish also instituted a new rule that forbade any American who was not a Roman Catholic from settling in Texas and required all Roman Catholic Americans to locate west of Nacogdoches, even those who had been living in the area east of the Spanish town for years. In the summer of 1805, the Spanish at Bayou Pierre stopped an American on his way to trade with the Caddo and confiscated his goods. The Spanish maintained that Bayou Pierre was part of their territory while the Americans claimed it as theirs.[18] On August 1, 1804,

Turner wrote General James Wilkinson, stating, "Our neighbors keep up that sort of conduct toward us, which a state of war alone would justify."[19]

Escape to Freedom

Those in Natchitoches also believed the Spanish were inciting rebellion among the enslaved population. In July 1804, John B. T. Palliet, a Natchitoches planter returning from Nacogdoches, reported to Captain Turner at Fort Claiborne that he had seen a royal decree in the commandant's office in Nacogdoches instructing the Spanish to use every means possible to weaken American control on the frontier.[20] The decree offered "a free and friendly asylum . . . in the Dominions of His Catholic Majesty, to such slave or slaves as shall escape from the territories of any foreign power."[21] The Spanish were encouraging slaves to flee and rewarding them with their freedom. This had not been such a problem before the coming of the Americans, when Natchitoches was still part of Spain.

News of this decree spread rapidly throughout the Natchitoches community, both frightening and enraging the white population, especially the planters. Many of the principal planters and all the syndics (justices of the peace) assembled and drafted a petition to present to Turner. People from as far away as forty miles came to sign it. The petition, dated July 29, 1804, listed the planters' concerns. The planters, most of whom were Creoles of French descent, stated that "our properties [the slaves] . . . and our personal security will be threatened with the most eminent dangers, if that decree be not suppressed in favour of the inhabitants of Louisiana." The planters claimed that the information about the decree "is now spread throughout all classes of men, so far as to produce the most dangerous sensation among our slaves. Its dreadful effects may be propagated through the whole province, & thus annihilate the prosperity of Louisiana, & soon make it a land of desolation." The petitioners wanted Turner to institute a program to carefully watch the slaves and to send their petition to the governor so that he could "restore our tranquility & secure our properties."[22] Turner set up night patrols of the militia to police the banks of the river to ensure that the enslaved population remained on their plantations, and he forwarded the petition to Governor Claiborne.[23] When Claiborne received the document, he endorsed the patrols and presented the matter to the Marquis de Casa Calvo, the

Spanish boundary official then in New Orleans. At first, Casa Calvo denied the allegations, but when Claiborne presented him with the wording of the decree, Casa Calvo doubted that the commandant at Nacogdoches had the authority to enforce such a decree and suggested that there must be some mistake. He acknowledged that such a decree had been put in place during the recent war between Spain and France but that it did not apply to the current situation. The commandant at Nacogdoches wrote Casa Calvo, saying he had not promulgated the decree but people knew about it.[24]

Then in October 1804, slaves from the plantations of the French Creoles Ambrose LeComte, Louis Derbanne, and Emanuel Derbanne attempted to flee to Nacogdoches and win their freedom. Several Spaniards had come among the slaves and told them that, if they reached Nacogdoches, they would be free. On October 14 at dusk, the slaves made their escape. As planned, they broke into a house and stole guns and munitions and also horses. Rather than going into the woods, which was the common choice for fleeing slaves, they took the main road to Nacogdoches and headed for Texas. They had used whistles as a signal for the escape but, unfortunately for the escapees, a patrol heard the signal and gave chase, firing on the fleeing people. One of the men who had escaped gave himself up the next day and informed on the others. Thirty people were implicated in the plot. Twenty men pursued the remaining escapees, apprehending three slaves who had turned back to see why others were not following and chasing the others as far as the Sabine River, arriving there the day after the fugitives had crossed. Nine slaves had reached Texas. Turner reported to the governor the escape of the slaves, the Spanish policy of freeing the slaves, and that the planters of Natchitoches were so enraged that "almost to a man" they were willing to go to Nacogdoches and "lay it in waste." The planters believed that, if something was not done, they would "not have a Slave left in three months." The planters wanted the U.S. government to take action.[25]

When Governor Claiborne learned of the event, he contacted Casa Calvo about the problem. Casa Calvo told Claiborne that he had sent a report of the incident to the King of Spain to learn his wishes concerning the royal decree. In the interim, Casa Calvo directed that any slave in Spanish territory be returned to his owner "under pledge not to injure his person."[26] But Casa Calvo blamed the people in Natchitoches for the runaways. He stated that it was obvious. The frequent commerce between Natchitoches and Nacogdoches resulted in people learning about the decree. If, however, the Natchitoches inhabitants had kept this information to themselves, the slaves would not have learned about it. Therefore, it was the planters' own fault if their slaves escaped. Alexis Cloutier along with five members of the militia and three others traveled to Nacogdoches and with the help of the commandant and Spanish soldiers retrieved eight slaves, including six men, one woman, and a two-year-old child.[27]

Turner returned the slaves who had been involved in the plot but had not attempted to flee to their plantations. Those who had escaped to Nacogdoches were deemed "dangerous persons of established bad fame; and" it was proclaimed "that their liberation would give alarm to the good Citizens." These were to be held over for trial. Undoubtedly, this was not in the best interest of the planters, who would lose their labor if the slaves were imprisoned. Sibley wrote to the governor about the outcome of this event. He explained that those in Natchitoches considered the slaves involved in the escape to be among the most valuable in the district. He claimed that the slaves "appeared much chagrined and very penitent for what they had done and uniformly said they never should have thought of it, if they had not been badly advised by free people that their only wish was to obtain freedom which every body said was a sweet thing." Sibley stated that the slaves were restored to their owners, who, Sibley pointed out, were the only people damaged by the escaped slaves. But "in order to satisfy the Public mind . . . each of them [the slaves were] tied down, with their faces to the ground, their legs and arms extended by bonds fastened to stakes drove down for the purpose to the utmost stretched, their posteriors exposed which with whips made of raw hide . . . every stroke of the whip bringing off pieces of skin and flesh. . . . it was done on the Public square."[28] Some people in the area apparently felt the slaves should be imprisoned but, when a public meeting was called to discuss this matter, only four individuals expressed any concern, according to Sibley.[29]

For a time, tranquility was restored, but it was short-lived. In April 1805, Turner learned that the Spanish commandant at Nacogdoches, who had returned the slaves, had been arrested for doing so and the new commandant was ordered to enforce the royal decree concerning slaves escaping to Texas. The planters of the Natchitoches District were once again alarmed about the security of their "property," and their "property" did flee.[30] This further added to the tension between the Spanish and the Americans.

Military Buildup on the Frontier

By October 1804, Turner's meager force had been augmented and the garrison stood at seventy-two with Turner as commander and an ensign, three sergeants, three corporals, fifty-four privates, four musicians (probably two drummers and two fifers) of the infantry, and for the artillery detachment a sergeant and seven privates. Considering the mounting tension on the frontier and the movement of Spanish troops into the area, Turner was no doubt relieved when Captain Wollstonecraft with his artillery company and Captain Francis Johnston and his infantry unit arrived. Major Moses Porter assumed command at Fort Claiborne in late 1805. With a crisis involving the Spanish over the Louisiana-Spanish border threatening, General James Wilkinson, commander in chief of the U.S. Army in the Mississippi Valley, dispatched Colonel Thomas H. Cushing and two companies of infantry from St. Louis and one company of infantry from Fort Adams to Natchitoches. The military presence in Natchitoches was growing.[31]

In the fall of 1805, the ongoing negotiations to settle the boundary question stalled, and the Spanish began moving troops into East Texas to strengthen their position. Manuel Antonio Cordero y Bustamante was the acting governor of Texas. Captain Zebulon M. Pike during his captivity in Santa Fe in 1807 met Antonio Cordero, was impressed with the man, and provides a description. According to Pike, Cordero was "fifty years of age, about five feet ten inches in height, fair complexion, and blue eyes. . . . in every part of his dress was eligibly written "the soldier." . . . He was universally beloved and respected. . . . He spoke the Latin and French languages well, was generous, gallant, brave, and sincerely attached to his King and country."[32] Cordero ordered the reestablishment of posts and reinstitution of patrols east of the Sabine. He sent a detachment of one corporal and nine men to Bayou Pierre and an officer and twenty men to the Murphy, Barr, Davenport, and Smith trading-company ranch called La Nana located along the Natchitoches-Nacogdoches Road east of the Sabine River.[33]

In November, the secretary of war wrote Major Porter, by then commanding officer at Natchitoches, directing him to request assurance from the Spanish commander at Nacogdoches that there would be no more activities by Spanish troops on the east side of the Sabine River. Porter was to guard the area and arrest anyone who entered the region without authorization and patrol around Bayou Pierre, which the United States claimed, but not to enter the Bayou Pierre settlement.[34]

Late in December 1805, Cordero ordered the La Nana detachment to reconnoiter the area between La Nana and the Arroyo Hondo and to establish a camp between the site of the old presidio at Los Adaes and the Arroyo Hondo. The Americans viewed this as an act of aggression. Porter demanded that Captain Sebastián Rodríguez, who was now the Spanish commander at Nacogdoches, recall all Spanish troops on the east side of the Sabine River immediately and asserted that the Spanish would not be allowed to established posts or patrol in the area. The Spanish commandant refused, replying that he would maintain his posts and continue his patrols. He also sent a letter to Governor Cordero at San Antonio. Rodríguez clearly viewed the American actions as a serious threat and issued a proclamation in Nacogdoches professing that the United States was attempting to seize territory that belonged to Spain, that the action of the United States was an act of war, and urged the settlers to prepare for an invasion.[35]

When Porter received Rodríguez's response, he ordered Captain Turner and sixty men from Fort Claiborne to remove the Spanish from the area east of the Sabine. Turner and his troops marched to the Spanish outpost, arriving at 11:30 the morning of February 5. The Spanish patrol had spotted the advancing American infantry. The Spanish cavalry halted the Americans at Bayou le Glese and demanded the reason for the presences of the Americans in Spanish territory. Turner asserted that he wanted to speak with the Spanish commanding officer and sent Lieutenant John DuForest, the interpreter, to arrange the meeting. When the officer did not return, Turner sent another messenger and then formed his battle line and marched to within forty yards of the camp. When the officer finally appeared, Turner demanded that the Spanish withdraw from their current position to the west side of the Sabine River. The Spanish officer Captain Joseph Maria Gonzalez consented to abandon his current position but to go only as far as San Juan Creek. After a great deal of arguing, the Spanish finally agreed to recross the Sabine but requested five days to do so due to the poor conditions of the horses and the fact that several were lost. Turner insisted that they leave. The next day, as Turner proceeded to La Nana as part of his patrolling efforts, he came upon the Spanish just three miles from their previous day's location. The Spanish used the same excuse, the poor conditions of the horses, to explain their slow progress. Turner, not trusting the Spanish, required Gonzalez to sign an agreement which stated that he would be across the Sabine within five or at the most six days. While retreating, Gonzalez reported to Rodríguez that he had been confronted by 150 American soldiers with two cannons, a much-inflated figure, and due to his much smaller force of only 18 men, of whom 5 were without arms, had been forced to retreat.[36]

When the Spanish governor Cordero heard of the American advance, he wrote Rodríguez to prepare to attack the Americans if they marched west of the Arroyo Hondo. Cordero planned to travel to Nacogdoches to take charge and sent 70 men as reinforcements. He then wrote Nemesio Salcedo, commandant general for the Interior Provinces, in Chihuahua, reporting the incident and his instructions to Rodríguez. However, Salcedo did not want to force the issue. He blamed the governor's actions of moving the La Nana post eastward to Los Adaes for the American hostilities and suggested the creation of a neutral ground for the contested territory. He did tell Cordero to inform the commandant at Natchitoches that Spain would not allow the establishment of any American posts between the Sabine and the Arroyo Hondo. By March 12, 1806, the area had reverted to the status quo. The Americans had returned to Fort Claiborne, and the Spanish had no other troops east of the Sabine except for those at Bayou Pierre and La Nana. Neither side had given up their claims, and both the Spanish and the Americans began to build up their forces in the area.[37]

Commandant General Salcedo informed Governor Cordero that he was sending two detachments of militia of 300 men each to the frontier. He assigned Colonel Simón Herrera, a well-respected, first-rate military officer and the governor of Nuevo León, to command the forces. Zebulon Pike, who met Herrera in 1807, described him as "about five feet eleven inches high, has a sparkling black eye, dark complexion and hair. He was born in the Canary Islands, served in the infantry in France, Spain, and Flanders, and speaks the French language well, and a little of the English. He is engaging in his conversation with his equals; polite and obliging to his inferiors, and in all his actions one of the most gallant and accomplished men I ever knew. . . . He had been in the United States during the presidency of General Washington, and had been introduced to that hero, of whom he spoke in terms of exalted veneration."[38] Salcedo directed Herrera "to preserve intact the dominions of the king by repelling and pursuing as far as the boundary line any American troops which may cross Arroyo Hondo."[39] In March 1806, there were only 801 Spanish troops in Texas. By the second week of June, the Spanish had over 1,000 men in Texas. By August, Herrera was at Bayou Pierre.[40]

The United States had not remained idle and was also moving troops into the area. The secretary of war ordered General James Wilkinson, then stationed in St. Louis, to the Orleans Territory to assume command of the troops and prevent any invasion of U.S. territory east of the Sabine or north or west of West Florida. In the event of such an invasion, Wilkinson was to meet force with force.[41] In early May 1806, Wilkinson directed Colonel Thomas H. Cushing of the Second Regiment Infantry to hasten to Natchitoches and take command. With Cushing went three companies of infantry, two companies from St. Louis and one from Fort Adams, two field pieces, and necessary supplies. If Cushing found upon arrival at Fort Adams that the Spanish had "assumed a menacing aspect at Nacogdoches," he was to add to his command all the troops at Fort Adams. Wilkinson ordered Cushing to ready the garrison at Natchitoches for an offensive operation and warned Cushing, "The sword must not . . . be drawn but in the last extremity, to punish outrage, to resist invasion, or repel an attack." The sometimes bombastic general added: "if a conflict must ensue, having previously animated your men by a strong exhortation, and sworn your officers in their presence to fall or conquer, make your onset with the bayonet; and your own glory, the honor of our arms, and the interest of the nation will be insured and maintained."[42] On May 19, two barges and a pirogue of the Freeman-Custis expedition reached Natchitoches.

The Freeman-Custis Expedition

President Jefferson had planned to explore Louisiana even before the Purchase. He wanted to find a route to the Pacific Ocean, and Meriwether Lewis had already begun preparations for the historic Lewis and Clark expedition. With the Louisiana Purchase, Jefferson proposed additional explorations, including ones of the Red, Ouachita, and Arkansas rivers. Jefferson dubbed the planned Red River effort "The Great Excursion." Its stated purpose was to acquire scientific knowledge of the Red River area, but the United States was also looking for a route to the Pacific Ocean and, at the time, the few maps available to the Americans suggested that the Red River had its headwaters in the western mountains. In addition, the United States wanted to gain influence over the tribal peoples on the southern frontier. Congress appropriated five thousand dollars for this endeavor. Thomas Freeman, a surveyor, would be responsible for compiling the data to map the Red River's course, and Peter Custis, a medical student and the naturalist for the expedition, would collect information on the natural history of the region, including information on the Native American groups. Captain Richard Sparks was to be in command of the effort with Lieutenant Humphreys; two noncommissioned officers, seventeen privates, and a Black servant accompanied the expedition. After a series of slow and costly delays, Freeman's party entered the mouth of the Red River, finally reaching Natchitoches on May 19, 1806.[43]

The expedition remained in Natchitoches until June 2. During this time, Freeman acquired from John Sibley, the Indian agent, and Thomas Linnard, the factor at the trading house, additional trade goods and gifts for the Indians. Sibley and Linnard also recommended guides and interpreters. Lucas Talapoon, a man fluent in the Red River Caddoan languages as well as Plains Indian sign language, and François Grappe, known as "Touline," who had grown up among the Caddo where his father, Alexis Grappe, acted as trader, joined the expedition as guides and interpreters. Freeman also acquired additional supplies and three American flags to present to important Indian leaders. The secretary of war had directed Colonel Cushing to provide a detachment of twenty soldiers from Fort Claiborne under the command of Lieutenant John Joseph DuForest to accompany the expedition. DuForest was to serve as Spanish interpreter if the need arose. When the expedition left Natchitoches on June 2, it consisted of seven boats and a military escort of forty men, four noncommissioned, and three commissioned officers. On the same day, a Spanish secret agent in Natchitoches sent a dispatch to Nacogdoches alerting the Spanish of the expedition's departure.[44]

Above Natchitoches the expedition faced the Great Raft. The Freeman-Custis expedition would have to work its way through this colossal series of logjams and tangled webs of tree trunks and brush. Navigating the Red River was always difficult but particularly during low water and, due to a dry spring and the expedition's late start, the men found the river level already falling. Bayou Pierre, an old channel of the Red River that hugged the west side of the valley, provided a detour around most of the Great Raft but, due to the Spanish presence at the Bayou Pierre settlement, the Freeman-Custis expedition chose to navigate the almost impregnable east side of the valley through its bayous, swamps, and interconnected lakes.[45] This was a much more difficult route, and people in Natchitoches openly mocked the idea that the expedition could navigate the raft by going up that way. And indeed, the explorers did find the route exceedingly challenging. As Freeman describes in his journal: "Next morning we came to the second raft, which crosses the river here 100 feet in width, and extends for 200 yards along its course. This raft rises nearly three feet above the water, and is covered with bushes and weeds: the trees . . . lie so close that the men could walk over it in any direction. With great exertions we opened a passage for the boats, through this raft on one side, by floating the large trees down the river.[46]

Above the second raft, Talapoon reached the expedition, having traveled overland by horseback, and brought news that Spanish troops had left Nacogdoches, intent on intercepting the Americans when they reached Spanish territory. Sibley, who arrived a short time later, provided additional information. Warned, the party continued upstream, pushing its torturous way through what was known by the Indians as the Great Swamp. Here the expedition became lost for several days. Finally, two weeks later, Freeman was able to write in his journal that, after "incessant fatigue, toil and danger, doubt and uncertainty, we at length gained the river above the Great Raft, contrary to the decided opinion of every person who had any knowledge of the difficulties we had to encounter."[47]

Continuing upstream toward the Coushatta village, the expedition encountered Talapoon and another man in a canoe coming to meet them. Talapoon had been sent with a request for Dehahuit, the great Caddo chief, to meet the expedition at the Coushatta village. The other man had a message for Touline informing him that about three hundred Spanish dragoons camped a few miles from the main Caddo village. He reported that a Spanish officer had met with Dehahuit. Touline sent the man back to the Caddo village, which was some thirty miles away, with a request that the chief meet the Americans at the Coushatta village. At sunset on June 26, the American expedition reached the Coushatta village, situated on a thirty-foot bluff on the east side of the river. The Americans camped about a quarter-mile below the settlement. Here they awaited the arrival of the Caddo chief.[48]

Echean, the Coushatta chief, had been given a flag by the Spanish. He willingly exchanged it for an American one, which he hoisted on a pole located in the middle of the village. At about noon on June 31 the great chief Dehahuit with forty young men and warriors appeared on the opposite bank of the river. The Caddo announced their arrival by firing their guns. The Coushatta sent all their canoes to the opposite bank to bring the Caddo to the east side of the river while the Caddo horses swam across. The Americans drew up in a single file to officially receive the Caddo. After settling their horses at an area at the upper end of the village, the Caddo men made their way down to the American camp, where the soldiers fired a salute in the chief's honor. Dehahuit remarked to Echean that "he never had been so respectfully received by any people before."[49]

Dehahuit and the expedition leaders sat in the shade with the young men and warriors of the Caddo Nation arranged in a semicircle behind them. Touline acted as interpreter. After a moment, Dehahuit commented on the difficulty that the Americans must have experienced passing through the Great Swamp with their boats and expressed amazement at their success. Freeman explained that they had "suffered much, but were not to be deterred by obstacles of that nature" from paying a visit to Dehahuit and the other chiefs and tribes on Red River. Freeman then explained the wishes of the president of the United States and the American people with respect to the Indians. He further delineated the route that the expedition proposed to take and the distance they planned to travel.[50]

As reported by Custis, Dehahuit told the Americans that the Caddo had been well treated by the French, and then by the Spanish, and now that they were under the Americans, Dehahuit hoped the Americans would treat them as well as the others had. He was pleased that the Americans had informed him of their plans, which was something the Spanish had not done. The Spanish had camped near the Caddo village and, in a meeting with Dehahuit, the Spanish commander demanded to know whether the Caddo "loved the Americans." Dehahuit reported that he had told the Spaniard he did but inquired whether it was proper for the Spaniard to ask such a question. Apparently insulted by the query, Dehahuit told the Spanish that he would not answer any more questions, no matter how trivial. He expressed his concern that the Spanish planned to attack the American expedition and stated that "it had been a law among his ancestors not to suffer the blood of whites ever to be spilt on their ground" and added that none would be "on his ground, rivers, lakes, or bayeaux; that if the Spaniards were desirous to fight he had not the least objection, provided that they would fight on their own land." Dehahuit then explained that he was sorry his village was too far away for the Americans to visit or he would invite the Americans to come "& though he could not take us to large, elegant & well furnished houses and treat us as well as we did him yet he could take us to a cool shade & make us welcome to such as he had."[51]

After the conference, the Americans distributed some provisions and liquor so that the soldiers and the young men of the tribe could drink together. The soldiers then formed a single line and the Caddo men went down the line shaking hands with each of the soldiers. The Caddos formed a line facing the soldiers, and the principal warrior standing opposite an army sergeant stepped forward and stated to the other Indians that "he was glad to see his new brothers had the faces of men, and looked like men and warriors." Addressing the sergeant through the interpreter he added, "here we are, all men and warriors, shaking hands together, let us hold fast, and be friends for ever."[52] The Caddo chief dined with the Americans and spent the day at the camp. The following morning, Dehahuit and his men left. The Freeman-Custis expedition remained in the Coushatta village until July 11, when they resumed their journey up the river. With them went three Caddo men to act as guides and spies.[53]

Meanwhile the Spanish, aware of the progress of the expedition, made ready to intercept it. In mid-July, Colonel Simón de Herrera and the Baron de Bastrop with a considerable force arrived in Nacogdoches. Herrera continued into East Texas to rendezvous with Juan Ignacio Ramón's force at the Caddo village and then with four hundred men headed for the Bayou Pierre settlement, while Bastrop traveled to Natchitoches to meet with Colonel Cushing to assess the Americans' intentions. At the same time, the Spanish governor Cordero was making plans to go to the Louisiana border.[54]

On July 26, three Caddo sent by Dehahuit overtook the Freeman-Custis expedition. The Caddos reported that between 1050 and 1060 Spaniards had entered their village, cut down the pole with the American flag, and taken the flag with them. The Spaniards had insulted the chief and boasted that they were going after the American expedition and, if the Americans did not turn back, would either kill them or carry them off in irons as prisoners. Freeman explained that he had orders to continue up the Red River until he was stopped by a superior force. The Caddo men estimated that Freeman's party would reach the Spanish position in three days. Dehahuit had directed the runners to accompany the Freeman expedition and, if there was a confrontation, to report back to him. The Americans continued up the river, passing one of the former Caddo villages and the location of La Poste des Cadodoquious, the old French trading post, both long abandoned.[55]

Freeman sent two men forward to reconnoiter and, on the morning of July 29, they returned, reporting that they had been fired upon. The expedition stopped and prepared their guns and equipment. Continuing upstream, they approached a Spanish picket of about twenty-two men who upon seeing the boats retreated into the woods. Advancing further, the boats rounded a bend and entered a stretch of river about a mile long. Here the shallow stream meandered back and forth through sandy beaches between two thirty-foot-high banks about two hundred yards apart. Canebrakes and heavy timber covered the banks of the river. The Americans spotted a Spanish sentry about a mile up the beach, and the Spanish encampment could be clearly seen on the bluff overlooking the river.[56]

After another half-mile, the Americans stopped at their usual time for dinner. They beached their boats and quickly built their fires and prepared their meal. Spanish horsemen could be seen galloping around the next bend of the river and returning. About a half-hour after the Americans had landed, a large party led by 4 Spanish officers rode along the far beach toward the Americans. When the Spanish prepared to cross the river, most of the American soldiers scaled the bank and positioned themselves in the brush above the beach. From this location, the soldiers could "give the enemy a severe reception." When the Spanish splashed across the river at a full gallop, the advance American sentry of a sergeant and 4 soldiers, positioned one hundred yards from the boats, commanded the Spaniards to halt. When the Spanish showed no evidence of slowing down, the soldiers again demanded that the Spanish halt, cocked their guns, and prepared to fire. The Spanish horsemen, about 150 in number, paused on the beach about 150 yards from the sentry. Thirty-seven foot soldiers could be seen across the river, and the 22 soldiers that the expedition had passed earlier positioned themselves about half a mile below. The Americans were outnumbered by at least four to one. Four Spanish officers, Captain Don Francisco Viana, Captain Bernard d'Ortolan, Lieutenant Juan Ignacio Ramón, and a fourth officer, probably Lieutenant Don José Flores, slowly advanced. They were met by Captain Sparks, Thomas Freeman, Lieutenant Humphry, Dr. Custis, the interpreter John DuForest, a Black servant, and the five-man sentry.[57]

Captain Viana, the Spanish commanding officer, stated he had orders to stop, by force if necessary, any armed troops or exploration party from passing through Spanish territory. Freeman responded that he was under orders from the president of the United States to explore the Red River to its source. Finally, after a conference lasting almost forty-five minutes, Viana asked if the Americans would return downriver and when. Because of his orders to avoid a confrontation with the Spanish, Freeman answered that he would remain at his current location for the remainder of the day and would start his return downriver the following morning. The Spanish had stopped the Americans. The Freeman-Custis expedition had ascended the Red River about 615 miles. On July 30, the expedition began its return trip, arriving at the Coushatta village on August 8. There they built a small building, left the boats, some of their supplies, and a small detachment of soldiers, and then using horses they traveled overland along the "Quechata Path," skirting the Great Swamp. Freeman reached Natchitoches on August 23, with the rest of the party arriving a short time later.[58]

Climax

By August 5, the Spanish force of about four hundred men camped on the Bayou Pierre Road about forty-five miles northwest of Natchitoches. They expected to arrive within twelve miles of Natchitoches in three days. A large body of Spanish regulars had allegedly passed the Trinity River and planned to join the other troops.[59]

An extremely anxious Colonel Cushing sent Major Porter to Colonel Herrera, the Spanish commandant, with a strongly worded letter. Cushing demanded to know why the Spanish had crossed the Sabine River and insisted that their troops withdraw immediately. He explained that the recent increase in the number of American troops in the area was to secure the American territory, which extended to the Sabine River and should not be viewed as a hostile move against Spain. But Cushing warned that, if the Spanish "should attempt to continue these [Spanish] troops within the territory of the United States . . . it will be my duty to consider you as an invader of our territory, and to act accordingly."[60]

Herrera in his response to Cushing acknowledged receipt of Cushing's letter and admitted he had crossed the Sabine with a detachment of troops. But he stated that his purpose was to protect the territory "as belonging, from time immemorial, to the King, and which is a dependence of the province of Texas."

He added that "I cannot permit, without violating my duty, any usurpation upon the land he [the king] possesses."[61]

On August 8, 1806, a very worried Edward Turner, now judge of Natchitoches County, sent an express message to Governor Claiborne alerting him to the deteriorating conditions on the frontier, reporting that the local militia had not been organized, and urging the governor to hasten to Natchitoches.[62] Having received Turner's letter, Claiborne traveled first to Fort Adams, where he expected to meet General Wilkinson and Cowles Meade, the acting governor of the Mississippi Territory, to discuss the defense of the Orleans Territory should the Spanish attack. Wilkinson had not yet arrived, so Claiborne proceeded to Natchez to await the general. Learning of the developing situation on the frontier, however, he hurried up the Red River, reaching Natchitoches on August 24.

By the time Claiborne arrived, the Spanish had returned to the Bayou Pierre area. But the situation was tense. Estimates placed the size of the Spanish force at over one thousand men, most of whom were cavalry with Spanish reinforcements expected daily. Wilkinson had directed Cushing not to take any action until he arrived. Claiborne had intended, if requested by Wilkinson, to call up the local militia.[63] He found the Americans who had settled in the area willing to serve in its defense, but as he reported to the secretary of war, "The same degree of patriotism does not exist among the French part of our society; many of the ancient Louisianans are still attached to the Spanish Government, and others are so fully impressed with an opinion that the United States are unable to resist "the mighty power of Spain," that in the event of War they would probably be disposed to take a neutral Stand, as the safest course."[64] This should not have surprised Claiborne since Natchitoches had been part of Spain for most of the previous forty years. People in Natchitoches had commercial ties to those in Nacogdoches and San Antonio, and Spain was not their enemy.

On August 26, Claiborne had written a strongly worded letter to Herrera, forcefully objecting to recent activities by the Spanish. He complained of the outrages committed by the Spanish troops when they turned back the Freemen-Custis expedition on the Red River and when they cut down the flagpole with the American flag that had flown in the Caddo Indian village. He stated that the Caddo had been under the protection of the French and, with the transfer of Louisiana to the United States, were now under the protection of the Americans.

He listed another "outrage," the seizure of three Americans within twelve miles of Natchitoches who had been sent as prisoners to Nacogdoches. Claiborne also brought up the issue of fugitive slaves who escaped to Spanish territory, where they were receiving protection. Claiborne acknowledged that Herrera was awaiting a ruling on this matter from the governor of Texas; otherwise Claiborne would have pressed for their immediate return to their owners. Claiborne also reminded Herrera of the ongoing negotiations concerning the boundary and concluded by stating that, "if the officers of Spain should persist in their acts of aggression . . . and if the sword must be drawn, let those be responsible, whose unfriendly conduct has rendered it indispensable"—meaning the Spanish.[65]

Two days later, Claiborne received Herrera's reply. Brief and to the point, Herrera declared that the Freeman expedition had been on a part of the Red River that had never belonged to the French; that the Caddo Nation was on land belonging to Spain; and that the three Americans were found twice spying on the Spanish and, when questioned, said that they wished to settle in San Antonio and, therefore, Herrera had sent them to the governor there under guard for their own protection. Herrera concluded by stating that his troops would not commit any hostilities that would affect the boundary negotiations but added that, if "I should be provoked to do so, I will endeavor to preserve the honor of his Majesty's troops and to fulfill the duties which are incumbent on my character and that of the officers under my command.[66]

By September 4, General Wilkinson still had not arrived. Reports placed eleven companies of 110 men each at Bayou Pierre, 300 regular troops at Nacogdoches, and unconfirmed, and possible unreliable, report of two regiments of regular troops expected in Texas shortly. Most of the Spanish troops consisted of militia cavalry. Claiborne had done what he could to prepare the settlement for a possible attack by the Spanish. The governor met with Dehahuit and 12 to 15 of his warriors. Claiborne wanted to convince the Caddo to remain neutral in any conflict between the Americans and the Spanish.[67]

Claiborne returning downriver toward New Orleans met Wilkinson coming up the Red River. Wilkinson stated, "I will observe that my orders are imperative, I shall insist on the Jurisdiction of the United States Westward to the Sabine River, and if the Spanish Commander resists this claim hostility must inevitably ensue."[68] Finally, on September 22, General Wilkinson reached Natchitoches to take charge of military operations on the frontier. After reconnoitering the area,

Wilkinson believed he could not only drive the Spanish across the Sabine but also take Nacogdoches. All he needed were gun carriages, vehicles, and animals before he could advance.[69] John Sibley was enthusiastic about Wilkinson's arrival. As he wrote his son, "Genl. Wilkinson arrived here last Sunday & is making every preparation to attack them [the Spanish] in their camp, he has now here nine companies of infantry & two artillery of the U.S. what cavalry can be raised in this part of the territory & I expect from Natchez—this territory there will be in the course of ten days from 800 to 1000 militia." Governor Claiborne gave Sibley command of the militia cavalry that he could raise locally. Sibley planned to join Wilkinson in two days. As Sibley wrote

> We shall drive the Spaniards (if we can) over the Sabine again. . . . Whether this will bring on a general war or not is uncertain, but the probability is that it will. . . . The territory they have lately taken possession of is beyond all doubt part of the country the United States have purchased & paid for, & we ought to defend it or perish in the attempt. I am highly gratified at the disposition & sentiments of General Wilkinson on the subject since his arrival here, they so exactly accord with my own views.[70]

Sibley claimed that he had received little support in his views until General Wilkinson arrived. This is not surprising. Arroyo Hondo, just a few miles west of Natchitoches, had been the international boundary between Spain and France and was known as such by the longtime residents of the area. The Bayou Pierre community, although it had commercial ties with Natchitoches, was always recognized as Spanish territory. The Americans were involved in a land grab.

General James A. Wilkinson

James A. Wilkinson (fig. 2) was born on March 24, 1757, into the colonial Maryland plantation class. His father died young, leaving the family ill provided; the relatively small plantation on which they lived was divided and most of it sold. Wilkinson trained for a time as a doctor but, when the Revolutionary War began, he quickly joined the Continental Army. He served under Benedict Arnold in the ill-fated invasion of Canada in the summer of 1776, was with George

Fig. 2. General James Wilkinson, by Charles Wilson Peale, from life, 1796–97. Courtesy of Independence National Historic Park.

Washington on that freezing winter night in 1776 when the Continental Army crossed the Delaware for its December 26 attack on the Hessians at Trenton, and was chief of staff to Horatio Gates during the American defeat of the British at Saratoga in the fall of 1777. Many considered Wilkinson a rising star in the army, and he quickly moved up through the ranks, but in 1781 he resigned. In the fall of 1778, Wilkinson married into an old, established, politically connected Philadelphia family and he and his wife purchased a large estate in Pennsylvania, mainly on credit. By 1782, the Wilkinsons, heavily in debt, were forced to sell the property. The next year, Wilkinson headed west across the Appalachians as part of the first wave of Kentucky pioneers. With his limited funds, he speculated heavily in land and opened a store in Lexington, and within three years he was one of the leading men in Kentucky and again heavily in debt.[71]

The logical outlet for the products of Kentucky was shipping down the Mississippi River to the port of New Orleans. Unfortunately, the Mississippi and New Orleans were under Spanish control. Many westerners felt the U.S. government, made up of men from the Atlantic seaboard, was more concerned with trade across the Atlantic than with western interests. Some felt that the West should secede from the United States and form a new country with ties to the Spanish to the west and south.

Wilkinson saw an opportunity in this movement. In 1787, with a flatboat full of cargo, Wilkinson traveled down the Mississippi to New Orleans. There he attempted to sell his freight to local merchants and negotiate with the Spanish governor. After several meetings, the Spanish granted Wilkinson a monopoly to trade through New Orleans in exchange for using his influence to encourage the Kentuckians to secede from the United States. Wilkinson swore allegiance to Spain and agreed to keep the Spanish well-informed concerning this separatist movement. Wilkinson developed an elaborate cipher system to communicate with the Spanish, and he became known to the Spanish as Agent 13. The Spanish agreed to pay him a "pension" of two thousand dollars a year for his services. Nothing came of this movement, known as the Spanish Conspiracy, but Wilkinson continued to provide information, and rumors began to circulate about his involvement with the Spanish.[72]

Wilkinson rejoined the army in 1791 and was second in command under General Anthony Wayne during the Northwest Indian War in the Ohio Valley (1785–94). When Wayne died, President Washington appointed Wilkinson to succeed him. President Jefferson selected General Wilkinson as the military commissioner to officiate at the transfer of Louisiana from France to the United States, which occurred in New Orleans in December 1803. Two months later, Wilkinson in his role as Agent 13 met with the Spanish officials in New Orleans. There Wilkinson pointed out that some fifteen years earlier he had been promised two thousand dollars annually for his services as Agent 13 but for the last ten years had received nothing. He asked for twenty thousand dollars, his back pay, and an increase of this annual pension to four thousand pesos, equivalent to his pay in the U.S. Army.[73]

Wilkinson also provided some "reflections" concerning the strategies the Spanish could adopt to arrest the waves of westward-moving Americans. He suggested that the Spanish exchange Florida for the American lands west of the

Mississippi River and that, pending the exchange, the Spanish should heavily fortify the Texas and Florida frontier. He alerted them of the Lewis and Clark expedition, shortly to leave St. Louis for its trip up the Missouri River, and recommended that the Spanish turn the expedition back. He warned that the Spanish should prevent any exploration of the Red or Arkansas rivers. Recognizing that, as commander in chief of the U.S. Army in the Mississippi Valley, Wilkinson was in a unique position to assist them, the Spanish paid Wilkinson twelve thousand dollars of his back pay. His pension increase was not approved. Wilkinson was once again being paid by the Spanish. After Congress divided Louisiana, President Jefferson appointed Wilkinson governor of the Louisiana District, which included all of the Louisiana Purchase north of the Thirty-Third Parallel, the current border between the states of Louisiana and Arkansas.[74]

In his role as a commanding general of the U.S. Army, Wilkinson was responsible for defending the United States' claims to land to the Sabine River and to act against the Spanish if they invaded the area. As an agent in the pay of the Spanish government, he was to protect Spanish interests and claims and provide information on American movements and intent—an interesting conundrum.

Two days after his arrival in Natchitoches, Wilkinson wrote the Spanish governor. Wilkinson contended that, regardless of whether a line of demarcation had ever been established between Louisiana and Texas, such a line was necessary for the "administration of justice, the security of property, and the prevention of hostile collisions." While stating that the United States had claim to more land, it had "adopted the Sabine river as the most obvious, most convenient, most natural, and least exceptionable, temporary boundary." Wilkinson explained that he had been commanded by the president of the United States to deliver a message: the Spanish were not to occupy any new posts east of the Sabine. If they did, it would be considered an "actual invasion" of the United States and would "be resisted accordingly." Wilkinson concluded by stating "that my orders are absolute, and my determination fixed, to assert, and, under God, to sustain the jurisdiction of the United States to the Sabine River against any force which may be opposed to me." He closed with "Retire then, sir, I conjure you, the troops of your command from the ground in controversy, and spare the effusion of human blood, without prejudicing your own honor, or the substantial interest of His Majesty your Royal master."[75] The Spanish governor simply replied that he was forwarding Wilkinson's letter to the commanding general. By this time the

Spanish had already moved their forces west of the Sabine, but they continued to claim the Arroyo Hondo as the international boundary. There were now over twelve hundred men, soldiers and militia, congregated around Natchitoches, ready to go to war against Spain. One can only imagine the impact that twelve hundred men had on the formerly sleepy community of Natchitoches.[76]

On October 4, Wilkinson wrote the Spanish governor, informing him that he was going to move the American troops to the Sabine River but that this was only to demonstrate the United States' claim to the lands east of the Sabine and should not be viewed as a hostile act. Colonel Herrera was concerned. As he explained to the Spanish governor, the Americans had three detachments of troops marching toward the Sabine. He emphasized how easy it was for the American forces to be resupplied by river to Natchitoches and the difficulty for the Spanish to receive reinforcements and supplies overland from San Antonio. He also pointed out the poor condition of his cavalry horses.[77] Salcedo had instructed Cordero not to engage the Americans without "absolute and positive certainty of being able to dislodge them."[78]

Then, on October 8, Samuel Swartwout arrived at Fort Claiborne with a coded letter for Wilkinson from Aaron Burr dated July 29, 1806, containing his latest conspiratorial plans. One might question why Aaron Burr would relay his plans to Wilkinson, but in fact Wilkinson had been a key player in organizing the venture. In the letter, Burr stated that he had obtained funds for his expedition and was promised the cooperation of a British and an American naval fleet. He intended to leave Philadelphia on August 1; travel down the Ohio River gathering men, supplies, and boats for the venture on the way; and arrive at Natchez by the middle of December to meet with General Wilkinson to finalize arrangements. What were Burr's plans? This is unclear. Some have suggested that Burr meant to pry the western states from the Union. Others contended that he intended to liberate all the Spanish provinces, including Texas. Still others believed that he would use the disruption along the Sabine River as an excuse to invade Mexico.[79]

For Wilkinson, in addition to his conflicting positions as commander in chief of the U.S. Army and agent in the pay of the Spanish, he was now worried about being exposed as a player in Burr's conspiracy. Wilkinson needed to get to New Orleans before Burr and hopefully capture him. On October 21, 1806, Wilkinson revealed Burr's plans to President Jefferson, thereby betraying his former associate.[80] On November 4, Wilkinson notified the secretary of war of his intent to negotiate a speedy agreement with the Spanish over the disputed border since he and his troops were needed in New Orleans, "where a deceitful calm at the present prevails." Wilkinson in typical melodramatic and self-serving terms wrote Claiborne: "You are surrounded by danger of which you dream not and the destruction of the American union is seriously menaced. . . . The Storm will probably burst on New Orleans, when I shall meet it & triumph or perish."[81]

Before he left Natchitoches for the Sabine, Wilkinson wrote the secretary of war that he planned to suggest to the Spanish that both parties move their troops to the area occupied when the territory was transferred to the United States, thereby creating a neutral ground between the two countries. This was something the Spanish commandant general for the Spanish Interior Provinces, Nemesio Salcedo, had suggested eight months earlier. Finally, on October 23, Wilkinson started his march to the Sabine River, arriving on October 31, and made camp across the river from the Spanish forces. About twelve hundred American troops faced about the same number of Spanish troops across the Sabine River.[82]

And then—it was over. The formerly bellicose Wilkinson became a peacemaker. On November 4, he wrote Governor Cordero that the letter Wilkinson had received from the governor had convinced him that no hostility existed on the part of Spain against the United States. Wilkinson wrote that, "After having fulfilled my orders for the assertion of the jurisdiction claimed by said States, it is my duty to show by an act no less unmistakable the spirit of reciprocal friendship of my government for the one which Your Excellency has the honor to serve."[83] This after months of mounting tension on the frontier. Wilkinson went on to explain that he planned to withdraw his troops back to Natchitoches within two days. He stated that he believed the Spanish troops would remain on the west side of the Sabine River until the Spanish and American governments completed the boundary negotiations.

Wilkinson also sent a copy of the letter to Herrera. Cordero opposed the agreement, but Herrera on his own approved it. As Herrera explained to the governor, the troops under his command were in a deplorable state and the cavalry horses would be unable to spend the winter in the area. Herrera decided that the agreement was a "timely and honorable opportunity to withdraw."[84] He sent Don Francisco Viana to the American camp to discuss the terms, and Colonel Cushing arrived at the Spanish camp the morning of November 5 and told Herrera that Wilkinson had left for Natchitoches at 5:00 a.m. and the American troops would return to Natchitoches the next morning. The Americans would fire a cannon notifying the Spanish of their departure.[85]

There is no surviving copy of a formal agreement, but Herrera summarized its contents in a letter to Governor Cordero: "We agreed that their troops are not to cross Arroyo Hondo, and ours are not to cross that [Sabine] river, but that settlers from both nations will be free to travel from one to the other provided they have the required passport."[86] In the end, the Spanish governor attempted to take credit for the resolution of the conflict. He presented it as a good solution for the Spanish, stating that, after deducting the men who acted as sentries and those guarding the horses, he had only about three hundred men available for any conflict. He claimed that the American army numbered two thousand veteran infantry, four thousand militiamen, and forty artillery pieces—an exaggeration.[87]

Wilkinson proclaimed that he had saved the country from war with Spain. He also contended that with the boundary question settled he and his troops could rush to the defense of New Orleans against the expected attack from a group of individuals led by Aaron Burr.[88] Wilkinson's temporary settlement of the boundary issue with the speedy negotiation of what became known as the Neutral Ground Agreement ended for a time the crisis on the frontier. More importantly, at least from Wilkinson's perspective, it freed him to hurry to New Orleans; whether to protect the city from the Burr conspirators or to ensure that his name was not associated with the movement, or both is up to interpretation. In the end the Burr conspiracy fizzled. Burr had been able to assemble only about eighty men for his enterprise, and he was captured near Natchez, Mississippi Territory. Burr was eventually tried for treason but found not guilty.[89] When Wilkinson was asked during the Burr conspiracy trial, "Was there any sum of money agreed to be paid on either side?" referring to the agreement creating the Neutral Ground, Wilkinson answered truthfully with an emphatic "Not one cent."[90] This apparently was true. However, on November 17, just twelve days after leaving Natchitoches, Wilkinson sent Walter Burling overland to Mexico City with a letter to the viceroy in which Wilkinson wrote:

> Although ignorant of what the United States might wish me to do, it was to withstand this revolutionary tempest [the Burr Conspiracy] that I recalled my troops so suddenly from the Sabine river to New Orleans. On my own responsibility and by my own private means I have taken and shall continue to take such measures as will enable me to check the commotion that threatens destruction to the realm of Mexico. . . . In order to ward off these calamities, from which sight and mind recoil in horror, I will hurl myself like a Leonidas into the breach, defending it or perishing in the attempt. . . . So far as I am concerned I am risking my life, my good name, and my property by the means I have adopted: my life by the change I have made in the military arrangements without the knowledge of my government, my good name by offering without orders this communication to a foreign power; and my fortune or possessions by draining my private purse and those of my friends in order to elude, frustrate, and, if possible, destroy the nefarious schemes of the revolutionists.[91]

He claimed that he had spent 121,000 pesos to protect Spain's interests, which he trusted would be reimbursed. The viceroy replied, thanking Wilkinson for his "interest in preserving the dominion of the king of Spain" but added that the information Wilkinson provided he had already learned from reading the newspapers. The viceroy went on to state that he had no authority to reimburse Wilkinson without an order from the king.[92]

Eventually Wilkinson faced several official inquiries and a court-martial with being a Spanish spy one of the charges made against him, but at the time the wily general was able to deflect all accusations. He wrote a multivolume memoir defending his reputation and patriotism. Wilkinson went on to participate in the unsuccessful attempt to invade Canada during the War of 1812, to purchase a plantation in Louisiana in 1817 which proved less profitable than he had hoped, and in 1822 to move to Mexico City. In 1823, he relocated to a less expensive area outside Mexico City, where he died in 1825 at the age of sixty-eight.[93]

Meanwhile the Wilkinson-Herrera agreement did not return things to normal on the frontier. Rather it created a no-man's-land, unpoliced by either the Spanish or the Americans, which became a haven for outlaws, runaway slaves, and filibusters. The people of both Natchitoches and Nacogdoches had to deal with the problems associated with this area, known as the Neutral Ground.

When General Wilkinson and Lieutenant Colonel Simón Herrera temporarily resolved the border issue, Fort Claiborne's garrison returned to one company of infantry and fifteen artillerists under the command of Captain Elijah Strong. Over the next few years, the size of the garrison fluctuated. The garrison increased to one company of infantry and three companies of artillerists or about two hundred men commanded by Lieutenant Colonel Constant Freeman in June 1807. In 1808, the garrison stood at eighty-nine men and remained at about that level through March 1815. In the summer of 1815, Major General Andrew Jackson, commander of the Division of the South, sent two companies of a rifle regiment to Natchitoches, and a year later two companies of the Eighth Infantry replaced the rifle companies.[94]

Military Life

During its existence, Fort Claiborne had a commanding presence in Natchitoches. Not only did the fifteen-foot-high stockade atop the hill on the north end of town loom over the settlement but also the influx of American soldiers, officers, military wives, and auxiliary personnel changed the ethnic makeup of the town. Two groups of men guarded the frontier: the military officers and the common soldiers. The officers formed an elite set. Most of the early officers had fought in the American Revolution and, after the establishment of the U.S. Military Academy at West Point in 1802, many of the younger officers trained there.[95] The army life, however, did not attract the more able and ambitious men to the ranks. Many of the men who enlisted became disillusioned when they learned that, rather than the adventure they had expected, they spent much of their time building forts and roads, raising crops, and doing other physical labor, a necessary component of the survival of the military on the frontier. One soldier stationed at a frontier post left behind his views on the soldier's life:

> I am deceived; I enlisted for a soldier; I enlisted because I preferred military duty to hard work: I never was given to understand that the *implements of agriculture and the mechanic's tools* were to be placed in my hands *before I had received a musket or drawn a uniform coat.* I never was told that I would be called on to *make roads, build bridges, quarry stone, burn brick and lime,*

> *carry the hod, cut wood, hew timber, construct it into rafts and float it to the garrisons, make shingles, saw plank, build mills, maul rails, drive teams, make hay, herd cattle, build stables, construct barracks, hospitals, &c.&c.&c., which takes more time for their completion than the period of my enlistment.* I never was given to understand that such duties were customary in the army, much less that I would be called on to perform them, *or I never would have enlisted.* I enlisted to avoid work, and here I am, compelled to perform three or four times the amount of labor I did before my enlistment.[96]

Desertions were common in the army, especially during the initial year of service. In 1823, for example, one-fourth of the men who enlisted deserted, some before they even arrived at their posts. In 1825, the situation was even worse, with about one-half of the new recruits disappearing during their first year. As the adjutant general reported to Congress in January of 1826, the "spirit of resistless unquietude" which caused a man to enlist in the first place also contributed to his tendency to leave. And any "restraint derived from the force of his oath to serve honestly and faithfully the full period" of his enlistment held little force.[97]

All soldiers, including those at Fort Claiborne, had to be at least five feet, six inches tall and between eighteen and thirty-five years of age. Those under twenty-one needed the written permission of their parents. The recruits received a signing bonus for enlisting, ranging from twelve dollars in 1802, increasing to sixteen in 1811, then forty dollars in 1813 during the War of 1812, returning to twelve dollars in 1815 after the conclusion of the war. In addition to those signing bonuses and their army pay, after 1811 soldiers also received a grant of 160 acres of public lands and three months of pay when they were honorably discharged. After December 1814, the honorably discharged soldier could select an additional 160 acres of public lands in lieu of the three months of pay.[98]

Military Duties

In 1806, the garrison at Fort Claiborne, along with other troops sent to the area, experienced tense moments when American and Spanish troops confronted each other during the border crises, and again with the English during the Battle of New Orleans in 1815 (during the War of 1812), but for most of the time the life of the soldiers at Fort Claiborne was neither glamorous nor exciting but rather mundane. The first task of the soldiers upon arrival was to clear the land and build the fort. Twenty soldiers did accompany the Freeman and Custis expedition on its exploration of the Red River above Natchitoches in 1806. But, except when the Spanish stopped the expedition, these soldiers spent most of their time hacking a path for the boats through the Great Raft or rowing, poling, or pulling the boats up the river. Soldiers from Fort Claiborne had performed similar duties during the explorations of William Dunbar in 1804 and 1805. The soldiers did participate in efforts to remove or capture squatters, outlaws, and deserters from the contested area between Natchitoches and the Sabine River. When the Indian agent called counsels with the Indians, the military attended as a show of force. The presence of the military soldiers in their uniforms with formal parades and military salutes provided the appropriate ceremonial flair for formal treaty signings, councils, and other events.

At other times, the soldiers worked at the government trading house, beating the skins and blankets or acting as guards. Many military officers found the tasks requested by the Indian agent and the trading-house factor inappropriate for a soldier and detrimental to a soldier's morale. They also resented being told what to do by an agent or factor.[99] For example, when in 1817 Factor Fowler asked for assistance from Lieutenant Colonel Trimble, then commanding officer at Fort Claiborne, for soldiers' help in building new factory buildings, Trimble denied Fowler's request. Trimble stated that he was unwilling to do so but might be able to assign some of the soldiers to the task in two months or so. Trimble explained that his regiment had done more duty than any other, that they had been actively engaged throughout the War of 1812, had since war's end been repeatedly assigned to different posts, and had been almost continually engaged in erecting temporary quarters, garrisons, and so forth. Trimble pointed out that the soldiers' enlistments would expire within the year, and he wished to give them as much rest from labor as he possibly could. Fowler believed that Trimble was hoping that men would reenlist.[100]

Garrison Life

Except for those tense moments in 1806 and 1815, life at the Fort Claiborne garrison was fairly monotonous. The soldier's day started at dawn with reveille, followed ten minutes later by the firing of the three-pounder morning gun. Assembly or roll call came next, then breakfast and sick call. The sick were sent to the post surgeon or surgeon's mate for treatment. At 8:00 a.m., the soldiers were mustered for morning parade. Then the guard was assigned and fatigue duties allocated. Another assembly and roll call occurred after the noon meal, and twenty minutes before sunset the bugler sounded retreat. The soldiers gathered for evening parade and their final meal. By "tattoo" at 9:00 p.m., all soldiers had returned to their barracks. The sounding of "Taps" ended the day. On occasion the soldiers were called for inspection. At those times, they would appear in full dress uniform for parade. They also assembled in dress uniform when dignitaries arrived, such as the Spanish bishop who visited Natchitoches in 1805, and for special holidays, such as the Fourth of July (table 2).[101]

Table 2. Annual clothing allocation for infantry soldiers in 1813

Coat	Frock	Socks, two pairs
Cap	Trousers	Shoes, four pairs
Vest	Gaiters	Blanket
Overalls, linen, two pairs	Shirts, four	Stock and clasps
Overalls, woolen, two pairs	Stockings, two pairs	Cockade and eagle feather

Source: ASP: MA 1: 436.

The daily guard manned the fort's front gate but would also protect the public boats or at times the Indian trading house. The guards assigned to the gate worked twenty-four-hour shifts with the soldiers alternately on duty or resting in the guardhouse. Any soldier moving in or out of the post, even if on fatigue duty, had to provide a written pass from the officer of the day or his commanding officer. These passes stated the purpose of the soldier's pass and expected length of his stay away from the fort. All passes for which the soldier would be gone for more than an hour or if the soldier was going into the town of Natchitoches required the commanding officer to countersign. Officers could leave the post only with the permission of the commanding officer and only after telling the acting adjutant where he would be. The guards also stopped all civilians entering the fort and would detain them until the officer of the day or the commanding officer gave permission for them to enter. Exceptions were made for known friends of officers. Unusual visitors such as Spanish officials required the commanding officer's approval before being allowed to gain admittance. At Fort Claiborne, the guard also oversaw the water cart. Since the brackish water of the Red River was undrinkable, men had to haul water to the fort from a spring about a mile away. The guard ensured that soldiers did not waste the water.[102]

While at Fort Claiborne, the soldiers assigned to fatigue duty performed a variety of tasks. They cleared the land and constructed the fort itself, including all the buildings, palisade, redoubts, and fortifications, and built and improved roads. They cut, hewed, and seasoned the timbers for repairs and new construction and made rails. They cleaned and whitewashed the barracks, tended the vegetable garden and the livestock, cut hay and fodder for the animals, mended tools, loaded and unloaded boats and wagons, as well as performing daily tasks such as gathering firewood and hauling water. The soldiers could, upon request, assist in the control of the Indians who became intoxicated while visiting the town of Natchitoches.[103]

Those not assigned to guard or fatigue duty or away on other assignments might drill. Colonel Thomas H. Cushing, commanding officer at Fort Claiborne in 1806, required that all soldiers exercise at reveille, and the soldiers practiced during parade the handling of their arms, including priming, loading, and firing their muskets, charging with bayonets, and marching, wheeling, and forming by sections, platoons, and companies. Cushing also instructed the artillerists to drill in maneuvering the artillery pieces and to practice with small arms. In 1815, Major General Edmund P. Gaines, commander of the Seventh Military Department, which included Fort Claiborne, ordered that the drill periods be extended to three or four hours in fair weather and that the soldiers' training include the construction of defense works. When Captain William C. Beard was commanding officer at Fort Claiborne, he required all noncommissioned officers to study the schooling and drilling of soldiers and to drill each other in the handling of arms.[104]

Officers were not exempt from work. They kept the company's orderly books, clothing and pay accounts, and muster rolls up to date. The commandant mailed monthly or quarterly reports to the regimental headquarters, oversaw the activities of the quartermaster and medical departments, and ensured that soldiers behaved appropriately and that the garrison functioned properly. The commandant also signed requests for rations submitted by the Indian agent for distribution to tribal dignitaries visiting Natchitoches.[105]

The soldiers and officers did engage in recreational activities. The town of Natchitoches sat at the foot of the hill on which the fort was located, and enlisted men found opportunities in town for drinking, gambling, playing billiards, and visiting the "ladies of the night" who were undoubtedly located in town. Gambling on the post, however, was a court-martial offense, except for backgammon. Other favorite pastimes included hunting and fishing. Soldiers also attended balls and dances in town. On occasion, the commanding officer granted furloughs if conditions on the frontier permitted it.[106]

Officers and their wives had a wider variety of social activities available to them. The officers hosted and attended private dinners and tea parties both at the fort and in the town. On New Year's Day 1810, Dr. John Sibley gave a dinner party attended by Fort Claiborne's commanding officer, Lieutenant Colonel Freeman and his wife; the post surgeon, Dr. William H. Emery; Factor Thomas Linnard; Captain Trudeau, and four others. When Don Manuel de Salcedo, the newly appointed governor of Texas, passed through Natchitoches in 1808, he dined one night with Sibley and one night with Freeman. In April and May of 1812, when the Mexican revolutionary José Bernardo Gutiérrez de Lara visited Natchitoches, the officers invited him to a banquet at the fort, which Gutiérrez described as "magnificent." The officers and their wives also attended balls, and the officers on occasion took leave.[107]

During the existence of Fort Claiborne, the term of enlistment for a soldier was five years, but soldiers, who were chronically ill and, therefore, unable to perform their duties, could be discharged earlier. This required a certificate from the post surgeon which was forwarded through the chain of command to the division commander or the secretary of war for action. Commissioned officers could resign their command by submitting their resignation papers to their commanding officers, who forwarded them to the secretary of war. Several officers did resign while stationed at Natchitoches, with some of them, Edward Turner among them, remaining at least for a time in the town to pursue other opportunities.[108]

The military attempted to keep soldiers healthy and well fed. Daily rations consisted of one and a quarter pounds of beef or three-fourths of a pound of pork, eighteen ounces of bread or flour, and one gill of rum, whiskey, or brandy. Officers received two or more rations. Vegetables from the post garden supplemented the diet. Prior to 1812, contractors represented by a subagent in New Orleans provided the rations, which were shipped to the posts quarterly. The post's assistant military agent could purchase fresh beef at Natchitoches, and the post subagent frequently manufactured the vinegar locally. After 1818, the newly established commissary general of subsistence procured the rations for the troops.[109]

Soldiers could buy food and personal necessities from the post sutler. Bartholomew Shaumburgh, an ex-soldier, maintained a store on the post in 1804. Food provided by the sutler at different times included turkeys, ducks, mutton, veal, venison, Irish and sweet potatoes, cabbage, turnips, parsnips, onions, shelled and snap beans, roasting ears of corn, pumpkins, carrots, watermelons, muskmelons, and cucumbers. The sutler operated under military regulations, and a board of post officers fixed the prices of the items. The sutler also sold articles to the Indians.[110]

By Louisiana standards, Fort Claiborne was considered a healthy post. The surgeon, surgeon's mate, or post doctor endeavored to maintain the well-being of the troops. This included disease prevention. To keep the post clean and the troops healthy, the soldiers whitewashed the barracks when needed, ensured that the barracks had good floors, and that bunks had mosquito bars and netting. Regulations forbade soldiers from cooking or keeping any uncooked food in the barracks during the summer months. The company commander inspected the quarters daily, and the post surgeon checked the provisions to verify that the food was fit for human consumption. Despite these efforts, the soldiers experienced intermittent attacks of fever during the "sickly season" (April through August), which often made them unfit for duty. Sporadic episodes of influenza occurred during the winter months, with the 1808 outbreak so severe that Lieutenant Colonel Constant Freeman reported almost the entire garrison as suffering from the illness. Other common ailments included rheumatism, gonorrhea, hernias, pleurisy, spleen trouble, sore legs, boils, and "simple hurts." The post hospital housed the sick enlisted men, while officers remained in their quarters. Equipment for the hospital included amputation instruments and trepanning sets and other medical supplies (see table 3). The surgeon or surgeon's mate had over eighty different medicines available to treat the soldiers. In addition, the hospital had its own supply of certain foods, including seventy pounds of chocolate in 1815. The hospital kept Madeira, port, and brandy for medicinal purposes. Generally, the post had its own surgeon or surgeon's mate but, when these men were away from the post or sick themselves, the commanding officer hired one of the civilian doctors in the town. Not all soldiers recovered. Most common causes of death at Fort Claiborne were attributed to drowning and shooting.[111]

Table 3. Medical equipment and supplies at Fort Claiborne, March 1815

Medical equipment
Amputating instruments
Surgeon's pocket trepans
Scales
Knives
Jars
Penis syringes
Brass balance boxes
Mortars and pestles
Phials
Stoppers
Brass pins
Thumb lancets
Trepanning sets
Arm syringes

Medical books
The American Dispensatory
Rush's Surgery
Hernia Trusses
Sydenham's Works
Cooper's Surgeon

Supplies	
Flannel	Tourniquets
Flint balls	Muslin
Lamb skins	Sponges
Bed sacks	Blankets
Pillows	Sheets
Wrapping paper	Pillowcases
Rugs	Blank books

Frequently used medicines (80 total)
Glauber's or Epsom's salts
Mercury
Gentian
Quassia
Calamine
Borax
Peruvian bark (cinchona)
Flower of sulphur
Barley
Benzoin
Basilicon ointment
Paregoric
Camphor

Foodstuffs
Chocolate (70 pounds in 1815)
Ginger
Sugar
Cinnamon
Tapioca
Liquorice extract
Pimentos
Bohea Hyson tea
Alum
Cream of tartar
Molasses
Rice
Madeira and port wines
Brandy

Source: Miller, "History of Fort Claiborne," 97–99.

In 1807, second lieutenants earned twenty-five dollars a month, with first lieutenants making thirty dollars, captains forty, majors fifty, lieutenant colonels sixty, and full colonels seventy. Officers also received other compensation such as additional rations and funds for forage, fuel, and housing (table 4). Those serving as adjutants, paymasters, military agents, and those performing other duties received extra pay. An enlisted man earned seven dollars a month in 1807, with corporals making eight and a sergeant ten dollars. During the War of 1812, pay increased to eight dollars for a private and eleven for a sergeant. When the war ended, the pay returned to prewar levels. After 1819, a soldier could earn an extra fifteen cents and a gill of whisky a day for work such as building fortifications and roads if the activity continued for more than ten days.[112]

Table 4. Compensation of infantry in 1807

	Pay per month ($)	*Forage per month*	*No. of rations per day*
Colonel	75	12	6
Lieutenant colonel	60	11	5
Major	50	10	4
Surgeon	45	10	3
Surgeon's mate	30	6	2
Captain	40		3
First lieutenant	30		2
Second lieutenant	25		2
Ensign	20		2
Sergeant	10		1
Corporal	8		1
Musician	8		1
Private	7		1

Notes: Officers with a rank above captain received compensation for forage for their horses. Twenty-five cents a day was allocated for rations for officers, while the value of the rations provided the noncommissioned as well as rank and file was sixteen cents. The artillery had similar compensation with the addition of artificers (a skilled mechanic) at $12 per month and one ration.

Source: ASP: MA 1: 225.

On payday, the paymaster computed each soldier's pay based on the number of days present on duty. Then at a table with the paymaster in the middle and the commanding officer on one side and the sutler on the other, the paymaster called each private up in alphabetical order and the noncommissioned officers by rank. The soldier approached the table, and the commanding officer noted the amount due based on his rolls, and the paymaster consulted his records. The sutler provided his bill for supplies purchased by the soldier since the last payday. The paymaster deducted this amount from the soldier's pay prior to distributing the money to the soldier, who then signed a receipt. Officers drew their own pay and certified the amount on their honor.[113]

According to regulations, the soldiers received their pay monthly. All too often, however, the pay arrived late despite legislation stipulating that it should not be more than two months late; it could be longer between paydays. The commanding officers at Fort Claiborne repeatedly complained about late pay. In July of 1810, in response to a complaint from Captain Wollstonecraft at Fort Claiborne, the adjutant general of the army admitted there was a problem in the payment of the troops. In one case in 1817, the captain of a ferry robbed the paymaster on his way to Natchitoches. The amount stolen included three thousand dollars of pay for the troops and two thousand for the Quartermaster Department. In June of 1817, Lieutenant Colonel Trimble reported that his men had not received their pay since August 1816.[114]

The Rules and Articles of War

The Rules and Articles of War formed the basis of the military justice system in the army after 1806. Punishment for offenses could result in up to fifty lashes with a whip, with officers determining the amount. For very serious offenses, confinement with hard labor substituted for the whipping. The rules required that three commissioned officers presided at trials, but small garrisons such as Fort Claiborne that might not have the requisite number of officers often used two noncommissioned officers to assist the presiding commissioned officer. If found guilty, the soldier usually received his lashes in front of the entire garrison at the morning or evening parade. After 1812, the army replaced the whippings to restricting to the post, wearing a ball and chain, confinement to the guardhouse, or loss of whiskey ration for a stated length of time.[115]

At Fort Claiborne, the commanding officer usually scheduled the trials between nine and eleven o'clock in the morning. The most common offense at Fort Claiborne was drunkenness, either while on duty or on leave. Other transgressions included absence from roll call; stealing; smuggling liquor into the post; selling, stealing, or losing public clothing (uniforms); and neglect of duty, such as not closing the blockhouse at night, permitting a soldier to leave the post without a pass, and, if assigned to the hospital, not caring properly for the sick. Less common crimes included gambling, lying, disorderly conduct, insolence toward one's superiors, and not properly caring for one's weapon.[116] A serious offense occurred in 1814 when George Strickland, a soldier at Fort Claiborne, was convicted of murdering Ross McCabe. Judge Josiah S. Johnson ordered that Strickland be executed and told him "that you will be hung by the neck, between the heaven and the earth, until you be dead, dead, dead, and may the Lord have mercy on your soul."[117]

Desertions were a problem at Fort Claiborne. Captain Turner reported in 1805 that the troops were "possessed of such a Mania for Desertion" that he was forced to punish the deserters by using the "severest example the Law will admit," which in 1805 was one hundred lashes. Turner further reported that the guardhouse was full of deserters. Some soldiers, such as Elijah Adams, Robert Carson, and one other man, climbed over the palisade to visit in Natchitoches. Adams and Carson were captured and, although they were considered good soldiers, they were charged with desertion, the only option allowed at the time. And on a night in July of 1805 after receiving their pay, privates James Ford, William Hollingshead, Levi Smith, and Andrew Christian scaled the stockade wall to spend an evening in Natchitoches. The first three were caught, but Christian avoided capture, stole a horse, and escaped to Nacogdoches. The commanding officer would send a detachment of two or three men under the command of a noncommissioned officer to pursue deserters. If the detachment captured the deserter, the men received a monetary reward of between twenty and thirty dollars or more, which the paymaster deducted from the fugitive's pay. After 1806, deserters often escaped into the Neutral Ground between the Rio Hondo and Sabine River. The army pursued the deserters into this area over heated objections from the Spanish.[118]

By August 1816, the garrison at Fort Claiborne stood at two companies of the Eighth Infantry and a company of artillerists under the command of Brevet Lieutenant Colonel Joseph Selden. Selden needed these troops to start the construction of a new fort five miles north of Natchitoches on Bayou Pierre, about a mile from the Red River. By February 1817, Lieutenant Colonel William A. Trimble had assumed command, with the Natchitoches troops numbering 154 men of the First and Eighth regiments of infantry, most assigned to construct Fort Selden.[119]

Fort Claiborne with its cadre of officers, soldiers, support personnel, and families was not the only federal institution in Natchitoches. In addition, the federal government designated Natchitoches as the site for a factory or government trading house and for an Indian agency. Many of the older residents did not welcome the Americans or, more accurately, the federal institutions into their predominantly French Creole community. Many of the French Creoles found the presence of the governmental trading house and the Indian agency particularly objectionable. Not only did these entities expropriate land belonging to members of the community but they also resulted in large numbers of Indians coming to the town. In addition, the trading house financially affected the French Creole merchants who, in the past, had been heavily involved in the Indian trade. There would be ongoing conflicts between the fort, trading post, agency, and many of the local residents until all three institutions were removed.

3

RELATIONS WITH THE NATIVE PEOPLES

The Indians come here to trade. . . . You see them coming down the hill, leading fur-laden horses . . . carbine under arm and bow over their shoulders. Around them dart the children. . . . Next come the women . . . their tiny nursing infants sleeping peacefully in the folds of coverlets slung over their shoulders. . . . The Indians . . . open haversacks where they store the silver rings they hang from their noses and ears, others paint their faces red and black. . . . Bedecking themselves with brilliantly embroidered headbands, garters [armbands], bracelets decorated with porcupine or sewn with parakeet heads or the beaks of black woodpeckers [and] with a tomahawk at the waist and a bow in hand, they march proudly toward the village making their cougar quivers rattle as the tail sweeps the dust.

—THEODORE PAVIE, Natchitoches, ca. 1829–30

U.S. Indian Policy

As early as 1775, the Continental Congress had established a department to deal with treaties and the appointment of Indian agents. After the Revolution, the new government passed a series of acts, known collectively as the Indian Intercourse Laws, designed to facilitate the orderly advancement of the frontier. Men like President George Washington and Secretary of War Henry Knox knew that force could be used to subjugate the tribes, but such an approach needed an army, could result in a protracted war or wars, and would reflect badly on the ideals and reputation of the new nation. A more pragmatic strategy, Washington and others thought, was to uphold treaties previously negotiated with the tribes, keep peace between the tribes and white settlers, and encourage trade with the Indians. They believed that this policy would result in peace, which was critical during the infancy of the new nation. By the early 1800s, the United States' Indian policy had four main goals.[1]

The first goal, the establishment and maintenance of alliances with the Native tribes, was particularly important on the Louisiana-Texas frontier. American officials understood Indian alliances, and the manpower that tribal warriors represented could be critical during any confrontation between the United States and its neighbor, the Spanish, in Texas. Therefore, the United States quickly began to apply the same method of building alliances that had been practiced among and between the tribes and first the French and later the Spanish powers—gift-giving and trade. For Native peoples, the ritual smoking of the calumet or peace pipe and the formal giving of gifts were essential prerequisites for any economic and/or diplomatic transactions, including the formation of alliances.

The policy's second goal, that of maintaining peace among the various tribes and between the Indian populations and newly arrived Americans, involved the Indian agent. The Indian agent acted as an intermediary to resolve problems between tribes and would also handle disagreements between white settlers and Indian groups, often related to land ownership and use. The military on occasion assisted the Indian agent in resolving disputes.

Introducing European-style farming, the third policy goal, served two functions. It was partly for humanitarian reasons, and missionaries were instrumental in introducing plow agriculture to the tribes. It did not, however, escape the notice of men like Thomas Jefferson that, if the Indians adopted European agricultural methods such as raising livestock, they would not require extensive hunting areas and would need less land on which to live.[2]

The fourth goal, and for many Americans the most significant, was to acquire land cessions from the Indians. The Spanish had insisted that previous treaties with Indians be honored. But many American settlers saw the tribal hunting grounds as vacant land begging to be turned into productive farms and plantations. As a tidal wave of land-hungry Americans rolled westward, they increasingly encroached on Indian lands. Ostensibly, the United States' policy aimed to protect both the tribes and the white pioneers by separating the Indians from the intrusion of the white settlers. The method selected was to relocate the Indians to lands further to the west. However, many tribes had no interest in abandoning their traditional homelands on which they had lived for centuries and to which they held title through previous treaties with the Spanish and the U.S. governments. When the tribes showed little interest in moving, Americans would often employ Machiavellian methods to push the Indians out of the way. President Jefferson, for example, advocated establishing among the Indians government trading houses which would provide the Indians "all the necessaries and comforts they may wish (spirituous liquors excepted)" and encourage the tribal members, particularly the chiefs, to run up large debts which they would be unable to pay. Then, as Jefferson noted, the Indians would "always cede lands to rid themselves of debt."[3] This approach proved successful with the Chickasaw, Creek, and Choctaw. The Indians sold thousands of acres of land in Mississippi and Alabama to settle debts, and the land was opened to white settlers.[4]

With the Louisiana Purchase, President Jefferson saw the expanse of "vacant" land in Louisiana as a place to remove all the tribes east of the Mississippi River. The U.S. government immediately began targeting the Cherokee, Creek, Chickasaw, and Choctaw, all tribes in in the southeastern United States, to exchange their lands and move west. Some of the Indian nations were unwilling to leave their ancestral homes, and many successfully blocked the government's efforts to remove them—at least for a time. Governmental programs and increasing pressure from white settlers, nonetheless, forced many small bands to relocate, and increasing numbers of small groups of Shawnee, Delaware, Cherokee, and Chickasaw began to cross the Mississippi River into Louisiana.[5]

In 1804, somewhere in the neighborhood of five thousand tribal people lived in what had become the Orleans territory. Both the Americans and the Spanish needed the support or at least the neutrality of these Native peoples during their boundary disputes and went to considerable lengths to forge alliances with the various tribes. The Spanish, to create a barrier against the seeming tsunami of Americans washing over the country, actively recruited Louisiana tribes to relocate west of the Sabine River in Texas. Members of several of the tribes living along the lower Red River around the rapidly growing town of Alexandria already experiencing the pressure from the influx of Americans did move to Texas. The Spanish also tried to get the tribes to join them to fight the Americans. The Spanish warned all the tribes that they should not forsake their old friends, the Spanish, and that Louisiana would soon once again belong to Spain. To further elicit the support of the Native peoples, the Spanish held a series of conferences, one in 1805 attended by the Towakoni, Taovayas, and Wichita chiefs, where

Governor Cordero distributed a large quantity of gifts and the tribes pledged loyalty to the Spanish. The Spanish also sent envoys to other tribes in attempts to cement tribal allegiance. In December 1805, Daguariscara, the chief of the Taovayas, along with 6 lesser chiefs, 120 men, and 24 women arrived in San Antonio for a conference with the Spanish governor.[6]

To advance its efforts, the U.S. government selected Natchitoches, located on the border with Spain, as the site not only of a military post but also of two other institutions—a government factory or Indian trading post and an Indian agency. The factor and the agent in charge of these entities attempted to develop productive relationships with the Native peoples. These governmental institutions, particularly the trading house, did not bode well for the French and French Creole merchants and traders who already had their own commercial ties to the tribes.

Despite its understanding of the importance of tribal alliances, Spain's inability to provide the resources necessary to support the Indian trade proved no match against the wealthy and vigorous Americans. Texas tribes traveled to Natchitoches to trade. Most tribes would remain neutral during the confrontation between the Spanish and the Americans at the Sabine River in 1806, and most would remain so during the subsequent years.[7]

The Indian Factory System

In 1795, Congress passed legislation that established the government-run Indian trading system. This system, through a series of trading houses called "factories," provided items such as guns and blankets to the Indians in exchange for pelts, hides, skins, and other products of the forests and prairies. Some have ascribed altruistic motives for the development of the factories such as protecting the Indians from unscrupulous traders or teaching the Indians European farming methods, but a more cynical view suggests that the U.S. government's reason for setting up the system was to buy the loyalties of the tribal peoples with low-cost trade goods. Since there was no effort to make a profit from the trade, the government could undercut the prices charged by most of the independent traders and merchants. It was reasoned that this would make the Indians dependent upon the U.S. government for goods. Those in Washington felt it would be more cost-effective in the long run to sell goods to the Indians even at a slight loss than to fully garrison all the forts on the frontier that would be needed if the tribes engaged in hostile activities. If the Indians did participate in aggressive behavior, the government could apply sanctions. It could simply withhold the trade goods to which the Indians had become dependent. These sanctions could be very damaging. Without guns, powder, and shot, the Indians would be unable to hunt or protect themselves against attacks from better-armed Indian groups.[8]

The government's factory system, which operated from 1795 to 1822, resulted in a total of twenty-eight factories or trading houses. As the Indians moved further west, the government closed the eastern factories and opened ones near the tribes' new locations. The factor, the person in charge of the factory, had to take an oath and furnish a bond. The government paid the factors well, with some making as much as thirteen hundred dollars a year plus rations.[9]

In 1807, John Mason, the superintendent of Indian trade, issued a circular with instructions for the factors. Mason directed that the price for the goods sold should be based on the purchase price plus a 68 percent markup to cover the cost of transporting the goods to the factory. The trade goods could only be sold to the Indians. If there were goods carried by the factory not needed for the Indian trade, they could be sold to a white person with an additional markup of 10 percent. Factors could not extend credit to any white person but could provide credit "with caution" to "principal chiefs with good character." The price offered to the Indians for their peltry and other products Mason left to the discretion of the factors. He cautioned the factors to be at the trading houses as much as possible. If the factor needed a guard, the commanding officer of the nearby garrison would provide aid. The interpreter selected was to be "a person of sober, discreet, and temperate habits, and attached to the interest of the United States." Mason reminded the factors that they could not by law trade for their own benefit. He further instructed them to "on all occasions so demean yourself towards the Indians generally, and towards the chiefs in particular, as to obtain and preserve their friendship, to be conciliatory in all your intercourse with them, and, by every proper means in your power, to secure their attachment to the United States." Mason directed the factors to "take the greatest possible care to ascertain and examine the quality of the furs and peltries . . . , see that their quality is fairly proportioned to the prices allowed, and that their condition is good."[10]

Initially, the factors exchanged the trade merchandise for deerskins and other items, but they soon learned that the Indians expected to receive goods on credit. The Indians found the withholding of credit insulting and would take their trade elsewhere. The no-credit policy was changed and, in time, those in some of the tribes ran up huge debts which they had difficulty paying.[11]

By 1811, the Office of Indian Trade managed the Indian factory system. Each fall the factors sent their lists of merchandise that they felt would sell well with the local tribes to the superintendent of Indian trade. His office purchased trade goods from different suppliers. For example, gunpowder came from Shipping Port, Kentucky, and the DuPonts in Delaware; guns from Philadelphia; blankets and strouds from England; and mock garnets from Baltimore. Principal redistribution centers such as New Orleans, St. Louis, and Detroit acquired goods and then repacked them for shipment to the factories. The factors needed the goods delivered before the start of the trading season. The Indians would begin arriving in the spring with skins, hides, pelts, beeswax, tallow, bear oil, and other products to exchange for merchandise. The tribal people needed to get supplies, particularly the ammunition, and have their guns repaired before the fall hunt.[12]

Popular items of the Indian trade included blankets and other textiles; guns, shot, and powder; kettles and knives; and items of personal adornment. Three-point, woven, twill blankets made up 75 percent of the blankets sold with two-and-a-half-point blankets representing the rest. The Indians preferred white wool blankets with dark blue stripes; blankets with red or black stripes would not sell. Well-dressed blankets had a long shag on one side, making them better able to shed water. Those with twilling visible on both sides the Indians considered inferior. Each year the factory system sold about twenty thousand blankets. The Indians also purchased stroud and calico. The Indian trade offered over 150 different types of textiles.[13] Guns were unquestionably the most important metal item traded. Except for those destined as gifts for major chiefs, however, the guns sold to the Indians were generally inferior and the quality of the gunpowder varied. The Indians found one-quart to four-gallon brass and copper kettles the most useful.[14]

The Indians also bought goods for personal adornment. Popular items included silver and sometimes brass arm, wrist, and head bands, ear bobs, nose wheels, brooches, crescents, gorges, and rings (fig. 3). The Indians favored black, gray, white, and blue wampum beads, made from clam and conch shells. These

Fig. 3. Stimafutchi, by John Trumbull. This Coushatta man is wearing trade goods, including cloth head wrap, ear bobs, nose ring, necklace, gorgets, arm band, shirt, and vest. Swanton, *The Indians of the Southeastern United States,* plate 26.

were considered an essential commodity at all the factories. The factories also stocked vermilion, a red pigment used to decorate the body, and mirrors with German-made ones coming in a wooden case with a drawer that contained the mirror, as well as agricultural implements such as hoes, spades, scythes, plows, harnesses, cotton gins, spinning wheels, or any other item the Indians expressed an interest in receiving. Many trading houses carried seeds such as white Spanish onion, radish, Dutch turnip, red beet, drumhead cabbage, pea, bean, cucumber, squash, melon, and cantaloupe. The only things the government forbade the factors from selling to Indian customers were liquor and playing cards.[15]

The Indians brought all types of pelts and hides to the trading house to exchange for goods, including, in the southern United States, many deerskins. The Indians sold the deerskins either "in hair," that is the flesh removed on the inside with the hair remaining on the outside, or "shaved," skins where both the flesh and the hair had been removed. Sold by the pound, the "in hair" skins weighed around two pounds and the "shaved" skins about one-and-a-half pounds. Other products the Indians brought included peltry of beaver, bear, buffalo, mink, otter, and other mammals as well as bear oil, beeswax, deer tallow, corn, horses, and cattle. The Office of Indian Trade directed the factors to "buy anything that could be sold again without loss."[16]

Before acceptance, the factors inspected the skins and pelts to ensure they were clean and in good condition. All flesh had to have been removed and the skins fully dried and free from "worms." If not cleaned and stored properly, "worms" or "caterpillars" could heavily damage the skins or the skin could "rot." To protect against worms, especially during the summers, the factors had the skins "beaten," sometimes as much as once a week. This was expensive due to the labor involved and was detrimental to the skins. When it was time for shipment, the factors packed and pressed the skins and pelts in boxes, bales, hogsheads, and other containers for shipment by flatboats, keelboats, or barges or overland by wagon or packtrain to the agent at the nearest Office of Indian Trade at a major port, such as New Orleans. The agent there would sell the skins and pelts at public auction, store the skins, or repack them for further shipment.[17]

The Natchitoches Indian Factory or Trading House

In August 1804, the great Caddo chief Dehahuit and a number of warriors visited Natchitoches to meet the newly arrived Americans. Dehahuit expected to receive the usual gifts as a preamble to establishing relations with the Americans. Unfortunately, Captain Turner, the commandant at the post, had little to offer. Dehahuit was at first offended at this diplomatic gaffe, but Turner quickly assured the chief that he expected the U.S. government to establish a factory or trading house at Natchitoches shortly.[18]

In 1805, Congress authorized four new trading houses to be added to the factory system, including one in Natchitoches. Thomas M. Linnard, the son of the quartermaster general of the War Department, accompanied the first load of trading goods to Natchitoches and was charged with maintaining the trading house until the factor arrived. The president of the United States appointed two men in succession to serve as factor at the trading house, but neither man ever made it to Natchitoches, and in 1807 Linnard was named factor. He took his oath to perform his duties faithfully and executed a bond of $8,000 dollars. His salary was $1,000 per year and $365 for subsistence. The government spent about $2,000 for construction of the factory and over $15,600 for the first shipment of goods. In September 1807, Linnard purchased what he believed to be public land near the fort and began construction of the necessary factory buildings.[19]

From its beginnings, the Indian factory had been unpopular with people in Natchitoches. The town merchants, many of them Creoles, saw the factory as competition. In the past the merchants had been the center of most of the Indian trade, and the factory would affect their business. The land Linnard selected for the factory was also an issue. The 118-acre tract including the area selected for the factory had been granted to Father Dagobert, who had served as the priest in Natchitoches from 1743 to 1744. The members of the Church of St. Francis viewed the land as belonging to them. Despite this claim, the U.S. factory was built on the property.[20] Bishop Dubourg, who visited Natchitoches in 1821, wrote, "I saw with sorrow the decadence of everything pertaining to religion: the church and the presbytery threaten to collapse; the ornaments are in tatters, the zeal and the Faith singularly turned cold, ignorance in nearly all classes—these deplorable ills are the result of an unfortunate litigation which has robbed the church of her properties and lack of instructions which for more than 15 years afflicts the parish."[21]

John Sibley, the Indian agent at the time, also objected to the location of the trading house in town. He felt that the numbers of Indians coming to the trading house and the ease of obtaining liquor at establishments in Natchitoches would result in drunkenness and disorder. He forecast quarrels among the people and between the townspeople and the Indians. But despite Sibley's concerns and those of others, construction began on the factory on the hill south of the main gate of the fort. Linnard completed the main factory buildings within their 120-by-140-foot enclosure by the middle of 1810. The factory complex consisted of a pine log building with the store on one side and the dwelling for the factor on the other, a skin house to store the deerskins and other pelts, and probably a building to house the trade merchandise until it was needed. Many trading houses had a home for the Indian interpreter and a blacksmith shop where the Indians could bring their guns and other metal items to be repaired by a blacksmith or gunsmith.[22]

To have the trade goods available for the spring, the factors placed their orders with the superintendent of Indian trade in the fall. In Natchitoches, the major trading season began in March and continued into September. In 1811, Linnard submitted his request for one hundred pairs of three-point blankets, one hundred pairs of two-and-a-half-point blankets. He also ordered stroud, a coarse woolen cloth usually manufactured in England. The Indians preferred red stroud but also bought blue stroud. Because of the red dye, red stroud cost a little more than the blue. Stroud was usually sold in pieces of twenty yards in length. Other textiles he ordered included three thousand yards of calico (a plain-weave fabric of unbleached cotton), as well as lesser amounts of scarlet cloth (a fine woolen broadcloth), humhum (a coarse imported cotton cloth), German checks (a large plaid with alternating colors forming a grid of large squares), Irish linens (a woven fabric of flax fibers imported from Ireland), blue gurrahs (a coarse Indian cotton muslin), white plattillas (a white linen fabric made in Silesia), ramals (a silk plain-woven Indian fabric often used as scarfs or handkerchiefs), and assorted bindings as well as needles, scissors, and sewing thread. Clothing included both English and French black silk handkerchiefs, calico shawls, calico shirts, and wool hats. Linnard ordered twenty guns, twenty rifles with barrels four feet long, as well as gunlocks, gunflints, and gunpowder. He also requested butcher knives, small brass kettles, iron pots, wood axes, brass wire, and twelve cowbells. The Indians also liked items they could use for personal adornment, and Linnard asked for mirrors, half-moon silver gorgets, small and large brooches, mock garnets, armbands, wristbands, head ornaments, and earbobs. He also requested fifty pounds of vermillion (see table 5 for items requested in 1814).[23]

People from different tribes speaking different languages traveled to Natchitoches to trade. They arrived with packhorses or canoes laden with the products of the winter and spring hunts and brought them to the factory compound. There Linnard examined the condition of the skins and pelts. The factory's in-

Table 5. Merchandise requested for the Natchitoches factory in 1814

Textiles			
60 pairs	3-point blankets	2,000 yards	Furniture calico
40 pairs	2 ½-point blankets	500 yards	American stripes
1,000 yards	Blue stroud	10 pieces	Plattillas
400 yards	Red stroud	100 pieces	Custah
4 pieces	Scarlet cloth	50 pieces	India check
40 pieces	Humhum or gurrahs	6 gross (?)	Scarlet garters (?)
10 pieces	Blue gurrahs	10 dozen	Black silk handkerchiefs
100	Calico shirts	6 dozen	Janey handkerchiefs
50	Linen shirts	72 dozen	Pullicat handkerchiefs
300	Calico shawls	20 pieces	Romauls handkerchiefs
20 lbs.	White tread	50 gross (?)	Quality binding in assorted red, yellow, blue, green
Other trade items			
30	Rifles	25	Common brass mounted hangers
5 doz.	Gun locks	25	Beaver traps
5 doz.	Gun flints	20	Brass kettles
50	Small hatchets	6 doz.	Ivory combs
50 doz.	White handle knives	6 doz.	Large brown combs
6 doz.	Cow bells	10	Silver gorgets
3 doz.	Common plated spurs	25	Head bands
6 doz.	Scissors	12 pairs	Arm bands
3 (?)	Needles	25 pairs	Wrist bands
6 doz.	Looking glasses with drawers	100 pairs	Ear bobs
16 doz.	Small looking glasses	50 lbs.	Vermillion
6 doz.	Pint tin cups		

Note: Blankets were ordered in "pairs." These could be cut in half to make two blankets or to use as one blanket for sleeping with part used as a bottom blanket and half used as a covering (Kapoun with Lohrmann, *Language of the Robe*). A "piece" of cloth usually measured twenty yards in length (Linnard to Mason, Natchitoches, December 6, 1814, "NSFFLB," 79–80).

terpreter, Gaspard Philebere, reputed to have spoken seven different Indian languages, translated any questions or concerns. After agreeing on the value of the peltry, the Indians selected their merchandise. Often the Indians spent some time in town visiting, eating, and drinking before returning to their villages. Some came just to trade while others combined their trading trip with an opportunity to speak with the Indian agent at Natchitoches about their concerns or complaints.[24]

Deerskins were the most abundant item in the Natchitoches trade. On February 9, 1808, Linnard shipped over 12,700 pounds of "shaved" deerskins and over 19,500 pounds of skins "in hair," along with 80 bear skins, to the agent of the Office of Indian Trade in New Orleans. The next year, on February 11, he sent over 4,100 pounds of "shaved" and almost 8,500 pounds of "in hair" skins. Despite the value of the skins and furs purchased and the seemingly large amount of skins shipped, Natchitoches along with many other factories lost money. In only one year between 1808 and 1811 did the sales cover the costs of the merchandise. The other three years, the value of the merchandize provided the factor far exceeded the value of the skins and furs purchased. The Natchitoches factory was not the only trading house experiencing this problem, which had several causes.[25]

The factory system itself did not always provide the required trade goods in a timely manner. To have enough trade items on hand, Linnard had to have his delivery by March, but this didn't always happen. In September of 1807, for example, Linnard sent his list to the Office of Indian Trade for the 1808 trading season. The agent in New Orleans received forty casks of gunpowder to forward to the Natchitoches factory in January 1808, with a promise that the rest of the order would be provided by the spring. The balance of the order was not shipped from Washington until August—too late to equip the Indians for their fall hunt. Then, when the shipment did arrive, it was incomplete. The shipment included no red stroud, the brass kettles were too large, and many of the popular ornaments were missing. The 1809 shipment was no better. It again arrived well into the trading season with essential items such as guns, blankets, and strouds missing. The shipments were again late and incomplete in 1810, 1811, and 1812. The failure to provide the key trade goods in a timely manner mortified Linnard and harmed the relations between the tribes and the factor, a representative of the federal government. Indian agent John Sibley expressed his concerns. As he wrote to the secretary of war, "The factory here has scarcely an article in it left necessary or [of] importance for the Indians. I wish it could be kept better supplied, whoever furnishes Indians the best and most satisfactory trade can always control their politicks [*sic*]," and the loyalties of the Native peoples were especially important on the Louisiana-Texas frontier.[26]

Although the factory and military personnel and Indian agent were supposed to work together, this did not always happen. Trading houses were often placed close to military establishments for protection and so the soldiers could assist the factor with the beating and packing of skins, transportation of goods and skins, and erection of buildings. But it was common that requests for assistance from the factor went unmet. Many commanders felt soldiers should not be subjected to orders from the factors. The soldiers themselves showed little enthusiasm for this type of work and apparently found the gill of whiskey and the fifteen cents a day, the common pay, inadequate compensation for their nonmilitary services. Linnard, the factor at Natchitoches, aware of the value of the trade goods and hides, asked the commanding officer at Fort Claiborne for soldiers to guard the trading house twenty-four hours a day. The commanding officer denied this request, stating he had no orders to provide guards and further believed a guard was unnecessary. Linnard contacted the superintendent of Indian trade, who contacted the secretary of war, who ordered the commander at Fort Claiborne to provide not only the requested guard but also two or three men to help with the beating of the skins, packing of the skins for shipment, and other tasks as needed.[27]

Linnard faced other problems with the military. In 1810, Captain Wollstonecraft, the new commanding officer at Fort Claiborne, refused Linnard's request to keep the factory's gunpowder in the fort's magazine. Linnard again contacted the superintendent of Indian trade, who contacted the secretary of war, who ordered Wollstonecraft to store the factory's powder. Then, when Linnard asked for soldiers to assist in the packing of the skins for shipment, Wollstonecraft at first refused unless the military could stop providing a guard for the factory. A short time later, Wollstonecraft modified his requirement and did provide soldiers to assist. But different soldiers appeared each day and then, after about nine days, the soldiers stopped coming. In 1812, the commanding officer at Fort Claiborne once again withdrew the military guard at the trading house. Linnard hired a boy as a guard, but several days later someone broke into the store and stole nine and a half-dozen black silk handkerchiefs, five yards of blue stroud, and seven dressed deerskins. Linnard believed the soldiers were responsible and, indeed, some of the stolen items were found among the soldiers' belongings, but the military took no action against the men. Linnard once again wrote the superintendent of trade to request that a guard be provided at the factory and not be withdrawn except in an emergency.[28]

Without adequate help to air and beat the skins and woolen textiles such as blankets, the factor found it difficult to protect them from deterioration, especially in the hot and humid climate of Louisiana. In 1809, some of the skins shipped to New Orleans from Natchitoches arrived damaged and the agent warned Linnard that shipping such skins was "worse than nothing."[29] Again in 1811, skins reached New Orleans in poor condition and the agent informed Linnard that, unless he provided the necessary care to the skins, that the losses would destroy the factory. Linnard replied that in the fall he had had an attack of bilious fever and, since he had no one to supervise the beating of the skins, the beatings might have been inadequate, but he doubted that the skins were badly damaged as he was present at their packing. He declared to his superiors that he expected on the average to lose somewhere between fifty and one hundred skins per year from the action of worms. He further explained that he had only a small, inadequate pack screw to press the skins prior to shipment. He often found it necessary to press the skins more than once.[30]

International events, particularly the Embargo Act of 1807, affected the markets for the skins and furs, interrupted the supply of some trade goods, and had a devastating impact on the U.S. economy, including the trade in pelts. The government sold most of the deerskins to individuals representing European markets and, although the U.S. hatter industry used some of the furs, furs were selling at a much lower rate than previously. Soon the domestic market for furs and skins became saturated. The superintendent of Indian trade directed the factors not to send their skins to New Orleans since he believed the skins could be better cared for at the inland trading houses. However, factors continued to ship their skins to New Orleans, and before long the agent had 217,013 pounds of deerskins to store in the city. In 1809 the president of the United States signed a bill revoking the Embargo Act.[31]

Difficulties returned with the outbreak of the War of 1812. The superintendent of Indian trade found it almost impossible to obtain some trade goods, especially blankets, and found virtually no market for the skins and pelts. The British attacked the factories in the north destroying those at Michilimackinac, Chicago, and Sandusky. The British and their Indian allies also struck other factories and ships transporting furs on the Great Lakes. In total, the factory system lost over $43,350 in property during the war.[32]

The Indian Agency

For the tribes, the Indian agency represented the U.S. government on the frontier. The agent served as spokesman for the government. He negotiated treaties between the tribes, settled land disputes between Indians and whites, licensed traders to go among the tribes, hired blacksmiths and gunsmiths to repair guns and metal agricultural tools for the tribal peoples, and, through his discussions with the Indians who arrived at the agency and the traders he sent among the tribes, kept the government informed of activities and developments on the frontier. But the agent had little enforcement power. He could revoke the licenses of individuals authorized to trade with an Indian group but, other than that, his power was limited. His approach was more persuasion. Few agents were fluid in the various tribal languages, and one or more interpreters would assist the agent in his discussions with the Indians. In some cases, a statement had to be translated several times between the original Indian languages and English and then back again. The agent depended on the language abilities of his interpreters to communicate his wishes and positions. Good interpreters were key to any negotiation.

The United States had great concern over the role that the tribes might play in any border dispute between it and Spain and viewed the tribes as critical in maintaining the balance of power on the frontier. Shortly after the acquisition of Louisiana, President Thomas Jefferson sent out a query asking for information about, among other things, the tribal peoples within the new territory. Early responders included Governor W. C. C. Claiborne.[33] Claiborne offered his services as Indian agent, but Jefferson felt the governor should not leave New Orleans at such a critical time. Instead, he authorized Secretary of War Henry Dearborn to appoint John Sibley as "acting agent" for the United States and directed him to hold "such conferences with the chiefs and others of the several Indian tribes in the vicinity of Natchitoches" to secure the friendship of the Indians. Dearborn instructed Sibley to "assure the Indians of the confidence they may at all times place in the justice and friendship of the Government of the United States, as long as they conduct themselves in a peaceable and friendly manner towards the Government and citizens of our Country." He also instructed Sibley to tell the tribes to break off any relationships with any other nation, such as the Spanish, "and rely on their father [the president of the United States] for such friendly aid as he extends to all his other red children within our extensive territories."[34] On October 17, 1805, Dearborn formally named Sibley to be Indian agent for that part of the Territory of Orleans west of the Mississippi River. Sibley received one thousand dollars a year and a subsistence allowance of four rations as pay and three thousand dollars' worth of goods to distribute as presents to the Indians. Sibley used his home just south of the gate of Fort Claiborne for the Indian agency. Most of the gifts the agent gave to the Indians during their official visits came from the factory, and the military provided the rations the agent distributed to his Indian visitors during their stay. The military also provided a "presence" during important meetings and would enforce some of the agent's rulings on the frontier.[35]

John Sibley

John Sibley (fig. 4) was born in Sutton, Massachusetts, on May 19, 1757, the son of Timothy and Anne (Waite) Sibley. He and his twin brother were third and fourth of the fifteen children in the family. The Sibleys had deep roots in New England, the first Sibley arriving in the Massachusetts colony in 1629. John Sibley studied medicine and served as a surgeon's mate during the Revolutionary War. After the war, he settled in Great Barrington, Massachusetts, where he practiced medicine and in 1780 married Elizabeth Hopkins. Then around 1784 Sibley moved to Fayetteville, North Carolina, with his wife and two sons following in 1788. In Fayetteville, Sibley practiced medicine, acquired property, became active politically, and published a newspaper. After his first wife died in 1790, he married the widow Mary White Winslow in November 1791 and had two more children. It seems that Sibley lost both his printing shop and a new home in a town fire in 1794. In 1802, Sibley, at the age of forty-three, left North

Fig. 4. Dr. John Sibley. Artist unknown.
Courtesy of Sanders Hearne.

Carolina for Louisiana. His family remained in North Carolina until the death of his second wife in 1811.[36]

In September 1802, John Sibley arrived in New Orleans. While there and later in the Natchez area, Sibley became acquainted with many of the men who would have significant roles in the development of Lower Louisiana, including the future Louisiana governor William C. C. Claiborne. In March 1803, Sibley reached Natchitoches and purchased his first house and tract of land in the town. He was to become a large landowner in the area. Sibley was an avid writer, corresponding with, among others, Thomas Jefferson, to whom he provided vocabularies of the Caddo and Natchitoches languages. He also wrote an account of the Red River and provided information on Indian tribes in the Red River and adjacent areas. When the military arrived in 1804, Sibley received the appointment as contract surgeon for the post. Rumors circulated concerning Sibley's private life. As Governor Claiborne wrote President Jefferson in January 1805, "I learn that the Doctor is not happy in domestic life, and that as a husband his conduct is not approved, indeed it has been such as to have lessened his standing in society," but the governor went on to write that in other respects he found Sibley's character to be exceptional.[37]

A forceful and litigious individual, Sibley and his business practices did not endear him to the Creole community in Natchitoches. In April 1805, for example, members of the Creole community complained to Captain Turner, who served as civil as well as military commander, that Sibley had begun to erect a building on property owned by the Church of St. Francis. This was the same tract of land, 118 acres, part of which was used for the construction of the factory. Earlier, according to the complaint, François Rouquier Sr., Jean Baptiste Buard, and Fois Pernault, all three Creoles and leaders of the St. Francis Catholic Church, had gone to John Sibley requesting him to stop building on property, which they believed could be as much as ninety feet outside his property line, until the land could be surveyed. Despite their request, Sibley continued to build. The committee then asked Turner to deal with the matter.[38] Apparently the matter was not resolved to the satisfaction of the committee because, nine days later, François Rouquier Jr., acting on behalf of the church, appointed Emanuel Prudhomme to represent the church as its attorney in legal negotiation concerning the encroachment of Doctor Sibley upon church land.[39] Sibley would be involved in many lawsuits in Natchitoches in the early 1800s as both plaintiff and defendant.

A Year in the Life of an Indian Agent

John Sibley kept a journal in 1807 of his activities as Indian agent. As he recorded, members of at least twenty-five tribes or bands arrived at the agency that year (table 6). According to Sibley, he received all his Indian visitors in a "welcomingly manner," giving them rations during their stay and small presents. For meetings with tribal dignitaries, Sibley hosted elaborate events, which included smoking the calumet, giving speeches, and distributing gifts. The gifts could include everything from cloth, tobacco, and silk handkerchiefs to guns and saddles, and to major chiefs, regimental coats, U.S. flags, and gorgets engraved with an eagle surrounded by the words "United States of America."[40]

Table 6. Tribes visiting the Natchitoches Indian Agency in 1807 and 1809

Visiting Natchitoches in 1807	
Immigrant tribes from east of the Mississippi River	Nacogdoches—part of the old Hasinai Confederacy
Kadohadacho (Sibley's Caddo)	Nadaco—part of the old Hasinai Confederacy
Yatasi (Sibley's Yattassee)	Adai (Sibley's Adaize)
Natchitoches	Ais (Sibley's Aiche)
Hainai (Sibley's Inies)—part of the old Hasinai Confederacy	Kichai (Sibley's Keyshie)—southern Kichai allied with the Caddo
Nabedaches—part of the old Hasinai Confederacy	
Immigrant tribes from east of the Mississippi River	
Apalache (Sibley's Appelaches)	Coushatta (Sibley's Conshetta)
Pascagoula	Choctaw (Sibley's Chacta)
Biloxi	Chickasaw
Alabama	Cherokee
Wichita-affiliated tribes (Sibley's Pani)	
Taovaya (Sibley's Tawiache)—part of Sibley's Pani	Kichai (Sibley's Keychie)—northern Kickai allied with the Wichita
Wichita—part of Sibley's Pani	Iscani
Tawakoni (Sibley's Tawakenoe)	
Comanche (Sibley's Hietan)	
Kotsoteka	Yamparika
Additional tribes/bands visiting Natchitoches in 1809	
Coastal Texas Bands	Karankawa
Atakapa	Bidae

Source: Based on Sibley, *Report from Natchitoches,* and Smith, *Dominance to Disappearance.* For the coastal tribes and bands, see Sibley to Secretary of War, Natchitoches, July 5, 1809, in Garrett, "Dr. John Sibley," 47, 323–24.

Some Indians visited Natchitoches to establish relations with the Americans or to trade at the factory; others came seeking justice for actions by other tribes or by white settlers. From querying these visitors, Sibley learned what was happening in the surrounding area. For example, in January, two Caddo men, who came to trade at the factory, informed Sibley that a party of Osage had stolen seventy-two horses and a quantity of buffalo robes. In February, another party of Caddo arrived and told Sibley that game was scarce due to the lack of acorns (deer fed on acorns); that Indians had attacked a group of Caddo returning from a trading trip to the Wichita; and that they could not travel to the prairies to hunt buffalo due to the scarcity of horses. In March, Sibley heard from an Alabama Indian that a party of Alabama and Apalachee came upon the Osage who attacked the Caddo in January and the Alabama and Apalachee killed and scalped five of the Osage. The Alabama man also told Sibley that several tribes had collected at the Coushatta village to hold a war dance.[41]

In April, Captain Sam, a Choctaw chief, requested from Sibley permission to settle a small group of seven men and seven women with children on a prairie near the Adai tribe. He provided a certificate, signed by some of the residents in the Rapides area where he had recently lived, attesting that he was peaceful and honest. Captain Sam stated that he wanted to live "quietly & have his little stock about him & not have them in the way of white people." Sibley gave him permission and seven hatchets, seven hoes, and one ax plus some seed corn, peach stones, and garden and melon seeds.[42]

In June, John S. Lewis and Jeremiah Downs arrived in Natchitoches with a Wichita chief, eight tribesmen, and a herd of horses. They had left four other white men with the Wichita to catch additional wild horses. From Lewis, Sibley learned that one of the Wichita chiefs had recently returned from San Antonio, where the Spanish had showered the Wichita with gifts, including a Spanish saddle and two or three horses or mules for each Wichita man present. Lewis also reported that he visited a Comanche camp, which he estimated contained two thousand people and more than five thousand horses and mules. The Comanche had also been to San Antonio and received presents from the Spanish governor.[43]

In September, John Homo, a Chickasaw chief, with thirty men met with Sibley to complain that men from the Red River Coushatta village had robbed him of "sixty shav'd deer skins and one hundred unshav'd ones, and two horses, the whol [*sic*] valued at two hundred dollars." John Homo asked Sibley to tell the Coushatta that, unless they returned the horses and an equal number of deerskins within three months, the Chickasaw would "take satisfaction of them." The Chickasaw chief asked for a certificate from Sibley stating that he had notified Sibley of the robbery. In November, when Echean, the chief of the Red River Coushatta, arrived at the post to trade, Sibley questioned him about the robbery. Echean stated that he believed the allegations to be true but thought the number of skins taken to have been less. He did agree that the horses or ones of equal value should be returned to the Chickasaw as well as the skins but asked for more time than three months. It would take longer than that to collect the requested number of skins.[44]

Sibley also attempted to settle land disputes between tribal peoples and recent American settlers. In April 1807, Francis Bossier, John Veron, and the Pascagoula chief with several other members of the tribe sought out Sibley to resolve a land dispute between the Pascagoula and Joseph Gillard. The Pascagoula chief explained that some years previously the tribe had sold some of their land to the late Mr. LeCour. LeCour's widow had since married Gillard, who was now claiming more land than the Pascagoula had originally sold, including the land the Pascagoula had expressly reserved for their village. Gillard was demanding that the Pascagoula move. John Veron said that he had acted as interpreter at the sale of the land to LeCour and that what the chief said was true. Sibley responded that, since the Pascagoula had been settled on the land when the United States took possession of Louisiana and, since Gillard had never had possession of it, Gillard could not demand that they move. If Gillard's claim came before the Board of Commissioners of Land Claims, Sibley promised to submit to the commissioners the objections of the Pascagoula and the evidence of their claim and stated that he was sure their claim would prevail. He suggested that the Pascagoula plant their crops for the year and he would inform Mr. Gillard that any claim he might have to the land would not be affected by the Indians living in their village. Sibley emphasized the importance of avoiding all disputes between the Indians and the white settlers but, if Gillard was able to prove his claim, the Pascagoula would have to move.[45]

On January 13, a serious incident came to Sibley's attention. Captain John Burnett reported that Tom, a Coushatta man, and Samuel Watson, a recent arrival from Kentucky, had gotten into an argument at the saltworks near Natchitoches. Tom had pulled a knife and Watson went to a boat that was loading salt and returned with a gun. As Tom advanced, Watson shot him, killing him instantly, and then Watson returned to the boat, reloaded the gun, and left. The sheriff had been sent to find Watson but was unable to locate him. Sibley immediately sent two Indians to Tom's family, asking them to come to the agency. He wanted to explain what had occurred. Sibley worried that the Coushatta might retaliate by killing someone. Sibley also wrote the governor, asking him to issue a proclamation to apprehend Watson.[46]

On March 18, the uncle and brother of Tom arrived at the agency. Sibley described what had happened and stated that the efforts taken to capture Watson had so far been unsuccessful. Sibley asserted that, when apprehended, Watson "would be brought to trial & if found guilty would be punished . . . , and that our government would always afford them [the Indians] protection & we were as ready to render them justice. . . . we would punish an injury done to them as soon as to a white man." Sibley hoped the Coushatta had sufficient confidence in the justice of the U.S. government "to preclude in them all idea of retaliation.[47] The Coushatta men replied that they considered the U.S. government to be just, that it appeared that Tom might have been at fault, and they believed the American government would do what was right. Sibley stated that he had treated them well, given them provisions, and that "they went away & appeared to be satisfied and talked rationally."[48] But on April 5, Pia Mingo and Red Shoes, two Coushatta chiefs, and thirty-three men from the Sabine Village of the Coushatta arrived at Natchitoches. Red Shoes said Tom was his brother and he had come to demand and expected satisfaction for his death. Sibley explained what was being done. Watson had been captured but escaped and, if he was caught again, would be brought to trial. Sibley reported that Red Shoes seemed satisfied and left but returned demanding some presents. Red Shoes claimed that presents would keep the Coushatta from doing "any mischief" and he "could not think of loosing [*sic*] his brother for nothing." Sibley wrote in his journal that "I did not disguise from him that I was not well pleased at the manner in which he had expressed himself, that we were not to be menaced into compliance with his unreasonable demand." The chief said no more, but before he left Sibley gave him a hat and a half-regimental blue coat faced with red. The governor had been slow at issuing the proclamation for Watson's arrest, and Watson was known to be on the Ouachita River.[49]

In June, White Meat, a Choctaw, reported that he believed a young Coushatta man had recently killed a white man about thirty to forty miles from Natchitoches. Sibley sent two men to investigate. They returned three days later, reporting they had found a man's body mostly underwater where they believed he had laid for twenty days or more. Sibley formed a "Jury of Inquest" with himself as coroner, and two days later they left for the scene of the crime. When they arrived at the site, Sibley empaneled a six-person jury and the men examined the body. The head was missing, and the body was in a bad state of decay. Small fish had been feeding on the flesh, but the men did discover five holes on the left side of the abdomen, which appeared to have been inflicted by a knife.

Both White Meat and Tombolin, another Choctaw, through the interpreter William Rollings, gave evidence to the jury. Tombolin testified that, while he was at the Coushatta village on the Sabine, he heard a young Coushatta man admit to killing a white man after a hard fight. This Coushatta man was at Natchitoches when Sibley and the Coushatta chiefs discussed the killing of the Coushatta Tom by Samuel Watson. At the time the Coushatta man said he wanted to kill a white man but the chiefs would not let him. He waited in the area around the fort for two days, hoping to kill a soldier, but had no opportunity. White Meat reported that a white man came by his home on his way from Opelousas to Nacogdoches leading a roan horse loaded with goods. White Meat's description of the clothes the man wore fit the clothes found on the dead man. White Meat's son-in-law Charles reported that, when he was returning from a trading trip to Natchitoches, he met the same young Coushatta man on the road. They traveled together for a while and passed the white man. The Coushatta man wanted to return and kill the white man. Charles argued that the "path was clean & was their trading path & it should not be bloodied."[50] The two continued to travel together. Then the Coushatta said he had to stop for a few minutes, that Charles should continue, and he would catch up with Charles shortly, but he never did. White Meat reported that the next day he saw the Coushatta ride by with his hand bandaged and his face badly bruised. Since the event, several Coushatta had told White Meat that the young man bragged about the killing and described the incident in detail. Sibley learned that a white man named O'Neal had been to Opelousas several times and that he was from somewhere in the Mississippi Territory. The jury ruled that the Coushatta man from the village on the Sabine River had killed O'Neal.[51]

Sibley sent William Rollings to the Coushatta village with a request that the Coushatta chiefs come to Natchitoches and bring with them the man who had killed O'Neal.[52] In September, Rollings returned with the Coushatta chiefs' reply. As reported by Rollings, the chiefs stated that

> they were fully sensible of our goodness towards them, and were greatly distressed at what had happened and they would never let go our hands or throw away our talks; but they had been sent for by Governor Cordero of San Antonio, & had promised to go & see him, they did not know for what; but that they would come to Natchitoches as soon as they returned from San Antonio . . . ; but they could not then think of giving up the young man who had committed the murder the fact they did not pretend to deny.[53]

Sibley also attempted to mediate conflicts between different tribes. In early May 1807, eight Choctaw from the east side of the Mississippi under the leadership of Stamelachee attacked a camp of Nadacos located at a salt spring high up the Sabine River. The Nadaco men had been away hunting while the women made salt. The Choctaw killed and scalped two women and wounded others. Sibley and Captain Edward Turner, the commanding officer at Fort Claiborne and the civil commandant of the District of Natchitoches, had brokered a peace treaty between the Caddo and Choctaw in May 1804, and the murders represented a serious breach of that treaty. The Nadacos were under the protection of Dehahuit, the great Caddo chief. Dehahuit demanded satisfaction for the murders as provided for in the treaty. Learning of the event, Sibley quickly sent for all the Choctaw chiefs who had participated in the peace negotiations three years earlier. Over the next few weeks, a total of two hundred Choctaw men, including Tombolin, Tuscatoga, Neuchema, Chechemastubba, Biachubby, Captain Sam, Mucklehei, and White Meat assembled in Natchitoches. When all the chiefs and head men had arrived, Sibley met with them at the "Indian House" along with an interpreter and a group of the townspeople.[54]

Sibley explained why he had called the chiefs together. He characterized the murder of the two Nadaco women "as unprovoked, cruel, & cowardly, and disgraceful to warriors." He noted that, according to the treaty, "they were bound to make a just retribution." He then recommended that a delegation of Choctaw be sent to tell the Caddo chief that they condemned the murders, regretted they had occurred, promised to do what they could to ensure the people responsible were punished, and wished to live in peace. Tuscatoga and two other Choctaws offered to go to the Caddo village, and Gaspard Philebere, the agency's interpreter, who spoke both Caddo and Choctaw, agreed to go with them. Sibley gave Tuscatoga a medal for himself and one to give Dehahuit along with other presents. While waiting for the reply from the Caddo, the Choctaw remained in Natchitoches. They were afraid to go hunting for fear of retaliation by the Caddo.[55]

Three weeks later, the delegation to the Caddo returned. Waiting at Natchitoches were 111 Choctaws, 55 Pascagoulas, 51 Apalachees, and 5 Caddos. Some had come to learn if the Caddo and Choctaw were at war, others to get outfitting for their hunts. The interpreter, Philebare, reported to Sibley that, when the delegation arrived at the Caddo village, they found that Dehahuit was away, but the old chief, Carody, received them with "great kindness and civility." Carody "expressed a great desire to be at peace" with the Choctaw and promised that the Great Chief would come to Natchitoches as soon as he returned home. Dehahuit would arrive in Natchitoches for the Grand Council in August.[56]

Dehahuit, the Great Caddo Chief

Dehahuit became chief of the Caddo upon the death of his uncle Bicheda, probably a victim of a particularly virulent smallpox epidemic that swept through the area in 1800–1801, killing perhaps a third of the Caddo population. A particularly astute and capable political leader, Dehahuit became a strong and influential force on the Louisiana-Texas frontier during the first three decades of the nineteenth century.[57] Sibley portrayed Dehahuit as a "very fine looking man" with a "strong mind," who had "more importance than any other ten chiefs on this side of the Mississippi within my agency."[58] Governor Claiborne recognized Dehahuit's contributions in maintaining peace on the frontier and in 1813 presented him with a sword "to a Chief, a Man and a Warrior, nothing could be more acceptable."[59] During the War of 1812, Claiborne described Dehahuit to General Andrew Jackson as "a man of great merit, he is brave, sensible and prudent—You may rely on whatever he may say to you."[60] The Spanish governor also recognized Dehahuit's importance. Eight tribes—the Yatasi, Nadaco, Nabadaches, Hainai, Nacogdoches, Kichai, Adai, and the Natchitoches—allied themselves with the Caddo, and Dehahuit would speak on their behalf. Dehahuit worked closely with Sibley during Sibley's time as Indian agent and successfully kept many of the tribes, including those in Spanish territory, neutral during tense periods when war appeared eminent between the Spanish and the Americans in 1806, 1811, and again during the War of 1812; when summoned to serve during the Battle of New Orleans, Dehahuit would answer the call.[61]

Although generally loyal to the Americans, Dehahuit was not above cultivating favor with the Spanish as well, especially if it was advantageous to the Caddo and the affiliated tribes. He freely accepted the gifts the Spanish lavished on him and, in 1809, he traveled to San Antonio with the chiefs of the Nadaco and the Nacogdoches to impress on the Spanish governor the importance of sending traders to these Texas tribes. Dehahuit would serve as chief until his death in 1833.[62]

The Grand Council

In June, Joseph Gillard arrived in Natchitoches and told Sibley the Coushatta were preparing to abandon their village on the Sabine and move westward into Spanish Texas. He reported that the Coushatta had "sent to the Appalache & Pascagoula a Belt & War Talk, to convince these tribes to join them [the Coushatta] in a war against the Americans." Sibley immediately sent a message to Layssard at the rapids (today's Alexandria area), near where the Apalachee and Pascagoula lived, to see what he knew about this matter. Sibley wrote the governor about the report. He also learned that both the Wichita and the Comanche had been to San Antonio, where the Spanish governor treated them royally, and they had returned to their villages loaded with presents. The Spanish were working hard to cement the alliances of these tribes to the Spanish cause.[63]

Meanwhile, Sibley attempted to align the tribes of Spanish Texas with American interests. In the summer of 1807, Dehahuit, undoubtedly at Sibley's request, arranged a Grand Council in Natchitoches with Sibley, the Caddos, the Wichitas, and the Comanches. Dehahuit arrived on August 9 and announced that three hundred Indians from different tribes would be coming in the next few days to participate in the Grand Council. Two days later, eighty Kotsoteka Comanche with four great chiefs rode into Natchitoches. The Comanche were nomadic hunters who followed the great herds of buffalo across the southern Great Plains and had traveled many miles to participate in the council. Sibley distributed provisions and cooking utensils to them. In total, Sibley would provide provisions for the over three hundred people who attended the council. As Sibley recounted, he invited the Comanche chiefs to his house and entertained them by giving them tobacco, which they smoked with him, and offering them liquor, which they refused, and a sweet drink made of honey or molasses and water, which they enjoyed, and gave each of the chiefs gifts. Sibley also sent for a tailor and had each chief measured for a scarlet coat with black velvet trim and white buttons.[64]

On August 11, the Hainai chief reached Natchitoches with 16 of his tribe. Two days later, members of the Tawakoni, Kichai, Nabedache, Nacogdoches, Nadaco, Ais, Adai, and Yatasi with their chiefs arrived at the American outpost. All these tribes, according to the Spanish, resided in Spanish territory and were technically under Spanish rule. The issue of the boundary between the United States and Spain was still unsettled, and Sibley was attempting to shift any allegiance the tribes might have from Spain to the United States. Some of the tribes came to participate in the Grand Council and to learn what the United States had to offer. Members of the Natchitoches and Chickasaw tribes were also present. Over 320 Indians assembled in Natchitoches. As presented by his interpreter, Sibley records the tribes with the number of members at Natchitoches who wanted provisions as 80 Hietans, 18 Tawakenos, 8 Keychies, 45 Nabedaches, 90 Caddos, 34 Nadacos, 16 Inies, 24 Nacogdochettos, and 4 Chickesaws.[65]

On August 16, Sibley invited two of the Tawakoni chiefs to his house. They had never been to Natchitoches before or met an officer or agent of the United States. Sibley told them how pleased he was to receive them and that "their Great Father & friend the President of the United States would hear of it." As a token of "their Great Father's" friendship, Sibley gave each chief an officer's fully trimmed blue and buff regimental coat with epaulets and lace, a hat with a plume, a shirt, and other gifts, including a gorget engraved with an eagle with the words "United States of America." He also provided gifts for each of the chiefs' wives, and other items to be divided among the other Tawakoni. On the same day, Sibley entertained the Kichai chief and his party. He gave them sweet drink, tobacco, and gifts.[66]

Two days later, Sibley received the entire Comanche party at his home. He delivered the scarlet coats made for the chiefs, as well as other gifts. As the Comanches were leaving, the principal chief produced a Spanish flag which, through an interpreter, he said that he had received from the governor at San Antonio and now wished to exchange it for an American flag. Sibley explained that the United States was not at war with Spain, and he worried that, if he gave a flag to the Comanche, it might upset the Spanish and, in the end, create difficulties for the Comanches. The chief replied, saying the Comanches wished to have an American flag and did not care what the Spanish thought. If Sibley would give the Comanches a flag, it would "wave through all the Comanche Nation, and they would all die in defense of it before they would part with it." Sibley got a flag and wrapped it around himself and then gave it to the chief who in turn wrapped it around himself. As Sibley reported, the chief "embraced it with great earnestness in [the] presence of all his people." Sibley also bestowed on the chief an elegant belt which Sibley wore himself; the chief put it on and, as Sibley reported, "had a good effect, as it was done in [the] presence of a large number of Indians of different nations."[67]

The same day, the Grand Council was held. For this event, the chiefs and head men of the Comanche, Caddo, Tawakoni, Nadaco, Nabedache, Kichai, Hainai, and Ais assembled in the Grand Council Room. Sibley had the council fire ceremonially lighted, and those attending smoked the calumet. Then Sibley delivered his message.

> Brothers,
>
> By arrangements with France and Spain two nations beyond the great water we the people of the United States have become your neighbors, and all the great country called Louisiana as formerly claimed by France now belongs to us, the President of the United States, the great friend & father of all the red people, assures you he is your friend and will continue to be so, so long as you are his friends, & friends to the people of the United States.

Sibley then addressed the relationship between the United States and Spain. "[W]e are not at war with Spain, we therefore do not wish, or ask you to be less their friends for being ours, the world is wide enough for us all, and we ought all of us to live in it like brothers." He cautioned the tribes "against opening your ears to the bad talks of any people whatever who may wish to make us enemies;

but be always persuaded that we have not come to this country to do harm to any of our red brethren, but to do them good." Sibley encouraged the tribes to return to Natchitoches and trade with the Americans: "[A]s you have come a long journey to see your new neighbors, it is my wish that you rest yourselves a few days & accept of our hospitality in such as we have to offer you, and a few presents which I shall present you in the name of your great father, the President of the United States, as a token of his good will towards you; and as you have now found the way here, you will be inclined to come again." Sibley added that the Americans wanted to trade with the tribes to everyone's mutual benefit and asked that "when any of our people visit you in your own country you will receive them as friends." He ended by stating, "Brothers, these are the words I have to say to you, when you return to your friends, tell them we take them all by the hand, repeat to them our words and forget us not."[68]

Daguariscara, the Tawakoni chief, then rose to speak. He supposed that "time will determine whether this days talk will prove true," but he was pleased with Sibley's statements and said he would carry Sibley's words back to his tribe. He invited Americans to visit his village so they could all become better acquainted and could trade. The chief then uttered a complaint. There "is a man of your nation, he comes from Nacogdoches who is a trader amongst us, he is too dear with his goods. If he is one of your nation can't you write him a letter [and] direct him not to impose so much upon us, and make him sell his goods to us cheaper." Sibley replied that he didn't know the man or whether he was from Nacogdoches, although he might be American by birth; he should be considered a Spaniard and, as such, the Americans would have nothing to do with him. Sibley assured Daguariscara that, if traders from the United States came to his tribe, the Tawakoni would have no cause to complain.[69]

Pisinampe, chief of the Kotsoteka Comanche, spoke next. He asserted that, as soon as the Comanches heard the Americans had come to Natchitoches, the Comanches wanted to come and see their new neighbors. They were all "highly pleased" they had come. Pisinampe then stated that his people needed trade merchandise and would gladly trade with the Americans on friendly terms. The Americans seemed to have the things the Comanche wanted, and the Comanche would probably visit again.[70]

Then Castor, the Kichai chief, stood to speak. When he heard from the Wichita of the arrival of the Americans, he had planned to come to visit and let the

Americans know of the Kichai's needs and how they could help each other. He was "charmed" with Sibley's words and stated that, "although I live in the dominion of another Nation, that makes no difference. I receive your talk like a brother, and wish to live with you in [the] future in peace and friendship as good neighbors, and I promise you that our Nation shall be the last who will transgress the treaty of this day. I hope we shall be better acquainted, that we shall trade together for our mutual advantage, and when you know our wants will be able to be of service to us."[71]

Dehahuit, the great Caddo chief, spoke last. He began by saying he was happy to have accompanied the various tribes to Natchitoches and was pleased that they had been well received. Even if he had not accompanied them, he would have come anyway. He stated that the tribes with whom he was allied complained that the peace made with the Choctaw was done on his accord and he wanted now to establish that the peace had been negotiated on Sibley's wishes. He asserted that the conditions of the treaty between the Caddo and Choctaw stipulated that whoever broke the treaty should make restitution. He declared that the Choctaw had broken the treaty by murdering two Nadaco women and he was at the council to see whether the conditions of the treaty were to be honored.[72]

This was undoubtedly not a topic Sibley wanted to discuss in front of the gathered tribal leaders. Ten days earlier, Sibley had admitted in a letter to Secretary of War Dearborn that he did not believe that the murderers of the Nadaco women would ever be punished.[73] Nevertheless, Sibley emphasized to the gathering the importance of the peace treaty and "that it had been made on fair & honorable terms for their general good, that it was the wishes of their great and good father the President of the United States, that all his red children should be at peace with one another."[74] He explained that, upon learning about the murder of the two women, he had sent for all the Choctaw chiefs and headmen on the west side of the Mississippi River. All the chiefs had been alarmed and distressed by the news and disavowed any involvement in it. Sibley had suggested the Choctaw send a messenger to the Caddo, which they did. The murderers had fled to the east side of the Mississippi River, and the Choctaw chief Chechemastubby was selected to go to the Choctaw Nation on the east side of the river with the accusation against the murderers. Chechemastubby did set out but became ill. Also, the river was high and traveling became difficult. Sibley said he felt the

Caddo should be patient a little longer. He added that the Choctaw considered the murderers to be vagabonds.[75]

Dehahuit replied that he "thought there had been time enough since the murders were committed to have had something done about it, that he could readily believe they were vagabonds, and that other Nations punished such vagabonds instead of protecting them." The Caddo chief had learned the leader of the murderous party was Stamelachee and he had recently been commissioned a chief by the U.S. government. He further stated that, unless the Choctaw gave Stamelachee up and had him punished, then the murders must be regarded as an act of the entire Choctaw Nation. However, he agreed to wait "three moons longer, or until cold weather" and during this time not to take any action. "But if satisfaction was not then made he would be answerable no longer."[76]

Discussions followed concerning a delegation of chiefs to visit Washington, DC. The Comanche and Tawakoni said they would go, but their people were waiting for them on the Trinity River and they had to return. The Caddo chief said he would be willing to travel to Washington but hesitated to do so until the affairs between the United States and Spain were settled, and the difficulties with the Choctaw prevented him from leaving home. However, when the other chiefs were ready to go, he would go with them. The council finished and the various tribes returned to their homes.[77]

"Silver Ore"

On October 15, members of the Wichita Confederacy, who had not attended the Grand Council, and members of the Yamparika Comanches rode into Natchitoches. Sibley provided his visitors, who numbered seventy-five, with provisions, tobacco, and cooking equipment. He entertained the four Comanche chiefs led by Quilvalparica in his house on the sixteenth and the entire Comanche party on the eighteenth, liberally distributing gifts (table 7).

Also, on October 16, Sibley met with two chiefs of the Wichita Confederacy. On October 25, Sibley saw Awakahei, the great Iscani chief (the Iscani were part of the Wichita Confederacy) and "the first man in the nation." Sibley presented Awakahei a medal like the one he had given Quilvalparica, the Comanche chief; a "handsome, welted, Philadelphia-made saddle"; and an officer's uniform coat.

Table 7. Gifts distributed to the Hietans (Comanche), by John Sibley, Indian agent, October 1807

	October 16, 1807	
	TO THE FOUR HIETAN CHIEFS	
4 scarlet blankets	8 oz. of vermillion	4 braggys*
4 hats and plumes	4 looking glasses	4 combs
	4 shirts	
	October 18, 1807	
	TO THE FOUR HIETAN CHIEFS	
4 stroud blankets	1 lb. vermillion	16 lbs. of balls
4 white blankets	4 bells	16 flints
4 fire steels	4 tin cups	4 braggys
8 knives	4 guns	4 pieces of binding
4 tomahawk pipes	8 lbs. gunpowder	
	TO THE SEVEN GREAT (HEAD) MEN OF THE HIETAN NATION	
7 blankets	7 braggys	7 handkerchiefs
2 lbs. vermillion	7 combs	7 fire steels
7 tin cups	14 knives	7 pieces of binding
	TO THE REST OF THE HIETANS	
12 knives	10 handkerchiefs	10 flaps*
10 pairs of scissors	10 looking glasses	2 pieces and 6 yds. of binding
100 needles	2 tin cups	10 combs
2¼ lbs. beads	10 hatchets	12 blankets
17 yards of calico	1 lb. thread	
	2 lbs. vermillion	

* "Braggys" and "flaps" are both terms used for breechcloths.

Source: Sibley, *Report from Natchitoches,* 70–71.

He also gave each chief a uniform coat along with other gifts to those present.[78] Sibley was particularly interested in what the Comanche chief Quilvalparica had to say. Speaking in Spanish, Quilvalparica told Sibley that Natchitoches was too far for the Comanches to come and trade but, if Sibley would send traders to them, they would be welcome. Quilvalparica declared that horses were to them "like grass" and they had buffalo robes to trade. In addition, he informed Sibley that they knew where there was silver ore. These things they wished to trade for guns, lead, and powder so they could fight the Osage. Sibley advised them that, if they returned with horses, mules, buffalo robes, and silver ore, they would be able to trade for as many guns as they wanted. Sibley knew that unbroken Texas horses could sell from ten dollars or more in Natchez and Kentucky and was intrigued by the mention of silver ore.[79]

In the spring of 1808, Awakahei, the Iscani chief, sent a message to Sibley notifying him that the Wichita planned a large trade fair at their villages that summer. He requested that Sibley send traders to the fair, where many of the neighboring Indian groups would participate. Sibley mentioned this to Anthony Glass, a merchant from Natchez, Mississippi. Glass expressed interest in the trading venture and indicated that, if he could get suitable trade materials at Natchitoches and a trading license from Sibley, he would go to the Wichita villages to participate in the trade fair. Glass posted the requisite bond of one thousand dollars, and Sibley issued the license. Sibley also contributed a five-hundred-dollar note toward the purchase of the necessary trade goods. Rumors spread rapidly about the "silver mine expedition." Judge John C. Carr in Natchitoches reported to Governor Claiborne that Anthony Glass with twenty-five to thirty men had left Natchitoches for a trading expedition among the Wichita, but Carr believed the real reason was to locate a silver mine reported to be in the area. Claiborne feared that Glass would pass himself off as an Army officer and official government representative and worried how the Spanish would respond to what appeared to be a military expedition into Spanish territory.[80]

Spanish officials had learned of the expedition from Juan Cortes, a resident of Natchitoches, who at this time was informing the Spanish of activities in the Natchitoches area. Cortes wrote to Simón de Herrera that sixty men from Natchitoches, twenty-eight well-armed men from Natchez, and one hundred more assembling in the Illinois country would work two silver mines and that

Glass was assembling the equipment needed to smelt silver. However, the Spanish had a new policy. Francisco Amangual with two hundred men had left for Santa Fe with orders to instruct the Indians not to trade with any other nation, and Marcel Soto had gone to the Wichita villages in April to tell the tribes of new trading opportunities at the Spanish Bayou Pierre community. Both the acting governor of Texas and the commandant general of the interior provinces knew of the Glass expedition but felt any action by the Spanish could destroy the shaky peace between Spain and the United States and decided to do nothing.[81]

In June 1808, Anthony Glass along with 10 other men, sixteen horses packed with trade goods, and thirty-two other horses gathered at the saltworks twenty miles east of Natchitoches to set out for the Wichita villages. The Glass party journeying overland arrived among the Wichita on August 11. The next day, at the Wichita council house, Glass speaking through the interpreter Joseph Lucas told the 150 head men and women of the tribe, "Your Great Father the president of the United States is still your friend and at peace with all nations and wishes you to be so likewise and will be your father and benefactor so long as you remain dutifull [*sic*] children." He went on to state that the border dispute between Spain and the United States was still not settled but should be resolved without a confrontation. If there was a conflict, the United States was strong enough to handle the dispute. He encouraged the tribe not to become involved. Glass then stated that the purpose of his visit was to acquire horses from the Wichita and the Comanche (fig. 5).[82]

For the next seven months, Glass and his men traded with these Native groups. The Comanche did take him to see the "silver ore," and he obtained a sample. Glass returned to Natchitoches the first week of May and deposited his journal and the "silver ore" sample with John Sibley. Sibley wrote to the secretary of war reporting on Glass's trip and included a description of the "silver" ore.

> [Glass] was conducted by the Indians to a place where he saw in large masses of many thousands of pounds weight a singular kind of mineral, it in color resembles iron but whiter, it is hard as steel, yet [malleable] of gold or silver, it is obedient to the magnet, but less so than iron. Neither the nitric sulphuric nor muriatic acid will touch it, it is not flexible in the greatest heat than can be produced in the blacksmith's furnace, it will neither corrode nor rust by

Fig. 5. Wee-ta-ra-sha-ro, head chief of the Wichita tribe, by George Catlin (1834). Courtesy of Smithsonian Institution, American Art Museum. Gift of Mrs. Joseph Harrison Jr.

> exposure to the atmosphere, it receives a polish as brilliant as a diamond & of a quicksilver color, it is found in a limestone country & entirely unmixed with any mineral or other matter.[83]

Sibley thought the mass might be platinum and sent a piece of it to Philadelphia to be analyzed.[84]

In 1809–10, three different expeditions attempted to retrieve the "silver ore." Almost as soon as Glass returned, several members of the expedition, including Schamp and McCall, arranged a trip to recover the rock. Joined by other men and backed by several wealthy individuals, including Sibley, the Schamp-McCall expedition acquired enough trade goods to purchase the "silver ore" from the Indians and in June 1809 set out for the Wichita villages. A second group of about ten men headed by John Davis, who had also been on the Glass expedition, formed in Natchez, Mississippi. They intended to travel directly to the rock and steal it while the Natchitoches group was at the Wichita villages trying to purchase it. A third and much larger expedition formed in San Antonio. Spanish officials had concluded that their policy allowing Americans to enter Texas was proving ineffective and they could not permit Americans to mine platinum or work silver mines in Spanish territory. On October 5, 1809, a fifty-two-man cavalry unit left San Antonio for the north.[85]

The Davis group arrived first but had brought no method to transport the rock and tried to hide the stone until they could return with the means to move it. The Schamp-McCall expedition with a number of Indians arrived a few days later, located the hidden rock, and using saplings as levelers loaded it into a wagon and made their way toward the Red River. By the time the Spanish arrived at the Wichita villages, most of the Wichita had left to winter with the Comanche. After exploring the area and finding no Americans, the Spanish force returned to San Antonio. The Schamp-McCall expedition having reached the Red River built a large canoe to transport the stone and waited for the river to rise with the spring floods. This group with the "silver ore" reached Natchitoches on June 4, 1810.[86]

Their arrival created quite a sensation. No one in Natchitoches had seen anything like the "ore" before. The rock, roughly cone shaped, measured forty inches by sixteen inches by twenty-four inches.[87] As reported by John Maley in his journal, "People crowded in from all quarters to see this wonder. Such a solid mass as this to sound like a church bell—it was surprising. Who would not be curious enough to go 100 miles to see [it], especially if [being] formed by nature? There was great prices offered these men for there [*sic*] shares but they refused selling at any price."[88] Eventually the whole rock was sent to New York for study. Analysis showed that the "silver ore" was an iron-nickel alloy and undoubtedly arrived in Texas as a meteorite.[89]

Indians and the War of 1812

In June 1812, the United States declared war on Great Britain. The Spanish in Texas and the Americans in Louisiana expected Spain to join Great Britain in the conflict. In 1813, Sibley learned that the Spanish were once again encouraging the Caddo, Yatasi, Coushatta, and other tribes to attack the Americans. Spanish and American officials on the Louisiana-Texas frontier redoubled their efforts to influence the tribes in the area.[90]

In early October 1813, Sibley reported that Creek Indians had sent "a talk and tobacco" to all the tribes on the west side of the Mississippi River and some of the tribes had "smoked their tobacco." A concerned Sibley sent a request to all tribes to come to Natchitoches for a "talk." On October 5, 1813, Sibley met with ninety-two Caddo chiefs and head men, twenty-four Alabama, ten Coushatta, and chiefs from the Yatasi and Apalachee tribes under an arbor specifically constructed for the event. As Sibley reported, he told the chiefs that the United States was not at war with Spain but was at war with England, that the British provided guns and ammunition to a segment of the Creek Nation in its fight against the United States, and that some of the Creek Nation had attacked white settlements in Mississippi. He ended by stating that the "Great Father the President of the United States continued his friendly disposition towards his red children, that he wished them all clean paths, good crops of corn, good hunting & happiness." Sibley recorded Dehahuit's response: "In such times many false reports were spread, they [the Caddo] were never sure of the truth of what they heard, Red people not having the Arts of Writing and Printing were more liable to be Imposed on than white people, . . . that he had learned to be very cautious not to be led away by idle reports, [that] he was not a child to open his ears to all he heard, that although his skin was red he trusted he had some of the sentiments & discretions of white people."[91] Dehahuit ended by stating that, if an enemy of the United States invaded, his tribe as well as all those under his influence would come and fight "as long as one warrior remained." Sibley seemed pleased with the Caddo's response. The next day he sat down in his office with Dehahuit and asked him to visit all the tribes to the south on behalf of the United States. The Caddo chief agreed. Sibley wanted Dehahuit to try to convince the various Texas tribes not to get involved with any conflicts between white men—here he was referring to the unrest in Texas between the royalists and the revolutionaries.[92]

Governor Claiborne returned to Natchitoches in October 1813. While there he sent a "Talk" to Dehahuit. Addressing the chief as friend and brother, Claiborne reminded him of their meeting seven years earlier where they had both promised "to keep the path between our two nations white." After mentioning the "outrages" committed by the English, which could not be endured, Claiborne explained, "The hearts of the Americans have become cross: They have raised the tomahawk, & will not consent to bury it until the English are just towards them." Claiborne continued:

> [T]he English unwilling to fight us man to man, have called upon the red people to assist them.—With tongues, as forked and as poisonous as a snake, they have told the Indians many lies, and made fair promises which they will not, and cannot fulfill. Thus it is, many of the red men have been prevailed upon to throw away the peace talks of their father the President;—But the Americans have the power, and the will to punish all their enemies. . . .
>
> I hear the Creeks have sent runners with War Talks, to the Conchattas [Coushatta] and other tribes, your neighbors, but I hope all these people will look up to you, as an elder Brother and hold fast your good advice.[93]

At a meeting a week later, Thomas M. Linnard, the factor at the government trading post, declared to Dehahuit that neither the Creek nor the Spanish could be trusted. Linnard reported that Dehahuit promised "he was ready and willing to make common with [the United States] and that our enemies should be his enemies."[94]

By February 1813 Dehahuit had returned from an extensive trip among the tribes of Texas, which he had undertaken at Sibley's request. Dehahuit assured Sibley that, if the United States should be attacked and requested the help of the Indian nations, the tribes would come and fight "as long as there was one warrior remaining."[95] At first the secretary of war declined the Indians offer of assistance, but in March 1814 he accepted the aid of the Caddo and Choctaw but only if the English invaded Louisiana.[96]

In August of 1814, General Andrew Jackson reported to the secretary of war that he had "directed the agents of the different Indian tribes to enroll every warrior in their nation and put them under pay."[97] By the fall of 1814, with the invasion of Louisiana becoming more likely, Claiborne told Sibley they would probably need the help of the western tribes and to "keep them prepared for prompt cooperation."[98] In October 1814, General Jackson reported that the Caddo chief with twelve tribes offered the services of between five hundred and one thousand well-armed warriors. Jackson had ordered they be enrolled and put under the commanding officer at Fort Claiborne.[99]

By January 1815, with the British approaching New Orleans, the Natchitoches militia had been called up and, as Sibley informed the secretary of war, "we are all in bustle & confusion in getting them off. About 400 will embark from here in boats tomorrow morning and probably be down in six days." The Indian warriors had been arriving since Sibley had sent out his call, and about 150 were encamped about a mile from town. But many of the Indians had dispersed for the winter hunt. Sibley had sent out runners in all directions, and warriors were arriving daily. Sibley expected to have all the Indians gathered in ten to fifteen days. Meanwhile the gunsmiths were repairing the Indians' guns. Two white officers were attached to each company of Indians. They remained in Natchitoches awaiting the arrival of more men.[100]

Then news reached Natchitoches. The British had been defeated at New Orleans. The Indians would not be needed. The agency had spent $4,598 for equipment and rations for the tribal members while at Natchitoches. By this time Sibley had been removed as Indian agent, although he was not aware of this until his replacement, Thomas Gales, arrived at Natchitoches on January 25, 1815.[101]

Although no longer Indian agent, Sibley, now in his late fifties, remained very active. In 1813, he had married Marie Eulalie Malige of Natchitoches and, over the years, had four more children. He was not above utilizing the legal system. Beginning in 1813, Sibley was involved in numerous lawsuits—thirty-one times as the plaintiff and forty-six as the defendant. In 1819, as colonel of the militia, he joined Colonel James Long's expedition into Texas and, with the capture of Nacogdoches, became a member of the supreme council of the post. With the collapse of the Long movement, Sibley returned to Natchitoches. Sibley was appointed parish judge in 1821. He served as the Natchitoches representative in the state legislature in 1819–20 and was elected to the state senate in 1821. He ran for the senate again in 1826 and 1832 but lost. He was again elected to the state House of Representative in 1836. He continued to buy property, including large tracts of land in East Texas. He died on April 8, 1837, just one month shy of his eightieth birthday, a man with a large estate.[102]

Indian Agent John Jamison

Thomas Gales, Sibley's successor, functioned as Indian agent until his death less than ten months later. In January 1816, the secretary of war appointed John Jamison to succeed Gales. A Virginian by birth, Jamison had served in the army from 1808 to 1815 and in 1815 was assistant adjutant general. Jamison arrived in Natchitoches in June 1816 to assume his duties. He faced many of the same issues that Sibley had during his ten years as Indian agent.[103]

In July 1816, Dehahuit, the great Caddo chief, traveled to Natchitoches to complain to the new Indian agent about the encroachment of white settlers onto traditional Caddo hunting grounds. Of concern was an area along Red River that the buffalo used as a crossing. White settlers had recently invaded the vicinity, and many hunting parties entered the Caddo lands and killed the game that the Caddo depended on for food and skins. Dehahuit requested that the boundaries of Caddo lands be firmly established. He reiterated the Caddo's loyalty to the United States. Jamison reported to the secretary of war, suggesting that the request of the Caddo be honored.[104]

In the spring of 1817, Dehahuit again visited the agency at Natchitoches. Angered by the invasion of not only settlers and hunters but also whiskey traders, Dehahuit demanded Jamison have all these people removed from Indian land. In March, Jameson reported that "hordes of hunters and licentious traders [have] entered the Indian villages and camps on the Red River above Natchitoches."[105] John Fowler, the factor at the government trading house at the time, characterized the whiskey traders as being "generally the most unprincipled men, . . . who only practiced the most degrading and fraudulent impositions" upon the Indians by exchanging whiskey for skins.[106] Jamison feared losing the loyalty of the Caddo and requested that the commanding officer at Fort Claiborne send a force to evict the intruders.[107]

In April 1817, Jamison accompanied a military force led by Major David Riddle to Pecan Point (in present-day McCurtain County, Oklahoma, about five hundred miles by water above Natchitoches). The Americans found nearly a dozen families on the lands claimed by the Caddo and removed them to the north side of Red River. They also arrested several traders and seized all their goods, worth about five thousand dollars. The soldiers captured John Petty at

Pecan Point and his partner William Mabbet at the Coushatta village and chased the rest of the traders and hunters out of the area. Petty and Mabbet were taken to New Orleans, where Mabbet was indicted. He was tried and acquitted, and he then sued Jamison and Riddle, claiming damages of ten thousand dollars for illegal detention and loss of his merchandise.[108]

Jamison hoped his actions would restore confidence that the United States would protect the tribes from white intruders. The Caddo were initially pleased with Jamison's action, but the whiskey peddlers returned, and Pecan Point became a settlement of outlaws who sold whiskey to the Indians and cheated and robbed them of their furs and skins, horses, and mules. The men at Pecan Point claimed they were in Spanish territory and out of the jurisdiction of the United States. In fact, Pecan Point was within the jurisdiction of the Missouri Territory at that time.[109]

The Indian agent feared the Caddo would become so disgusted with the U.S. government that they would shift their allegiance to the Spanish. Dehahuit did make several trips to San Antonio to meet with Spanish leaders. The Caddo chief complained bitterly to Jamison about the whiskey traders and, in May of 1818, reported that eight tribes, including the Cherokee, Shawnee, Kickapoo, and Kaskaskia, planned to join forces and drive the whites out of the Red River country above the Great Raft. Both Jamison and Fowler, the factor, reported their concerns to their superiors. In October, the secretary of war asked the commander of the Eighth Military District for an evaluation of the situation and requested he remove the whites from Indian country.[110]

Jamison had to deal with other issues as Indian agent, including land disputes between whites and tribal groups such as the one between the Pascagoula and Joseph Gillaird, the same disagreement that Sibley had tried to resolve. Jamison also met with tribal representatives to discuss sending blacksmiths and gunsmiths to the tribes to repair tools and guns, licensing traders to go among them, and in the case of the Comanche a request for a doctor to administer inoculations against smallpox, about which the Comanche had learned.[111]

The presence of the three U.S. governmental institutions—Fort Claiborne, the trading house or factory, and the Indian agency—characterized Natchitoches for the first decade and a half following the United States' acquisition of Louisiana from France. Although the military commander, the Indian agent, and the factor did not always work well together, they did succeed in their geopolitical goals of establishing and maintaining the United States' claim to this portion of the Louisiana Purchase. But representatives of these institutions were not popular with all the local Natchitoches residents or even with most inhabitants during this time. In fact, many of the older Creole population would work to get all three entities removed from their town.

4

A TOWN ON THE FRONTIER

> On the river is located the city of Natchitoches. It is the abode of five hundred inhabitants, while a thousand others dwell in the country. . . . It is the residence of a priest and a district commander who renders zealous and paternal justice to all persons claiming it. The trade of a portion of the inhabitants of the city consists in pelts, cattle, hogs, and cheese; while the other portion is engaged in the chase . . . hunters, who gather all told more than twenty thousand skins in three or four months. . . . The inhabitants in the country engage especially in the culture of the tobacco so famed for its good taste. . . . The other products raised there by these inhabitants prove equally well by their abundant yield the richness of its soil.
>
> —PAUL ALLIOT, "Historical and Political Reflections on Louisiana," ca. 1804

In 1802, two years before the arrival of the American military force, the census of the Catholic Church of St. Francis enumerated 792 whites, 948 slaves, and 38 free people of color for a total of 1,778 parishioners in the Natchitoches area. No estimates remain of the non-Catholic residents, but they probably were not numerous. Since at least 1788, when the community built its new church, the commercial center of Natchitoches had been shifting northward from its earlier location along Bayou Amulet to a narrow plain about three hundred yards wide between the main channel of the Red River (now Cane River Lake) and a series of low pine-covered hills to the west. With the building of the new church, merchants such as Joseph Tauzin relocated their homes and businesses to the new area. By 1805, stores began almost at the foot of the hill east of the new Fort Claiborne.[1]

Since the town's French beginnings in 1713, trade in deerskins, pelts, and hides had been a major occupation for those living in the Natchitoches area. Some were hunters themselves; others, traders, who traveled to the tribes to acquire skins and pelts; and Indians came to Natchitoches to exchange their deerskins, buffalo robes, and other products of the forests and plains with the local merchants for guns, blankets, iron tools, beads, and other goods. The merchants in Natchitoches had commercial ties with the Spanish as well, earlier with those at Los Adaes, a Spanish fort and mission about twelve miles west, and later at Nacogdoches and San Antonio.

One large trading firm, known as the Edward Murphy Company in Natchitoches and the House of Barr and Davenport in Nacogdoches, began in 1798 and was heavily involved in the Spanish trade. The firm under contract with the Spanish government provided gifts and trade goods to distribute to the tribes in North and East Texas and delivered supplies to the Spanish troops and residents in Nacogdoches and San Antonio. A man of wealth and property, Murphy, originally from Ireland, had lived in the Opelousas–New Iberia area and for a time had a store and warehouse at the rapids near Alexandria before arriving in Natchitoches around 1785. Murphy managed the Natchitoches end of the operation. He purchased merchandise in New Orleans from the Royal Warehouse during Spanish times and then arranged for shipment up the Red River to Natchitoches, where he held the goods in his warehouse until ready for transport to Nacogdoches and beyond. Murphy's men loaded the merchandise on carts drawn by a yoke or two of oxen or on horse and mule packtrains. The carts and packtrains made the fifteen- to twenty-two-day trip over 130 or so miles from Natchitoches to Nacogdoches. In August 1808, for example, the firm transported in three carts five barrels of brandy, four barrels of sugar, four barrels of salt, two barrels of powder, four hundred pounds of lead, ten pieces of cloth, twenty pounds of vermillion, and one hundred pounds of beads to Nacogdoches. At the company's peak, Murphy was sending goods from Natchitoches to Nacogdoches once or twice a month.[2]

William Barr, another Irishman, reached Louisiana around 1786 and by 1793 was in Natchitoches, but he moved to Nacogdoches that same year. Samuel Davenport (fig. 6) from Pennsylvania reached Natchitoches about 1785–86, where he became a merchant and trader. In 1794, he too relocated to Nacogdoches. Barr and Davenport handled the Nacogdoches end of the operation with Barr

Fig. 6. Samuel Davenport. Courtesy of the Stone Fort Museum, Stephen F. Austin State University, Nacogdoches.

spending most of his time in Texas while Davenport traveled back and forth between Nacogdoches and Natchitoches. In 1803, the trading firm sent twenty-two men to the Indian villages with merchandise to exchange for skins, pelts, horses, and other goods. Tribal members also came to Nacogdoches to trade. The firm's carts and packtrains carried deerskins, buffalo robes, and other items back to Natchitoches. One shipment in 1808 involved six men on horseback and thirty mules packed with twenty-five hundred deerskins. In Natchitoches, Murphy stored the skins in his warehouse until he could load them and other items onto boats and send them downriver to New Orleans to be sold.[3]

The fourth member of the firm, Luther Smith from New York, ran the horse and mule part of the operation. In 1799, the Spanish governor allowed the firm to export animals from Texas to Louisiana. Two years later, Spanish officials permitted the firm to drive about three hundred horses and mules to Louisiana to exchange for supplies for the Indian trade. Smith sold the horses and mules in Louisiana and, after the Louisiana Purchase, in West Florida, which was still at that time part of Spain. This became a lucrative portion of the operation.[4]

Jefferson's Embargo Act of 1807 affected the firm. In November 1808, local officials stopped ox carts on their way to Nacogdoches and forced them to return to Natchitoches in adherence to the act.[5] When Congress repealed the act in 1809, the shipment of goods resumed. Spanish directed the firm to do what it could to keep the Indians friendly to Spanish interests and to discourage them from trading with the Americans. In late 1807 or early 1808 Smith died, followed in July 1808 by Murphy and Barr in 1810, leaving Davenport the sole surviving partner. By this time, the Americans had established their own trading house as well as an Indian agency in Natchitoches, and robbers occupying the Neutral Ground had made traveling through the area increasingly difficult.[6]

In addition to the skins and furs, Natchitoches exported large amounts of high-quality tobacco to New Orleans. In 1796, the Spanish lieutenant governor noted that all the tobacco in Natchitoches was of an excellent quality and recommended that the government purchase all that year's production.[7] Shortly before the Louisiana Purchase, cotton began to supplant tobacco as the major cash crop in the area. As Natchitoches native Emanuel Prudhomme explained to Pierre Clément, the commissioner for the French government, in May of 1803, "Although tobacco from Nakitoches [*sic*] has preserved its reputation, its cultivation has dwindled and has been taken over by that of cotton."[8] One observer wrote, "perhaps cotton and tobacco are raised on Red River in greater perfection than in any other quarter of the union; certain it is, that they command the highest prices in the market."[9]

By 1810 the residents of Natchitoches were contending with the disruptions resulting from the arrival of the Americans and their fort, trading factory, and Indian agency. Like those in the rest of Orleans territory, they also experienced the upheavals wrought by the U.S. government's efforts to reorganize Louisiana's administrative practices to conform to those of the United States. This included the Herculean task of authenticating land claims so that the government could identify the unclaimed land and offer it for sale to settlers. Initially the expectation was that this process would be completed by March 1, 1806. This proved incorrect.

Old Claims and Land Surveys

The rivers and bayous had been the main transportation networks during colonial times, and French officials made many of the early land grants along these waterways. The French used the arpent system of land survey, the arpent being both a linear measurement of about 192 feet and an area measurement equivalent to around 0.84 acres. (See map 3 for examples of both the arpent and the American Public Land Survey System.) The typical French land grant was two to four arpents along the river and forty to sixty arpents deep. This afforded the grantees access to the river, good alluvial land for planting along the natural levees, and often a backswamp area where they could graze their livestock and cut the rot-resistance cypress trees so important in building construction. The Spanish continued the arpent system but with the typical grant being six to eight arpents along the river and forty arpents deep. They also made larger grants, some exceptionally large, in the upland areas.[10]

The French and Spanish governments had granted land to the early colonists to encourage settlement. The crown assigned some of these grants, but colonial officials issued most of them. Some grants were made in writing by a local commandant, some with verbal permission of the commandant, and, in some cases, people simply settled on vacant land. Some grants had been settled and then abandoned. The land often went unsurveyed, the boundaries were often vague, and the owners seemed generally unconcerned about these niceties. Records of ownership, where they existed, were in French or Spanish. Fires in New Orleans in 1788 and 1794 had destroyed many of the official land maps, and the Spanish took many of their records with them when they left New Orleans. Over the years, numerous initial grantees had lost their documents and the older Creole community, not pleased with its abrupt transfer to the United States, did not always cooperate.[11]

Congress passed an act in 1805 to send surveyors into the Territory of Orleans. These men were to map all private lands before plotting the vacant public lands. The survey method to be used was the Public Land Survey System (PLSS) originally proposed by Thomas Jefferson. This method divided all land into townships of six square miles and then subdivided the townships into thirty-six one-mile-square sections with numbers assigned to each section. Sections could be divided further into quarter sections and quarter-quarter sections.

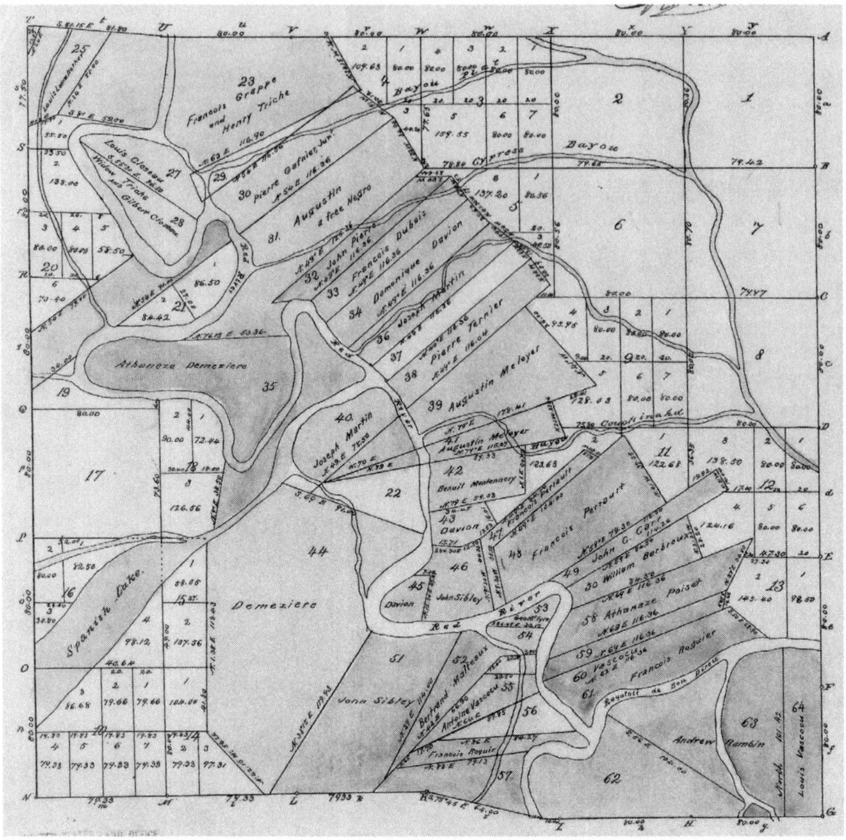

Map 3. Plat survey of Louisiana District Northwest, 10N, 7W, ca. 1825. Map shows both the French and Spanish arpent and the American survey systems. Louisiana Land Office, Old Plat Map.

The surveyors also assigned numbers to the arpent grants (map 3). Congress authorized the opening of a U.S. District Land Office in New Orleans for the eastern part of the Territory of Orleans and another office in Opelousas for the western part. Eventually offices would be added in Ouachita, Natchitoches, and Greenburg. The act also established a board of commissioners for each land office, made up of a register and two other people. The board divided the claims into three categories: those that met all the conditions prescribed by Congress, those that did not meet all the conditions but that the commissioners believed deserved confirmation in conformity with the Spanish laws and customs, and those that did neither. The inhabitants, who held land through French, Spanish, or British grants, were directed to appear before the board with witnesses and documentation to prove their land claims. If the board approved the claim, the information was forwarded to Washington, DC.[12]

The actual confirmation of titles proved to be a longer process than originally anticipated. Many inhabitants, even those who held valid land titles, seemed reluctant to appear before the commissions. Reasons given included not enough time to register their claims or it was too far to travel. Some lacked the funds to pay the registration fee. Others alleged that they did not understand the process or received bad advice. Still others had misplaced their records, or the records had been retained by the Spanish. And there were those who claimed that they did not understand the language, lacked knowledge about the new government, or were unaware of the requirement. Many feared that the complicated process to prove their claims was an attempt to deprive them of their rightful property. The result was that many missed the congressional deadline of March 1806.[13]

Certificates of land ownership could be issued under several different circumstances. In Natchitoches, for example, Pierre Joseph Maes's claim to 1,354.04 acres along Bayou Quissachie had been granted by the French commandant Juchereau de St. Denis under a French patent. Louis Clauseau received 181.94 acres as a Spanish grant. John Baptiste Davion Sr. received his title to 166.83 acres for his occupancy of the land for ten years. Manuel Rachal based his claim on an order of survey and settlement.[14] Edward Murphy filed a claim for a 119-acre tract of land on the right descending bank of the Red River across from the town of Natchitoches on December 27, 1806. He had purchased the land from Louis Buard. This claim was confirmed by Congress on March 3, 1807.[15] On the same date, Congress confirmed claims for several lots in the town of Natchitoches, including the property of Joseph Tauzin (lots 1 and 13), the heirs of Harvey Fontenot (lot 2), of Michael Casenave (lot 4), Evariste Lauve (lot 9), Charles Pavie (lot 10), John Nancarrow (lot 12), John Horn (lot 14), and François Rouquier (lot 19). A little over 118 acres, originally granted to the Reverend Dagobert, the Catholic priest in Natchitoches in 1743–44, was settled in favor of the Police Jury after "possession for ten years." It would be the 1820s before Congress approved some of the other claims in the town of Natchitoches, including those of Arnaud Lauve (lot 8 in February 5, 1825), Pierre Joseph Maes (lot 11 in March 31, 1826), and John Sibley (lot 15 in March 31, 1826).[16]

Governor Claiborne struggled to allay the inhabitants' fears concerning their land. Congress repeatedly extended the deadline for the inhabitants to prove their claims. It would be 1821 before the government sold any public land in Louisiana. Until then, potential settlers had no legal method to purchase the vacant public lands. Because of the complicated land inheritance laws in Louisiana, it would be 1879 before all the titles were finally settled. In the end, claimants filed nearly ten thousand private land claims in what became the state of Louisiana.[17]

The Neutral Ground

While most of the landowners in Louisiana had to deal with questions associated with land ownership, the people in Natchitoches faced another challenge, the wave of crime resulting from the Neutral Ground Agreement. This agreement, hastily arranged in 1806 by U.S. and Spanish military officers, remained in place until the final resolution of the boundary issue in 1819. In the interim it created unforeseen consequences for those living in the Natchitoches area and neighboring Texas. For the French Creole population of Natchitoches, it was just another example of the negative impact the Americans had on their community. The no-man's-land between the Sabine and the Arroyo Hondo became a largely unpoliced haven for squatters, runaway slaves, and outlaws who preyed on those traveling through the area. Several roads crossed the Neutral Ground, the most significant of these being the Natchitoches-to-Nacogdoches road in the north and the Orcoquisac-to-Opelousas road in the south. Secondary roads included those from Bayou Pierre to Natchitoches, from Bayou Pierre to Nacogdoches, and from Opelousas to La Nana, a large land grant west of Natchitoches. Additional trails also traversed the area (see map 1).[18]

A Spanish census in 1797 enumerated fourteen families living in what became the Neutral Ground, most of these around the old Spanish settlement at Los Adaes and in the Bayou Pierre community. These people farmed and ranched, raising cattle and hogs in the uplands. By 1805, twenty-eight families resided in the area. The trading firm of Barr, Davenport, Murphy, and Smith had two large land grants in the area—La Nana, which straddled the Natchitoches-to-Nacogdoches road, and Las Ornigas to the north along the Sabine River.[19]

To protect the Spanish border from encroachment by Americans, Nemesio Salcedo, the commandant general for the Interior Provinces, which included Texas, ordered Governor Manuel Antonio Cordero of Texas in 1805 to issue a proclamation stating that at any sign of hostility by the United States all slaves who fled to Spanish territory would be free. Despite repeated requests from the Americans, the Spanish officials refused to change this policy. Slaves escaped from the Red River plantations to the Neutral Ground and from there to Texas and freedom, much to the alarm of the planters. Then, in late 1808, Manuel Maríe de Salcedo, the new governor for Texas, arrived in San Antonio.[20]

Manuel de Salcedo, the son of Juan Manuel de Salcedo, Louisiana's last Spanish governor, had assisted his father and returned with him to Spain after the Louisiana Purchase. When appointed the new governor of Texas, the younger Salcedo journeyed with his family across the Atlantic, landing in New Bedford, Massachusetts, and spent three to four months traveling to Natchitoches. The family stayed there four days before leaving for San Antonio. While in Natchitoches, Salcedo dined with the Fort Claiborne commander, Colonel Constant Freeman, and with John Sibley. He also met with John C. Carr, civil judge for Natchitoches. Carr and Salcedo discussed the problems Natchitoches planters faced, including the October 1804 escape of slaves into Texas. According to Carr, Governor Salcedo favored the return of all slaves but doubted the commandant general would allow such an action.[21]

On October 9, 1808, between thirty and forty slaves fled from several area plantations and headed for the protection of the Neutral Ground and Texas. Some Americans returning from Nacogdoches captured eight of the escapees who had crossed the Sabine, and some of the other slaves turned back. Others were still missing. Judge Carr contacted Governor Salcedo, reporting that Louis Derbanne, one of the Creole planters, had entered the Neutral Ground to search for the runaways. Carr asked for the governor's help in recovering the slaves. Carr also wrote Governor Claiborne, telling him that he had contacted Salcedo and that the Texas governor had promised while in Natchitoches to return any runaway slaves after he became governor. Carr warned Claiborne the planters were so concerned that they had asked him to authorize a posse of two hundred men to invade Texas and recover the fugitives. On November 22,

Claiborne wrote the commandant general for the Interior Provinces to demand the immediate return of the fugitives to Louisiana. Claiborne offered to send back any slaves who were the property of Spanish subjects that might escape to the Territory of Orleans. This reciprocal solution had been suggested before, and both sides realized this agreement benefited the Americans much more than the Spanish since the Spanish had few slaves in Texas. However, an agreement was reached and, by early 1809, the slaves were returned to their owners. With Spanish Texas no longer a safe haven for the escapees, the number of slaves fleeing the Red River plantations near Natchitoches declined.[22]

Because the Neutral Ground was policed by neither the Spanish nor the Americans, it quickly became the home of thieves, robbers, and murderers. As the Spanish commanding officer at Nacogdoches wrote in 1807, "Without at least one hundred well-mounted men to keep a patrol continually guarding the territory between this point [Nacogdoches] and the Sabine, and visiting the ranches and crossings, it is impossible to prevent the outlaw citizens of the United States who have over-run the disputed territory [Neutral Ground] from crossing the river and pillaging our country for there is no horse they will not steal and no crime they will not commit."[23] The outlaws were raiding the farms on the west side of the Sabine River and then retreating east across the Sabine to the Neutral Ground, where the Spanish could not follow. The Spanish settlers were abandoning their homes to escape the attacks.

The outlaws also harassed those traveling through the area, and the deprivation had become serious. A gang led by James Elliot robbed both the whites and the Indians of horses. John Sibley's views probably reflected those of many in the Natchitoches area when he wrote to Governor Claiborne, "No one I believe calculated that the famous Sabine Expedition [the Wilkinson-Herrera confrontation at the Sabine River] was to have such consequences. Some government ought to exercise jurisdiction on this side the Sabine, we either ought to suffer the Spaniards to do it or do it ourselves. What can be more ridiculous and more in opposition to Common Sense than that the commanding officer of Fort Claiborne shall prevent armed Spaniards from crossing the Sabine & tell them at the same time he is prohibited from going within 50 miles of it?" Sibley ended by suggesting that volunteers offer their services if the military was unwilling or unable to act.[24]

Conditions became so serious that the commandant at Nacogdoches wrote Judge Carr, suggesting a joint effort to evict the outlaws from the Neutral Ground. Carr ignored the request but sent armed men to capture the horse thieves active in the area. But in 1810, a joint Spanish-American expedition of fifteen Spanish and fifteen American soldiers and officers with Samuel Davenport acting as translator entered the Neutral Ground and over a two-week period in August destroyed all the houses between the Sabine River and Arroyo Hondo except for Miguel Crow's ranch. The military found many of the houses abandoned, their owners having already fled.[25]

The robbers returned. In December 1811, José Zepeda with three hired men was traveling from Nacogdoches to Bayou Pierre with twenty-five head of cattle and some money. Bandits attacked the group, killing one of the men, wounding two others, and taking the livestock and equipment. Zepeda and the two wounded men slowly made the rest of their way to Bayou Pierre on foot. In January 1812 about thirty robbers with "faces blacked, and otherwise disfigured" attacked another Spanish convoy on its way to Bayou Pierre, killing one man and wounding several others, and stole the Spanish horses, mules, baggage, and the equivalent of about six thousand dollars. A month later, Apolinar Masmela was sent from San Antonio with between fifteen thousand and twenty thousand dollars in funds to Louisiana to purchase supplies for the Spanish. When he reached Nacogdoches, the commandant there warned him that robbers infested the Neutral Ground and advised him not to cross the area. However, San Antonio desperately needed supplies. The commandant provided Masmela with an armed escort of eleven soldiers and fifteen settlers. As predicted, outlaws attacked the Spanish convoy. The Spanish force successfully defended itself, killing several of the robbers and wounding others. The bandits fled, and the Spanish party continued to Natchitoches. The Spanish purchased the necessary supplies and, in June, as they prepared to recross the Sabine River, the bandits attacked the Spanish again, capturing all the merchandise and pack mules. The Spanish counterattacked and retook their property. The raids in the Neutral Ground continued. Conditions became so serious that it threatened all the commerce between Natchitoches and Texas. Samuel Davenport wrote the Spanish governor at San Antonio that, because of the outlaws in the Neutral Ground, he was afraid to risk his company's resources in the trade with the Spanish in Texas.[26]

Local authorities had been unsuccessful in stopping the robberies, and the Natchitoches merchants—including firms of Compere & Hertzog, Vienne & Landray, C. Pavie & C. Jos. Tauzin, and A. Sompayrac, John Cortes, Ambrose Duval, and Etien Lauve—appealed to the territorial governor for aid. As the merchants, many of them French or Creoles, explained, the local militia did not want "to leave their houses and risque [*sic*] their lives for as they conceive," to be "the exclusive interests of the merchants," and in any case the local public prison was inadequate to hold the outlaws. This, the merchants argued, required the intervention of the army. If the deprivation was not stopped, the merchants claimed, the raiding "will annihilate the most valuable part of the commerce of this parish" and eventually of the territory. The merchants suggested the army send a unit from Baton Rouge to deal with the outlaws and the commandant at Fort Claiborne be instructed to house in the fort's prison any outlaws apprehended. Governor Claiborne forwarded the merchants' request to General Wade Hampton, the commanding officer of the U.S. troops in the Orleans Territory, with the suggestion that the military set up three posts in the Neutral Ground.[27]

Hampton replied that, until the boundary issue was settled, he could not establish posts within the Neutral Ground. He believed a joint military effort of the Spanish and United States like the one undertaken in 1810 would suffice. Hampton sent Lieutenant Colonel Zebulon M. Pike to Natchitoches and directed him to suggest to the Spanish a joint expedition to remove the outlaws. If the Spanish did not agree with this, Pike was to undergo the operation without Spanish participation. Pike arrived in Natchitoches and contacted the commandant, suggesting the joint effort. The commandant replied that he was not authorized to undertake such an enterprise on his own, but he would immediately forward Pike's request to the governor at San Antonio. Pike did not wait for the Spanish governor's response. On March 5, 1812, he ordered two officers and forty men to enter the Neutral Ground and destroy all houses and camps that they discovered. The force captured sixteen men, thirty-five horses and mules, and merchandise, guns, and ammunition. When the Spanish governor replied authorizing the joint expedition, the commander at Fort Claiborne agreed to cooperate with the Spanish in the future, if the situation required a joint expedition, but said there was currently no need for Spanish troops to enter the Neutral Ground since the outlaws had been apprehended. The Spanish launched its own expedition anyway but found only the charred remains of the houses burned by the Americans. In April, Sibley reported that the bandits "are pretty nearly broken up. Now nine of them are to be tried at the Superior Court at Rapids."[28] This proved to be the last expedition by the Spanish into the Neutral Ground. Spain's involvement in the Peninsular War and rebellions and revolutions brewing in the New Spain colonies proved of greater concern to the governing authorities than the strip of land between the Sabine River and the Arroyo Hondo. In 1812, the Neutral Ground would become the staging area for an armed incursion into Spanish Texas.[29]

Natchitoches in 1810

Seven years after the Louisiana Purchase, Natchitoches had changed. The American fort, factory, and agency dominated the town, and the number of people in the area had grown to almost 3,000, with whites representing 44.2 percent, slaves 49.7 percent, and "all others free persons" 6.1 percent of the population (see appendix table 1). These people lived in 261 households. Many households represented family units, but others, such as Louis Benin's and John Sibley's, contained large numbers of men. Louis Benin recorded twelve men between twenty-six and forty-four in his household and one between sixteen and under twenty-six. There were no women, children, or slaves living at the Benin residence. John Sibley listed twenty-eight men in his household between the ages of twenty-six and forty-four. The men listed in these residences may have been traders who spent most of the year at the various Indian villages, hunters, keelboat men, or some could have been boarders who worked in town.[30]

Slaves (1,476) made up the largest number of people. These bondsmen lived in 167 or 64 percent of the households in Natchitoches Parish. Most households had fewer than 20 slaves, many fewer than 5. Some listed more than 20 slaves, including the widow Fonteneau (37), John Sibley (30), Athanase Demezieres (28), Jean Louis Buard (24), Louis Buard *père* (33), François Rouquier (29), Ailhaud St. Anne (48), and Alexis Cloutier (23). There were several slaveholders who had more than 50, including Antonio Prudhomme (52), Emanuel Prudhomme (58), Remy Lambre (60), Ambrose Lecomte (54), and Madame Porter (50). The largest slaveholder was the planter and merchant Claude Thomas Pierre Metoyer with 103 enslaved men, women, and children. Almost all the large slaveholders were French or French Creole planters. Eight of the free people of color owned slaves, including the Metoyer brothers Augustin (17), Louis (15), and Pierre (12). Many of the enslaved people undoubtedly worked as field hands on plantations, reflecting the increasing importance of agriculture in the area.[31]

The 1810 census of Natchitoches listed 181 "others." Some of these were free people of color, freed former slaves or their children. Twenty of these people, including the Metoyer brothers, maintained separate residents with a total of 94 people living in these households. The others lived in the households of whites, with more than 36 residing with François Grappe near the Campti community on the east side of the Red River. These were probably members of the Natchitoches tribe who had relocated to the area from their former home in what had become the town of Natchitoches.[32]

During the early nineteenth century, Natchitoches Parish was primarily a fur-trading and agricultural center, but it did have several industries including, in 1810, a soap and candle operation, one of only four such manufacturing enterprises in the entire Orleans Territory. This Natchitoches operation produced 4,588 pounds of candles and 4,606 pounds of soap, with the candles representing almost half the total amount (9,902 pounds) manufactured in the entire Orleans Territory. The trading firm of Barr and Davenport provided candles for the Spanish army hospital and barracks in both Nacogdoches and San Antonio, which may have been a market for the Natchitoches manufactured candles. Another major industry was salt production. In 1810, Natchitoches had two saltworks that generated 9,600 bushels of salt, valued at $5,760. The only other saltworks in the Orleans Territory was one in Ouachita parish in the northeastern part of the territory, but it produced only 600 bushels of salt, valued at $350. Natchitoches also had 32 looms where weavers wove 1,624 yards of fabric. This was a relatively small amount when compared to the weavers in Rapides Parish south of Natchitoches who, with 125 looms, produced 22,810 yards of cloth the same year. The weavers in all of Orleans Territory manufactured a total of 133,180 yards of cloth. Natchitoches did possess a hattery that made three hundred fur hats, as well as five shoemakers who cobbled 650 pairs of shoes, boots, and slippers. Other industries included a sawmill that cut about 160,000 feet of lumber and a brickkiln that fired around 160,000 bricks. This was the Natchitoches that José Bernardo Gutiérrez found when he arrived in 1811.[33]

The Filibusters

In 1808, reports reached Louisiana of a revolutionary movement brewing in Mexico and rumors circulated of Napoleon's interest in Spanish America. Many on the American frontier believed that Texas had been part of the Louisiana Purchase and rightly belonged to the United States, that the Neutral Ground Agreement had been a mistake, and that events in Mexico might provide opportunities for Americans in Texas.[34] For their part, the Spanish feared Americans would take advantage of the upheavals in Mexico. A treaty existed between the United States and Spain, but Spanish officials worried about a possible American invasion of Texas. Nemesio Salcedo, commandant general for the Interior Provinces, judged "the restless, turbulent, covetous spirit of the Anglo-Americans on our borders, their roving character, and the looseness of their government, the rebellious spirits it harbors within its borders, and the weakness of its constitution and laws which make it impossible to rely upon its promise and good faith"; these qualities, he continued, "make me fear some aggression on the part of these Anglo-Americans; against the nearest provinces."[35]

On September 16, 1810, the priest Miguel Hidalgo y Costilla, one of the conspirators against the old Spain Imperial rule, rang the bell at the parish church in Dolores, Guanajuato, Mexico, and heralded in the Mexican War of Independence, a fight that would last for eleven years and end with an independent Mexico.[36] On the morning of January 22, 1811, the revolution reached Texas. Juan Bautista de las Casas, a former military officer, along with a number of soldiers, captured Governor Manuel Salcedo and his military staff at San Antonio. The Spanish loyalist staged a counterattack and seized Casas. He was tried, convicted, and executed. His revolution had lasted only thirty-nine days, but others picked up the standard. One of these was José Bernardo Gutiérrez de Lara.[37]

The Gutiérrez-Magee Filibuster

José Bernardo Maximiliano Gutiérrez de Lara was from an old pioneer family that had founded Revilla (present-day Guerrero, Tamaulipas, Mexico) on the Rio Grande in 1750. In 1810, he was a landowner, merchant, and blacksmith but, when he learned of the Hidalgo movement, he quickly joined the ranks of the revolutionaries. After the Casas Revolt, Gutiérrez, representing the insurgent cause, traveled to the United States via Natchitoches to solicit support for the independence movement. Gutiérrez along with Captain José Menchaca, another revolutionary, and fourteen other heavily armed men, with as much silver as Gutiérrez had been able to collect, made the difficult trek across Texas, avoiding the Spanish forces until the party arrived in the Bayou Pierre area. There the Spanish loyalists overtook them. In the fight that ensued, Gutiérrez's party lost almost all their supplies, about half the silver, and equally important, Gutiérrez's papers and dispatches. Gutiérrez, Menchaca, and most of the others managed to escape and made their way to the Rio Hondo. There the Americans, who had heard of the revolutionists' plight, found them. Gutiérrez arrived in Natchitoches in September 1811.[38]

The revolutionaries saw the unpoliced Neutral Ground as an opportune locale to assemble volunteers for their army and Natchitoches as an advantageous place to obtain supplies. At the time about fifty outlaws were believed to inhabit the Neutral Ground. Some felt that these men, seeking adventure and profit, would join Captain José Menchaca. Menchaca planned to attack San Antonio, overthrow the Spanish government there, establish a new government, and then send funds to purchase supplies. About three hundred Americans collected in the Neutral Ground and on October 15, under the leadership of Menchaca, crossed the Sabine and headed toward Nacogdoches. This effort proved unsuccessful. Menchaca joined the approaching loyalist troops, and the Americans in disdain returned across the Sabine.[39]

Meanwhile, Gutiérrez, remaining in Natchitoches, negotiated with the merchants for supplies to send to the mouth of the Rio Grande, where money would be waiting to purchase them. However, Gutiérrez's principal purpose in entering the United States was to travel to Washington to meet Secretary of State James Monroe and others to solicit U.S. support for the rebellion. After about a month in Natchitoches, Gutiérrez left for Washington with letters of introduction from Captain Overton, the commanding officer at Fort Claiborne, and John Sibley. Sibley also provided Gutiérrez with two hundred dollars to assist with his travel expenses.[40]

Gutiérrez arrived in Washington in December 1811 and met with officials of the War and State departments. He asked for money, troops, and ammunition for the revolution. Gutiérrez also visited with José Álvarez de Toledo y Dubois, a fellow revolutionary. Those in Washington, aware of conditions on the frontier, encouraged Gutiérrez to return and, after about three weeks, Gutiérrez left for New Orleans, believing the United States would help in his endeavors. The United States, interested in its own territorial expansion, viewed Texas as a worthy prize but still officially considered Spain a "friendly power." The United States' support would be covert.[41]

Back in Louisiana, Gutiérrez met with Governor Claiborne, who introduced him to William Shaler. Shaler had arrived in New Orleans in January to act as a special agent for the United States and to report on the activities of the revolutionary José Álvarez de Toledo y Dubois, but he would also assist the Gutiérrez expedition. In April, Shaler and Gutiérrez traveled together to Natchitoches.[42]

On his return, the captain at Fort Claiborne invited Gutiérrez to dine and threw him a "magnificent banquet." Many of the leading citizens in the town, including John Sibley, entertained Gutiérrez during his stay. Gutiérrez also met with the Caddo chief, Dehahuit. As he recounted in his diary, "Knowing that the Indian nations are doing damage to the soldiers and citizens of San Antonio, I summoned the chief of the Caddo, as the supreme chief of the Indian nations, and I rebuked him of this; I ordered him to go immediately to tell the said nations in my name to stop hostilities against the Spanish, and to await my orders as to what they should do in future. The said chief has recognized me as supreme chief, and has set out to comply with my orders."[43]

Dehahuit's thoughts on Gutiérrez's "orders" have gone unrecorded, but it is doubtful that he followed Gutiérrez's directions on this or any other occasion. Dehahuit had received an invitation from the Spanish at San Antonio who also wanted to solicit his support. Dehahuit discussed this with Sibley. Sibley advised him not to become involved in the conflict but decided to invite the Caddo chief to Natchitoches, thereby precluding him from going to San Antonio. Dehahuit and the tribes associated with him would take no part in the filibuster efforts; however, several Texas tribes, including the Lipan Apache and Tonkawa, would join the conflict.[44]

In June, Sibley informed the secretary of war about the increasing numbers of volunteers arriving to take part in the filibuster movement. These Anglo-Americans were flooding the formerly quiet French Creole community. A paper circulating in both the Orleans and the Mississippi territories invited men to join the effort and to rendezvous at the Sabine. Sibley reported that the revolutionaries were growing to such a number that, even if the United States wished to stop the volunteers, there was no military force in the area large enough to do so. He also worried that, if the revolutionaries wished to take the military equipment and supplies stored at Fort Claiborne, there would be no way to stop them.[45]

By early August, Sibley estimated that the nascent army, camped on the east side of the Sabine River in the Neutral Ground, numbered about two hundred, with new recruits arriving daily. In addition to the denizens of the Neutral Ground, Gutiérrez's army grew to include Anglo-American volunteers, Tejano settlers, Indian allies, and Spanish soldiers eager to change sides. The rewards promised for participating in the revolution were impressive. Each volunteer would receive forty dollars a month plus a league of land, a little over forty-four hundred acres, in the future Mexican Republic. Former military officers and civilians joined the effort, including Joseph B. Wilkinson, son of General James A. Wilkinson, and Owen, a merchant, and Hall, a lawyer, the latter two both from Natchitoches. In Natchitoches, Shaler convinced Lieutenant Augustus Magee, then stationed at Fort Claiborne, to join the movement. The twenty-three-year-old graduate of West Point resigned his commission in the U.S. Army and became the military leader of the expedition, known as the Republican Army of the North. Gutiérrez served as the nominal commander. Rumors circulated in Natchitoches that a force consisting of about five hundred men with ammunition and provisions was gathering in the Neutral Ground for the invasion. Spanish sympathizers in Natchitoches quickly passed this information on to the loyalists in Texas.[46]

Governor Claiborne, who was kept informed of the developments on the frontier, was well aware of the Neutrality Act of 1794. He, like many in the West, believed in the westward expansion of the United States. But the governor wrote Judge John Carr, the civil official in Natchitoches, on July 30 and again on August 7, reminding him that the Neutrality Act barred the formation of any filibuster or military expedition on American soil. Claiborne also asked General Wilkinson to instruct the commanding officer at Fort Claiborne to help prevent the expedition. On August 11, the governor issued a proclamation reminding the people of Louisiana of the penalties for those who would participate in an invasion of a country with which the United States was at peace; however, by this time, volunteers were streaming through Natchitoches on their way to the Sabine.[47]

On August 8, 1812, about 130 men, under the military leadership of the now Colonel Magee, crossed the Sabine River. Gutiérrez followed on August 10. A force of about 300 Spanish soldiers retreated in front of the advancing army. The filibusters reached Nacogdoches on August 12. There around 50 Spanish soldiers welcomed their arrival. About 190 of the townspeople joined the revolutionary cause. The Spanish, in their haste to leave, left behind valuable military stores, including flour, powder, ammunition, lances, and spears; about eighty thousand pounds of wool; and horses, mules, and species, much of which belonged to a Spanish merchant who had been on his way to Natchitoches to exchange these items for much-needed provisions for San Antonio. Soon packtrains of two hundred heavily laden horses and mules trod along the old Camino Real on their way to Natchitoches, where the busy merchants exchanged wool and other commodities for supplies. On the return trip to Nacogdoches, the pack animals carried flour, arms, and other goods for the Republican Army. Samuel Davenport, now working as quartermaster for the army in Natchitoches, oversaw the purchasing and shipment of goods not only from Natchitoches but also Natchez and other centers in the Mississippi and Orleans territories. Natchitoches quickly became a busy trading center crowded with merchants and with stacks of military provisions and supplies off-loaded from boats to be packed on horses and mules for their trek west.[48]

American recruits continued to join the movement. As Shaler reported to Secretary of State Monroe from Natchitoches in October 1812, "the business of volunteering for New Spain has become a perfect mania; I hear of parties proceeding thither from all quarters, and they are constantly passing thro' this village from Natches [Natchez]. . . . I suppose that volunteer force cannot now be rated under 600 americans."[49] So many laborers and militiamen volunteered from western Orleans and Mississippi territories that the residents of these areas became concerned there might not be enough men left to work the fields and protect their homes. Many of the volunteers brazenly passed through Natchitoches. Others, aware of Claiborne's proclamation, skirted the town. The new volunteers collected at the Sabine before being sent forward to Nacogdoches.[50]

On October 19, the army, with an effective force of six hundred, headed southwest toward La Bahía (present-day Goliad) and San Antonio. The Spanish withdrew from La Bahía and repositioned their forces on the road to San Antonio. The Gutiérrez-Magee expedition arrived at La Bahía, finding it virtually undefended. It easily fell to the Republican Army. Meanwhile, Spanish reinforcements arrived in San Antonio, bringing the Spanish Army to about eight hundred men. Then, led by Governor Manuel de Salcedo and Lieutenant Colonel Simón de Herrera, the Spanish laid siege to La Bahía, a siege that continued for four months. Rueben Ross went to Nacogdoches to recruit Indian and white volunteers for La Bahía. About three hundred Lipan and Tonkawa men joined the fight against the Spanish, along with twenty-five Coushatta, but most tribes decided not to participate due to the influence of the Caddo chief, Dehahuit. When Colonel Magee died under mysterious circumstances, maybe consumption, suicide, or murder, on February 6, 1813, Samuel Kemper assumed command. Under Kemper, the Republican Army attacked the Spanish. The Spanish—experiencing heavy casualties and a disastrous defeat—retreated toward the safety of San Antonio.[51]

Kemper and Gutiérrez followed them about a month later with a force of about eight hundred men. Herrera with about twelve hundred loyalists and six cannons attacked the Kemper army outside of San Antonio, but the filibusters routed the Spanish force and the Republican Army marched into the town. Several hundred men in San Antonio defected to the Republican Army, and Salcedo and Herrera had little choice but to surrender. The army took fourteen officers as prisoners, including Salcedo and Herrera. The revolutionaries charged these men with various crimes and convicted them. The Americans believed the prisoners would be taken either to Matagorda to be placed onboard a ship or imprisoned at La Bahía. However, on April 3, a guard of sixty soldiers marched the prisoners about six miles out of town, stripped them, stabbed them multiple times, and finally slit their throats. The soldiers left the bodies unburied. When the Americans learned of this action, apparently sanctioned by Gutiérrez, they were irate. On April 6, 1813, in San Antonio, Gutiérrez issued a declaration of independence. He gave the Americans little credit for the success of the Republican Army and insisted that Texas would be part of a new and independent Mexico and not affiliated with the United States. Angered by Gutiérrez's attitude and sickened by the killing of the Spanish officials, some of the Americans returned to Louisiana.[52]

Back in Natchitoches, William Shaler, Gutiérrez's former confidant and advisor, was appalled by the events. Shaler had been losing faith in Gutiérrez for some time and was planning to replace him with José Alvarez de Toledo. By May 29, Toledo, who had been in Nacogdoches, returned to Natchitoches, bringing with him his printing press with the first copy of *Gaceta de Texas,* ready to print. In Natchitoches, he published *El Mexicano.* Printed in both Spanish and English, the stated purpose of the newspaper according to Shaler was to provide an impartial account of the Mexican rebellion. It quickly became a vehicle to demonize Gutiérrez. The June 19 issue read: "The public voice accuses the GOVERNOR and PROTECTOR [Gutiérrez], as he stiles [*sic*] himself, of that state as responsible for a progressive series of the most frightful calamities. Since his entry there he has committed errors, weaknesses, and monstrous crimes that we shudder at in recording."[53]

The paper went on to "apologize" for "introducing to notice so insignificant and contemptible a character as José Bernardo Gutierres [Gutiérrez],"[54] but as stated, Gutiérrez's name was associated with major events. Toledo had this paper, along with broadsides, distributed widely in Texas, including San Antonio. He traveled to San Antonio and on August 4 took command of the Republican Army. Gutiérrez's activities and the propaganda resulted in his removal as governor. The junta sent a letter of credit to the "senior inhabitants" of Natchitoches, requesting that they provide accommodations for Gutiérrez and his family. Shortly thereafter, Gutiérrez left for Natchitoches, where he resided until 1824. After independence, Gutiérrez returned to Mexico. As Sibley would describe his departure, "Bernardo has sent in after his family who are at Grand Ecore, about a hundred horses & mules with a squadron of cavalry arrived yesterday to conduct his family out."[55] Gutiérrez would be elected governor of the state of Tamaulipas.[56]

The surrender of San Antonio shocked the Spanish into action. On August 18 the Republican Army of about 1,400 met the loyalist forces of 1,820 men under the command of Joaquín de Arrendondo and Ignacio Elizondo, and the Spanish army decisively defeated the revolutionaries at the Battle of Medina River. Arrendondo let most of the Americans still in the army return home, but he set in motion a reign of terror for the Spanish rebels. He executed 327 insurgents at San Antonio and imprisoned hundreds of others, and it is reported he shot about 100 more who were fleeing the country at the Trinity River. Meanwhile Elizondo swept toward Nacogdoches, destroying property and torturing and killing the rebels that he found. By September, Elizondo had executed 71 men, taken over 100 prisoners, and seized the property of the "traitor" Samuel Davenport.[57]

Rumors reached Natchitoches of the defeat. Joseph B. Wilkinson arrived on September 4 and confirmed the reports. Remnants of the Republican Army began flooding into Louisiana. Sibley told of approximately three hundred families escaping from San Antonio and La Bahía, including two hundred women fleeing on foot. When the news reached Nacogdoches, many abandoned their homes and headed for the Sabine River, Louisiana, and safety. The Lipan Apache, about five hundred warriors and their families, had crossed the Trinity River and were moving toward the Sabine. Sibley predicted that within "a few days this town will be crowded with hundreds of the most wretched of the human species, having fled from their own country to Save their lives."[58] On October 3, Sibley reported that about two thousand Spaniards had crossed the Sabine River—men, women, and children—along with several Indians tribes.[59]

About three hundred people along with their livestock and household goods flooded into Natchitoches, and another six hundred reportedly arrived at Bayou Pierre, Opelousas, and Attakapas. Governor Claiborne, writing from Natchitoches, believed that at least twelve hundred people had crossed the Sabine, "most of whom are wholly destitute of the comforts, & the necessaries of life—I learn however with pleasure, that the Citizens of this and adjoining parishes have extended to these strangers much hospitality and supplied with a generous hand, their immediate wants."[60] The condition of the refugees was serious. Fortunately, Louisiana crops had been particularly good that year and many of the planters hired the refugees to work in the fields. In October, Claiborne reported that the Spanish were offering the former inhabitants of Nacogdoches and San Antonio pardons if they appeared at Spanish headquarters within fifty days. Claiborne believed that few if any would accept the offer.[61]

Despite the failure of the Gutiérrez-Magee filibusters, there were those who still believed in taking Texas. In 1813, John Hamilton Robinson and the Friends of Mexican Emancipation, for example, although largely organized in Natchez, had supporters in Natchitoches, including John Sibley, John C. Carr, and John Nancarrow. If Robinson's effort proved successful, Sibley would be governor-general of the Interior Provinces and Carr, Nancarrow, and William Bullett would form a company that would have exclusive trading rights. Commercial interests seemed to be the primary consideration for those from Natchitoches. Toledo also attempted to organize an army to overcome the Spanish loyalists and accused Robinson of conspiring with the French. In Natchitoches, a committee composed of Samuel Davenport, Charles Slocum, William Bullett, John Galvin, John Sibley, John C. Carr, and John Nancarrow investigated the charge and, in the end, vindicated Robinson, but attempts to reconcile the rivals met with little success. Neither Robinson nor Toledo succeeded in their aims.[62] In 1815, Claiborne heard of rumors of another invasion into Texas but, as he wrote, "I must confess, I shall learn with regret that any portion of our Citizens should engage in enterprises which the government of the United States as far as I know and believe does not approve, and the laws positively forbid."[63]

The Adams-Onís Treaty

Ever since the Louisiana Purchase, the American and the Spanish governments had been negotiating over Louisiana's borders. Charles IV of Spain issued a royal decree for the collection of all data and maps relating to the matter. José Antonio Pichardo received the commission to undertake this effort, on which he labored diligently from 1808 until his death in 1812. To the east the Spanish claimed both East and West Florida while the Americans believed that at least West Florida had been acquired with the Purchase. West Florida was particularly important to the Americans because many of the rivers south of the Tennessee River drainage flowed through West Florida into the Gulf of Mexico. The Americans in the area needed ports such as Mobile to ship their goods to markets. To the west, the United States claimed the land all the way to the Rio Grande while the Spanish maintained that all of Texas and as far east as the Rio or Arroyo Hondo just a few miles west of Natchitoches belonged to Spain. Finally, the negotiations between John Quincy Adams, secretary of state under President James Monroe, and Luis de Onís, the Spanish ambassador in Washington, resulted in the 1819 Adams-Onís Treaty, also known as the Transcontinental Treaty, which set the Spanish–United States boundary. In the treaty, Spain ceded its claim to Florida to the United States and the United States gave up any rights to Texas west of the Sabine River. When Louisiana had become a state in 1812, its western boundary was set at the Sabine River and Americans had begun moving into the Neutral Ground, most probably in late 1813 and early 1814. By 1819, 208 land claims had been filed in the Neutral Ground. Of these all but 29 would eventually be ruled as valid.[64]

The Long Filibuster

Not everyone on the frontier agreed with the Adams-Onís Treaty. Many felt that Texas had been part of the Louisiana Purchase and resented the American government apparently trading Texas to obtain Florida. Among these men was Dr. James Long, who initiated a filibuster expedition into Texas. The center of the Long effort was in Natchez, Mississippi, but a number of those in Natchitoches became involved, including John Sibley and Samuel Davenport, who now lived in Natchitoches. To recruit men for the venture, the organizers promised each enlistee a league of land. On June 7, 1819, 22 men arrived in Natchitoches and left for Texas the next day. Another 120 men crossed the Sabine on June 8 and began to congregate at the rendezvous west of the Sabine, awaiting supplies and other troops. Men from various parts of Louisiana were making their way to Texas, and four barges of supplies had been sent up the Red River. Both John Sibley and Stephen Baker also provided goods.[65]

James Long, now General Long, left Natchez with about 70 men on July 17, traveled through Natchitoches, and arrived in Nacogdoches four days later. In Nacogdoches he established a provincial government with a 21-member council, with himself serving as president. On June 23, 1819, he declared Texas independent from Spain. Plans were made to move on to La Bahía and San Antonio. But supplying the army proved difficult, and Long was forced to break his army up into small detachments to hunt for food. In San Antonio, Governor Antonio Martínez learned about the Long expedition, and the viceroy in Mexico City again sent General Arredondo to San Antonio with a force of 500 cavalrymen. By the end of September, enough troops had reached San Antonio to start an offensive. Colonel Pérez left San Antonio with 550 men, and 100 additional soldiers joined his army. As they approached Nacogdoches, Pérez's troops began to attack small groups of the scattered American force. Long had gone to Galveston, and Major Hamlin Cook evacuated Nacogdoches, retreating toward the Sabine River. When Pérez arrived at Nacogdoches, he broke some of his troops into detachments to hunt for the filibusters and then pursued the fleeing troops toward Louisiana. Arriving at the Sabine on October 31, he found an American military force stationed on the opposite bank of the river. When questioned by the Spanish, the American officer said he had orders to arrest General Long and to stop the Spanish from crossing the Sabine River. The Long filibuster was over, and the Americans participants came scurrying back across the border into Louisiana. The Spanish fell back from the border and spent the next month burning some twenty houses and ranches and driving Anglo-American settlers from the area. East Texas became a "desert."[66]

The Removal of American Government Institutions from Natchitoches

Even before the transfer of Louisiana to the United States, the Spanish were concerned about the movement of Americans into Louisiana. In 1792, Louis Charles de Blanc, the Spanish commandant at Natchitoches, wrote the Spanish governor of Louisiana that the increasing number of Americans is "a thing that is not at all desirable. I for one fear the evil conduct of those depraved people whom we have just cause to suspect."[67] For some, the arrival of the American military, government trading house or factory, and the Indian agency in Natchitoches proved this statement all too true. The Creole community members saw the Americans building their fort on land that belonged to one of the longtime residents of Natchitoches, encroaching onto property owned by the Catholic Church, and expropriating land that belonged to the community. The local people, who were not happy about the American government's presence in their town, made a concerted effort to get all three entities removed.[68]

Fort Claiborne

Many of the townspeople wanted the fort removed from the town, but they were not the only ones. By 1810, Fort Claiborne was in a deplorable state of disrepair. Lieutenant Colonel Constant Freeman reported to Brigadier General Hampton that the fort's pickets were rotten, barracks and quarters were rapidly deteriorating, and general repairs were absolutely necessary.[69] Captain Walter H. Overton wrote Zebulon M. Pike in March 1812 concerning Fort Claiborne. He noted that the land-claims office had recently settled the ownership of the land on which the fort stood in favor of a resident who claimed ownership. He saw military disadvantages resulting from the location of the fort. There were hills to the west and south within easy musket shot of the fort, and the fort was nearly surrounded by a lagoon. He added that the proximity of the fort to the town gave "the soldier free scope to indulge himself in all the vices of the age, which is everyway calculated to seduce him from his duty & ruins his health and dissipates his morality." He also emphasized that the buildings at the fort needed repairs, which would require much labor and expense. Overton recommended the fort be abandoned.[70] In 1814, Inspector Major Daniel Hughes stated that the fort was almost a ruin, its stockade decaying and the barracks needing new roofs, but there was no funding to undertake the required repairs. In April 1816, General Andrew Jackson recommended that either the fort be repaired or a new fort built on the Sabine River.[71]

In 1816, the military decided to construct a new fort outside of Natchitoches. Both General Jackson and Governor Claiborne argued for a site nearer the Sabine River, but at the time the United States and Spain had not yet settled the boundary issue. The secretary of war felt that a fort located in what was still contested territory might harm the ongoing negotiations over the border. Instead, he directed that a new location should be chosen on public lands along the Red River below the Great Raft. Lieutenant Colonel Joseph Selden selected the site for the new fort about nine miles by land north of Natchitoches on a high bluff overlooking Bayou Pierre near its junction with the Red River. By August, soldiers were clearing the land for what would become Fort Selden, and by the end of the year construction of the buildings had begun. Unfortunately, in the summer of 1817, sickness struck the garrison. In June, Lieutenant Colonel William A. Trimble, by then commander at Fort Selden, reported that 47 of the 108-man garrison were sick, 40 suffering from intermittent fevers with 20 in critical condition. All the officers were also ill. By July, over 90 of the men, women, and children of the post had been affected. Trimble attributed the sickness to the fort's unhealthy location and recommended that it be abandoned. Also, there was a question as to whether the fort was on public lands. John Sibley claimed he owned the land within fifteen feet of the fort's buildings. Trimble believed Grand Ecore would be a better location for a fort. In late July, the secretary of war instructed that no additional funds be invested in Fort Selden except what was necessary to temporarily accommodate the troops until its future was determined.[72]

In late July, most of the troops returned to Fort Claiborne and, by October, the rest of the soldiers and all the public property had been transferred back to Fort Claiborne. In May of 1819, Captain William Beard, then the commanding officer at Fort Claiborne, received orders to reoccupy Fort Selden with authorization to relocate the troops if the sickness returned. Captain Robert A. Coombs and his company moved to Fort Selden to assist with repairs to the fort and the rest of the garrison with all the public property returned to Fort Selden by July 11, 1819, and Fort Claiborne was closed. But the stay at Fort Selden would be a short one.[73]

On February 22, 1819, the Adams-Onís Treaty set the boundary between Louisiana and Texas. With the border issue finally resolved, Captain Beard in June received orders to proceed to the Sabine River and establish a military presence in the area. Beard arrived at the Sabine on August 12, 1819, and construction on Camp Ripley began, but Camp Ripley's location proved unsatisfactory. It was thirty miles from one of the major crossings of the Sabine River, and it was costly to transport supplies from Natchitoches to the post. In the winter of 1821–22, the troops returned to Fort Selden. In March of 1822, Major General Edmund P. Gaines ordered Lieutenant Colonel Zachary Taylor to build a military post on a ridge near the Natchitoches-to-Nacogdoches road about eighteen miles from the Sabine River and about twenty-five miles from Fort Selden. This became Fort Jesup and would defend the frontier until its eventual abandonment in April 1846.[74]

In 1806, people in Natchitoches had begun submitting their land records to the authorities for review and approval, but it would be March of 1826 before the claim to lot 11, Pierre Joseph Maes's original lot and the location of Fort Claiborne, was certified in Maes's favor. Nancarrow, who had purchased the land from Maes, attempted to obtain rent from the U.S. government for the use of the land but with little immediate success. The government ultimately did pay John Nancarrow $4,404 for the use of the property to 1815. Six others eventually obtained similar payments from the government for a total of $3,360 with John Sibley receiving $1,035, while Pierrie Maes Jr. was awarded $741. In 1804, Turner had estimated that the site of Fort Claiborne was worth about $200.[75]

The Government Trading House or Factory

From its beginnings, the Creole community viewed the land on which the factory was located as belonging to their congregation—the Church of St. Francis. On December 13, 1811, the land office settled the church's claim in favor of the police jury for having been in "procession of the property for ten years," although the police jury had only existed for four years. In 1813 the members of the congregation submitted a claim for four acres of this tract, stating that the land had been used continuously by the church for over eighty years. The land office awarded the four acres to the church.[76]

Over the years, the locals made several attempts to have the factory removed from the village. In 1813, these endeavors became even more determined.

Thomas M. Linnard, the man in charge of the factory at the time, knew of these efforts and, in December, wrote to the superintendent of Indian trade, describing what he felt were the real reasons behind the complaints. Since the arrival of the trading house in Natchitoches, Linnard contended, the merchants of the town had lost probably between two thousand and three thousand dollars per year because the Indians were now trading with the factory rather than the local merchants. Linnard did admit that this had been exacerbated by what the "good people of Natchitoches" called an "improper & unprecedented act." A year earlier, Linnard had purchased bear oil from the Indians and found a good market for it. In 1813 he refused to accept the peltry from Indians who also had bear oil unless the oil was sold to the factory as well. Linnard maintained that his reason for buying the oil was to offset losses in the peltry. He stated that the amount of bear oil was not great and that he had sold it for the same amount he had paid for it, which he claimed was only three-quarters of what it was truly worth. He did not explain how selling the oil for what he had paid for it would offset losses from the peltry. Linnard pointed out that the merchants were "in the habit of getting it [the bear oil] at almost nothing when the Indians were in a state of intoxication." Linnard denied the accusation that he had bought the oil specifically to harm the merchants. He concluded by stating that the grievances were much exaggerated, and no one had complained about the Indian trade, "when the commerce in Peltries had been beneficial to one of the chief promoters of this clamor" and who had "realized a considerable fortune by this same commerce and which the establishment of the Factory obliged him to abandon."[77]

A few days later, Linnard learned the police jury had sent a petition to the president of the United States, the Congress, and the state legislature requesting that the factory be removed from Natchitoches. The reasons given included complaints about the trouble the Indians caused the inhabitants, citing: pilfering crops, killing livestock, and drunken and disorderly conduct. The petition also included specific instances of violence allegedly perpetrated by the tribal people.

At first Linnard had not been able to obtain a copy of the petition. When he did, he wrote the superintendent of Indian trade. As far as the specific allegations were concerned, Linnard argued they were "either much colored or mistaken" and addressed each of the charges individually. The person who was murdered, Linnard claimed, was a "poor discharged soldier" who was employed to "keep hogs at a lonely & infrequent place out of the jurisdiction of the Territory." This man had argued with the two Indians who had killed him. Linnard reported that, according to his interpreter, one of these Indians had never been to the factory. The other worked for one of the French planters and, therefore, the presence of the Indian in the area was not due to the presence of the factory.[78]

With respect to the incident of Mr. Smith, Linnard explained that Smith "was notoriously in the practice of selling liquor to Indians & always had a parcel about him." The Indian who threatened Smith with a gun had been "indulged in many liberties by him & when in town was most of the time at his house." On the day in question, Smith struck the Indian who "mortified in the extreme at the blow immediately drew his gun." Several people present kept the Indian from harming Smith. Linnard noted the Indian had not been drinking at the time.[79]

In the case of the drunken Choctaw Indians who insulted Mr. Malye and drew their knives on Malye and his son, the danger was so minor, according to Linnard, that the Malyes were able to beat off the threat by themselves. One of the Indians lived on the plantation of one of the justices of the peace and hunted to feed his family. At the time, the justice of the peace spoke of the general good conduct of the Choctaw man involved and obtained the release of both men from jail. Linnard pointed out the justice of the peace was now one of the individuals representing the event as one of "the insufferable grievances" resulting from having the trading house and agency in the town.[80]

With respect to the allegations that "vagabond Indians" were found behind the plantations, Linnard contended that the planters encouraged the Indians to stay there since planters employed the Indians to hunt, to tend their livestock, and to pick cotton. And regarding the vagabond charge, Linnard said not a single Indian had migrated to Natchitoches since he had been in the area. Linnard then addressed the problems with the Indians getting liquor. He blamed the "negligence or connivance" of the civil authority for the excesses and claimed the state laws were adequate but were not enforced. If they had been enforced, Linnard contended, the laws would have prevented the drunken excesses.[81]

Whatever the truth in these arguments, the police jury, the parish governing organization, requested that both the trading house and the agency be removed from Natchitoches. P. D. Cailleau, the parish judge at the time, who wrote the secretary of war with this request, also mentioned that the Catholic Church owned the land on which the trading house was built and would accept the factory buildings as payment in lieu of rent for the years the factory had utilized the land. The congregation planned to turn the buildings over to the police jury to use as a courthouse.[82] Linnard claimed "the eager and unjust wish to obtain the building without paying for it has impelled them [the police jury] beyond prudence."[83] In 1816, P. S. Compere, representing the wardens of the Church of St. Francis, sent a petition to President James Madison, asking for the removal of the factory from church land. He claimed the buildings had been constructed without the congregation's consent and suggested the buildings be turned over to the Church in lieu of payment for use of the property by the factory.[84]

On May 18, 1816, Governor Claiborne wrote the Indian agent, telling him that both the factory and the agency would be relocated. That October, the superintendent of Indian trade directed Linnard to begin looking for a new site for the factory. Linnard, however, had already sent his letter of resignation as factor, effective January 1, 1817. The superintendent appointed John Fowler of Virginia, a former clerk in the Office of Indian Trade, as Linnard's successor. It would be Fowler who oversaw the relocation of the trading house.[85]

By the time Fowler arrived in February 1817, a site had been selected for the new fort, Fort Selden. The factory was to be located adjacent to the fort, but Fowler felt this was not a good location for the trading house since unloading and loading trade goods and peltry would require negotiating a steep bluff. He preferred another site about one and a half miles from the fort on the bank of Bayou Pierre, about three-quarters of a mile from the Red River. But certain people in Natchitoches did not favor this new site. They wanted the factory moved further away, and there were questions about who owned the land.[86]

When the military decided to abandon the partially constructed Fort Selden, Fowler recommended moving the factory to a site further up the Red River. He noted that the Indians around Natchitoches were decreasing in number and could be easily served by local merchants and that the Indians to the north were much more numerous and the hunting better. Fowler pointed out that the Indians had to travel a considerable distance to trade at Natchitoches. Many unscrupulous traders had located closer to the tribes and preyed on the tribal people, plying them with liquor and cheating them out of their furs and skins. Fowler believed the new trading house should be established at the junction of Sulphur Fork and Red River, about 270 miles by water and 150 miles by land from Natchitoches (near the current Louisiana-Arkansas border). He noted that major villages of the Caddo, Coushatta, and Delaware were in that area. Although keelboats could not easily navigate through the raft at the time, Fowler felt that large pirogues could make the trip to the site year-round. In May 1818, Fowler moved the factory to Sulphur Fork.[87]

Fowler faced difficulties during his time as factor at Sulphur Fork. He reported that the military guard sent to assist him proved virtually useless. The sergeant in charge was prone to drinking and would not assign soldiers to help in the construction of the trading house. He protested that the soldiers broke into the store and stole fifteen gallons of whisky and other merchandise. The local Indians repeatedly complained about the white whiskey sellers and asked the factor to have these men removed from the area. The whites were pushing the Indians off their lands. The factor also informed the superintendent of Indian trade that the Caddo chief had become very insolent and threatening and, in April 1819, Fowler learned that Dehahuit had just returned from a long visit with the Spanish in Texas. The factor repeatedly reported his concerns but received no relief. In June of 1820, Fowler closed the factory, left the buildings and merchandise under the custodianship of Larkin Edwards, and returned to Natchitoches. Fowler had suffered several bouts of illness while at Sulphur Fork and in December 1820 died while in Natchitoches. In February 1821, William McClellan was named the new factor at Sulphur Fork and arrived in May of that year.[88]

The factory system always had its detractors. During its existence it was never authorized for more than three years at a time. By the end of the War of 1812, the Indian agents as well as the representatives of the independent fur companies were seriously questioning the factory system. The fur companies and others argued the government should not be competing with private enterprises. By offering trade goods at low costs, the government was injuring the private businesses that were also engaged in the Indian trade. Other people felt the factory system had failed in its purpose of making the Indians dependent on the government or of keeping the peace with the tribes, and there were those concerned with the cost of the program. The original investment had been completely depleted. People believed there was something basically wrong with the management of the program. The government failed to cover its cost while the private fur companies were making large profits. Supporters of the system, generally those sympathetic to the Indians, many public officials, and the factors, pointed out the benefits the system provided the Indians. But in 1822, opponents of the factory system in Congress passed an act authorizing the president to close the factories and settle all accounts.[89]

In the end, the entire factory system realized a total loss of $146,263. The Natchitoches–Sulphur Fork factory fared better than many. The factory did lose $11,719 between December 1807 and September 30, 1811, due in part to the disruption resulting from the Embargo Act, but between March 1812 and December 1816 the factory earned a profit of $16,406. The factory did not operate between April 1817 and June 1818 due to the preparation for the move to Sulphur Fork but, after the relocation until March 1820, it netted a gain of $20,394. Meanwhile, Indians continued to come to Natchitoches to trade but now again with the local merchants.[90]

The Indian Agency

There was also a concerted effort to have the Indian agency removed from the town of Natchitoches. For the trading house, the underlying concern may have been that economic interests of the local merchants who were losing business to the federal operation. In the case of the agency, the objections seem to have more to do with the Indian agent, John Sibley, than the agency itself, although some found the presence of large numbers of Indians in town worrisome.

John Sibley, the Indian agent for the first nine years in Natchitoches, was a wealthy and successful businessman with extensive real estate holdings and enemies and a somewhat spotty reputation. In 1805, Sibley began construction of a building that town residents claimed was partly on the property owned by the St. Francis Catholic Church. Several men went to Sibley requesting that he stop building until the land could be surveyed. Sibley continued to build. Then seventy community members submitted a memorial to Captain Turner to request that Sibley remove the building. They claimed that Sibley's building might be as much as ninety feet outside his property line. Sibley continued to build. François Rouquier Jr., on behalf of the church, appointed Emanuel Prudhomme to act as attorney for the church community.[91]

This was not the only grievance lodged against Sibley. In December 1813, Henry Harrison wrote the secretary of war to complain of Sibley's conduct, stating that the whites and the Indians disliked him, maintaining that the Sibley family had too much power and wealth, and asking that Sibley be removed as Indian agent. The secretary of war responded by asking for specific evidence to document Sibley's behavior. In May 1814, Harrison replied by accusing Sibley of abusing the Indians, cursing them, and treating them badly. He said Sibley had unjustly imprisoned some Indians and, when Harrison and the parish judge had tried to intercede on their behalf, Sibley had threatened him and the judge and told them not to meddle in Indian affairs. Harrison further accused Sibley of allowing the Indians to get drunk and doing nothing to control them. Several others in Natchitoches provided depositions concerning Sibley's behavior. James Bludworth claimed Sibley cheated his employees and treated the Indians badly, resulting in the Indians disliking and distrusting him. Daniel Eams, a brick mason, complained Sibley had not paid him for work he had done, was a ruthless speculator and a liar, and had called the Indians "damned brutes and dogs" to their faces.[92] Davidson Brown, a blacksmith, stated that, when Sibley had not paid him for work he had done repairing the guns and tools for the Indians, he had refused to do any more work. The Indians ended up paying for repairs for which the agent should have paid and were terribly upset over this. When Brown finally agreed to accept only 75 percent of the money owed, Brown accused Sibley of requesting reimbursement for the entire amount from Washington and pocketing the difference. The residents of Natchitoches also complained to the Louisiana legislature, and, in the fall of 1814, fifteen members of the legislature sent a letter to President Madison requesting that Sibley be removed from his position as Indian agent.[93]

Learning that Harrison and others had written Secretary of War James Monroe and the legislature, Sibley wrote Monroe: "Some time ago a man by the name of H. Harrison came here from the frontiers of South Carolina, & passed himself for a lawyer. The Judges refused to license him. . . . This man had taken it into his head that I have contributed to his ill success in the law, & to revenge had been publishing some false, defamatory pieces against me, which could produce no effect provided the circulation of them were limited to the extent of his acquaintance." Sibley claimed that Harrison had left the area some weeks earlier, but Sibley had learned that Harrison and another man had sent a petition asking for signatures in Natchitoches concerning Sibley's conduct. Sibley admitted that he had not seen the petition but believed it was "a tissue of falsehoods." Sibley in his letter to Monroe stated "I hope Sir that these things will excite no prejudice in your mind against me, until at least I have an opportunity to justifying myselfe [*sic*] & showing that I have conducted the business of my agency with propriety.

I know that my personal Influence amongst the Indians is great notwithstanding the attempts that have been made to injure it."[94]

Sibley's letter arrived too late. The secretary of war had written to Governor Claiborne, directing him to remove Sibley from his post, and authorized the governor to select a new agent. Claiborne failed to notify Sibley. Instead, the governor contacted General Andrew Jackson, asking him to select someone to fill the position of Indian agent.[95] Jackson recommended Thomas Gales for the position.

It is clear from Sibley's correspondence that he was extremely upset with his removal as Indian agent. Undoubtedly the way it was done was humiliating. He made several attempts to contact the secretary of war to learn the reason for his removal but, as far as is known, never received an explanation. Whatever the truth in the other accusations, the statements that Sibley treated the Indians badly and that they hated him appear to be untrue. Sibley had been influential in keeping the various tribes of western Louisiana and East Texas friendly to the United States or at least neutral during the confrontations between the United States and Spain in 1806 and again during the early stages of the Mexican Revolution. Gale served as agent until his death, less than ten months after his appointment.[96]

Like Sibley, John Jamison, who was appointed agent in 1816, ran into problems with some of the people of Natchitoches. In 1818, H. H. Bullard wrote the secretary of war about what Bullard viewed as Jamison's inappropriate conduct and asked for Jamison's removal as Indian agent. Bullard accused Jamison of issuing and then rescinding trading licenses to some traders and of licensing a trader that Jamison knew sold liquor to the Indians, in direct violation of U.S. policy. The secretary of war took no action against Jamison. Since 1816 there had been ongoing discussions in Washington about relocating the Indian agency along with the factory and military post. Several locations were evaluated for the agency, but Jamison was not to take part in this move. He died of typhus fever in the fall of 1819. It would be George Gray, the new Indian agent, who would oversee the relocation of the Indian agency to Sulphur Fork during the winter of 1820–21.[97]

In the end, the American government did relocate all three bastions of the American frontier—fort, factory, and Indian agency—but not due to pressure brought by the local people. Rather it was the changing nature of the frontier itself. The establishment of a new international boundary between the United States and Spain resulted in the removal of the fort. The decreasing number of Indians in the area and the need for a government presence farther north contributed to the decision to move the factory and Indian agency.

By 1820, Natchitoches was a far different place than it had been just ten years earlier. A portion of the Neutral Ground had been added to its borders, and people had been settling in the area. The parish now had a population of 7,372, compared to just 2,970 ten years earlier, an increase of 148 percent. The character of the town itself had changed. By the early 1820s, all three of the government institutions that had once dominated the town had been removed, and the town was booming, crowded with wagonloads of settlers heading west.

5

THE DEVELOPMENT OF A REGIONAL CENTER

> The village is compact, larger than Alexandria, and composed of Spanish, French, and American houses, and a population composed of these races together, with a considerable mixture of Indian blood. From its position, this must be a great inland town. At the head of steam-boat navigation, the last town westward towards the Spanish frontier, and on the great road to that country and to Mexico, it has already a profitable trade with that country. The Spanish come there for their supplies. . . . They pay in bars of silver and mules. I have seen droves pass of four hundred horses and mules. The relations of this place with the interior of the state, and of New Spain, must necessarily be extended, and this must ultimately become a place of great trade.
>
> —TIMOTHY FLINT, Natchitoches, early 1820s

Natchitoches in 1820

In 1820 the population of Natchitoches Parish stood at 7,372, an increase of about 4,400 in just ten years (see appendix table 2). In 1810 the enslaved people had represented almost half (49.7 percent) of the total population. In 1820 they contributed a little less than a third (31.6 percent). This did not indicate a decrease in the number of slaves. In fact, the enslaved population grew from 1,476 in 1810 to 2,326 in 1820. Rather, the growth of the white portion of the population reflects the large numbers of people who had settled in the old Neutral Ground, now known as the Rio Hondo District, and in other areas. In the 1810 census, the "other category" represented 6.1 percent of the population. In 1820, listed as "free colored persons," they contributed 4.0 percent. Again, this did not represent a decrease in this category. In actuality, this group grew from 181 in 1810 to 301 by 1820 (see appendix tables 1 and 2).[1]

The Town of Natchitoches

In 1820 the town of Natchitoches was booming, "full of strangers, & every place crowded with goods & wagons carrying things out to Sabine & Nacogdoches & droves of horses & mules packing for St. Antonio." Land-hungry American settlers were flooding into Texas and, as the last stop for provisions before the trek westward, Natchitoches was thriving.[2] The town had 857 people living in 104 households. More than two-thirds of the residents were white (589), and a little less than a third were slaves (240), with the rest (28) classified as "free colored persons." About a fifth of the town's white residents were foreign-born and non-nationalized. Seventy percent of the households, or 168 people, engaged in some form of agriculture, twenty-two people were involved in commerce, while fifty were occupied in manufacturing (see appendix tables 2 and 3).[3] Natchitoches' success was due in no small part to its role as a gateway to the West. As John Sibley noted in a letter to his son-in-law Josiah S. Johnston in June 1821:

> Texas is filling up with Americans as fast as the State of Alabama did, Mr. Austin has the permission of the Spanish Government to settle on the Brassos or Colorado three hundred families. Some officers are here instructed to escort him out & the governor will meet him. Young Austin is here & will start out in three days. Lafitte is still going on in privateering. He has lately brought in a slave ship with 200 Negros which he took near Havana. Red River continues up in fine order for steamboats. The Beaver and Arkansas are now here & will make several more trips. Our season has been a little rainy but not too much. I never saw a prospect of finer crops. . . . Considerable Building is going on.[4]

During the first two decades of the nineteenth century, the United States attempted to generate revenue through the sale of government land. To facilitate the sales, the government extended settlers credit for the purchase of the lands, which sold for $2.00 an acre. The buyer would pay one-twentieth of the price of the land on the day of purchase, with another quarter due within forty days, and the balance to be paid in two, three, or four years. After the economic panic of 1819, this changed. In 1820, Congress passed an act which required full payment at the time of sale for public lands but reduced the price from $2.00 to $1.25 per acre. Since the minimum amount of public land that could be purchased at the time was eighty acres, this meant the settler had to have access to at least $100. Texas provided an appealing alternative for settlers. Moses and Stephen F. Austin, as well as others, took advantage of this opportunity.[5]

Moses Austin, originally from Connecticut, early became involved in lead mining, first in Virginia and then in what would become Missouri. He was successful and amassed a considerable fortune but invested in the Bank of St. Louis. When the bank failed during the Panic of 1819, Austin faced substantial financial difficulties. To rebuild his fortune, he planned to establish an American colony in Spanish Texas. To this end, Austin and several companions traveled through Natchitoches in November of 1820 on their way to San Antonio, where they arrived in December. After an initial refusal, the Spanish governor endorsed Austin's plan and forwarded the request to higher authorities for final approval. During his return trip, the sixty-year-old Austin became ill with pneumonia and, even after returning to Missouri, he never fully recovered. Before his death, Moses Austin requested that his oldest son, Stephen, continue with the Texas project.[6]

Stephen F. Austin had been born in Virginia, worked with his father at his lead mines in Missouri, and after his father's business failure acted as a land speculator and as a merchant in Arkansas before moving to New Orleans to study law. The younger Austin arrived in Natchitoches on June 26, 1821, to participate with his father in his venture. There he found José Erasmo Sequin waiting for Moses Austin with confirmation of his land grant and permission to settle three hundred families in Texas. Austin remained in Natchitoches until July 6, writing letters to friends and associates about the enterprise, sending out announcements about the project to be published in newspapers, and buying mules and provisions for his trip. While in Natchitoches, he engaged in the social life of the community, dining with John Sibley and attending events such as a ball. Austin didn't hear of his father's death until after he had left for Texas. As Austin and his party rode into San Antonio in August 1821, he learned of Mexico's independence from Spain. Austin convinced the governor to continue with the colonization efforts. For his part, Austin would receive 12.5 cents per acre from the colonists. After riding over the grant area in Texas, Austin returned to Natchitoches, where he found awaiting him almost a hundred letters from potential settlers from Missouri, Kentucky, and other states as well as more than fifty families already in the Natchitoches-Nacogdoches area eager to join his venture. After spending time in Natchitoches dealing with his correspondence, Austin left for New Orleans to arrange transportation for supplies and some of his colonists. In addition to the original three hundred families, Austin would receive other contracts from the Mexican government in 1825, 1827, and 1828 to settle a total of nine hundred families.[7]

Austin was not the only American involved in the colonization of Texas. Another was Major Hayden Edwards, who, John Sibley wrote on October 1825, "with a large party of ladies & gentlemen," was "crossing the Sabine to settle at Nacogdoches." Five hundred families from Kentucky were to join them shortly. Edwards's contract with the Mexican government allowed him to settle eight hundred families on his grant in the Nacogdoches area. In time, fifteen men acting as impresarios brought American settlers to Texas. By 1830, over twenty thousand Americans with one thousand slaves had immigrated to Texas. Many of them traveled through Natchitoches.[8]

Sibley, for one, did not view the large numbers of settlers leaving the United States for Texas as desirable. As he explained in 1826, he had "witnessed hundreds of reputable families going into the Mexican country where they obtain the best lands for a bit [12.5 cents] an acre rather than settle on the vacant lands on this side & take their chance of purchasing at ten bits [$1.25] an acre." At the same time, he noted that in western Louisiana people lived "on what they call Congress lands, these people pay no taxes, exercise no right of suffrage, make no roads, bridges or mills. All their improvements are temporary & what public duties they are called on to perform are either neglected or complied with reluctantly, while at the same time the State is at considerable expense to protect them & administer justice." Sibley's solution was for the federal government to transfer the public lands to the state at a reasonable price and let the state deal with the settlers.[9]

Natchitoches was prospering. Then, on March 29, 1823, calamity struck. A fire broke out in the St. Francis Catholic Church. It was Saturday of Holy Week, the day before Easter Sunday. Robert Vaughn, along with several of his Spanish-speaking laborers, were working on the wall for the jail near the east end of the church. At about noon, he entered the church. The altar was decorated for Holy Week. There he observed Joe, the caretaker for the church, and several women extinguishing the candles on the altar. Vaughn helped before he and the others left the church by the vestry door, which Joe locked. The front door was left open to allow members of the congregation entry into the church. About an hour and a half later, one of Vaughn's workers spotted smoke billowing from the steeple of the church. Vaughn, running to the front door, saw flames two and a half feet high shooting up from the center of the altar. Joe and Jn Maria de los Santos, seeing the fire, entered the burning building to retrieve as much of the silver and church accouterments as they could carry. It was a very windy day, and the fire spread rapidly. Before the town's people could extinguish the blaze, the fire burned over sixty buildings in the downtown area of Natchitoches, including many of the buildings along Front and Second streets, the major commercial area.[10]

P. A. Rost, who owned a building adjacent to the church that the fire destroyed, sued the Catholic congregation for gross negligence and requested compensation of two thousand dollars for his losses. The church, a wooden structure, had been in a bad state of disrepair, its window sashes and shutters broken. At the time of the fire, the front door and windows were open. St. Francis Church had no resident priest. Joe, a free man of color, had been acting as sexton and beadle for the church for almost twenty years. He sang hymns and officiated in the church on holy days. The church wardens paid him one hundred dollars a year for his services. Rost claimed that Joe was a habitual drunk, that the church wardens knew of Joe's drinking problem, and that Joe had been intoxicated on the day of the fire. This last point was disputed by several witnesses, but the court ruled in favor of Rost, awarding him the money he requested. The members of St. Francis Church appealed to the Louisiana Supreme Court, which overturned the lower-court ruling based on a technicality.[11] By May 1826, the foundation of a new church had been laid where the old one had stood. This church would be brick, one hundred by fifty-two feet. The builder was a "Spanish Gentleman from Havana who it is Said has built 26 Churches."[12] Two years later, John Sibley wrote, "Our Town of Natchitoches improves slowly. We have a large tolerable handsome and well finished Catholic Church Nearly done a good looking Belfry and a good Bell. Several New Houses have been built . . . , but the destruction of the great fire is scarcely repaired."[13]

In the mid-1820s and 1830s, the merchants located their businesses along Front, St. Denis, and Washington streets. The market house, where greengrocers and butchers rented stalls, stood on the river near a cake shop and a store owned by Joseph Tauzin. The mercantile establishments in town sold a wide variety of goods. The Indian trade was still significant in Natchitoches, and one of the larger stores, that of DeBlieux and Trezzini, carried items of interest to the Native peoples, including three-, three-and-a-half-, four-, five-, and six-point blankets, beads, and vermillion. The store also stocked shoes for men, women, and children and hats for men and boys; men's and ladies' saddles, and bridles; a general assortment of dry goods, including fine and common cloth and coarse material for "negro" clothing, and handkerchiefs; hardware such as carpenter's tools and grindstones; and tobacco, Glauber salts, spices, tea, indigo, glue alum, brimstone, castor oil, coffee, tafia, claret, and white wine. In June 1826, DeBlieux and Trezzini announced they had been appointed agents to grant licenses to peddlers and traders. Those who were interested could apply at the store.[14] DeBlieux had a building on Washington Street in Natchitoches and ran a store and bank on the ground floor with his residence on the second (fig. 7).

At the time, most peddlers were young men in their twenties and early thirties who traveled a circuit by foot, horseback, or in carts and wagons, providing goods directly to rural households. Some traders used flatboats with a cabin and shelves to serve the farmers along the smaller rivers and streams. Both the peddlers and the traders often operated on the barter system, exchanging their trinkets—calico, handkerchiefs, and other items—for eggs, chickens, rags, skins, and other products. These they delivered to the merchants in town for more items to trade. Some peddlers and traders worked on commission with merchants such as DeBlieux and Trezzini. As the rural communities grew, the peddlers often established the first stores in emerging settlements.[15]

There were other merchants in town as well. Theodore Deterville, for example, carried a more restricted inventory than the DeBlieux and Trezzini store. He sold whiskey, coffee, sugar, rice, spices, chewing tobacco, castor oil, wine, tea, assorted garden seeds, writing ink, spermaceti candles, and playing cards as well as other items. Deterville advertised that these would be offered "at the most reduced prices." The store carried at least some items for the Indian trade, including blue and red stroud and vermilion.[16]

Fig. 7. Alexandre Louis DeBlieux's store along Washington Street. Library of Congress, Prints and Photographs Division.

J. Wiley and Company stocked an assortment of English and American goods, domestic goods, and ready-made clothing. It announced in the newspaper the arrival from the North of six trunks of gentlemen's dress and frock coats, vests, pantaloons, "of the most fashionable colors and latest patterns"; plaid and camblet cloaks; four trunks of shirts, "common and fine"; eight cases of gentlemen's and ladies' boots and shoes; nine cases of "gentlemen's castor and Rorem hats"; one truck of ladies' leghorn bonnets; plus a wide selection of fabrics; and a general assortment of crockery, glass, and hardware. The store also offered 150 suits of "stout" clothing for slaves.[17]

J. Coughlan in 1826 started a store at the former location of the Alexander Jackson Jr. establishment. Here he offered a variety of dry goods, groceries, and clothing, all "sold low for cash." He claimed that he gave the "highest price in cash paid for Beef Hides and Peltry." Other store owners included William H. Flagg, who carried clothing and groceries; Charles Duranco, who sold Havana and Puerto Rico coffee, sugar, salt, brandy, whiskey, hyson and imperial teas, sperm and mold candles, sweet oil, and an assortment of dry goods; and Pavie and Constantzi, who offered fresh flour and bacon and served as booking agent for the steamboat *Planter.*[18]

The enterprises of both Harrison & Hopkins and Cortes & Huppe catered to the cotton farmers and planters. In January 1826, Harrison & Hopkins advertised thirty-five hundred yards of forty-two-inch bagging along with twenty coils of bale rope, the materials needed to wrap cotton bales. Later that year, the store offered for sale sixty barrels of flour, twenty-two barrels of pickled pork, four thousand pounds of pork "salted in pieces suitable for smoking," six thousand pounds of bacon, one cask of "superior hams and shoulders," as well as other items. Some of the goods came directly from the North. For example, the firm received on the steamboat *Pilot* from Maysville, Kentucky, "229 bls. [barrels] Flour, 30 bls whiskey, 45 bls apples, 8 bls dried peaches, and 1 bls Irish potatoes." The store also sold pine planks and acted as a booking agent for the steamboat *Dolphin.* Occasionally it advertised real estate for sale. In 1832, Harrison and Hopkins obtained a contract from the U.S. Army to supply provisions to Fort Towson. Apparently, to suggest more local competition, both Harrison and Hopkins submitted independent bid proposals. The firm received six dollars for each barrel shipped to Fort Towson. The cost reflects the difficulty of getting the supplies around the Great Raft, which at the time began near Loggy Bayou. At first the firm attempted to ship the goods by steamboat, but finally resorted to keelboats to take the supplies upriver.[19]

The firm of Cortes & Huppe supplied the cotton farmers and planters with cotton bagging, bale rope, and woolsey for slave clothing. The firm also sold specialty items such as a coach and harness and acted as a real estate agent for both farmland and town property, including in April 1826 the Lafayette Hotel, located on the town's "principal street"; 640 acres in Kisatchie, an area in the uplands west of town; the plantation of Bernardo Gutiérrez, the Mexican revolutionary who lived in Natchitoches parish at the time; and property belonging to Antoine Cornu, the owner of several keelboats involved in the shipping trade. In July 1825, the firm listed for sale "A mulatto girl aged 13 years, of a good character, and promising to become a good servant."[20] Management of stores turned over rapidly. In February of 1827, G. T. Bostwick opened a new establishment in the space previously occupied by Mr. Deranco; Johnson & Wheless advertised as a "CHEAP CASH STORE" at the former location of the James Fleming & Co. store, while W. Harkins set up his store in the building formerly occupied by Taylor & Lee opposite the market.[21]

The hotels also changed management often. Cable and Johnson had operated a "large and commodious establishment," but in 1826 Benjamin Start assumed the running of this hotel. The three-story building, known as the LaFayette Hotel, measured forty-eight by sixty-six feet, with a cistern, kitchen, stable, and garden. Start informed "his friends and the public, that he is in readiness to accommodate Travellers and Boarders." He claimed that his bar or tavern was supplied "with the most choice liquors and every exertion will be used to furnish his table with the best the country . . . market affords." He promised "plenty of good forage" and an attentive hostler to look after his customers' horses and that every exertion would "be made to render comfortable all those who may favour him with a call." By May 1827, J. Cable had taken over the management of another Natchitoches establishment, the Union Hotel, and undertook "several improvements . . . calculated to make the establishment much more comfortable." He assured his old friends and customers "that the same attention which he has been in the habit of showing, may still be confidently expected."[22]

The town had professional men. Dr. Charles George Lewis worked as one of the local doctors and in 1827 could be found at Dr. Long's Apothecary Shop during the day. W. Long had just recently opened a drugstore where he offered "Cheap and Fresh Medicines." He promised high-quality medicines "compounded with great care, to give the fullest satisfaction." Long pledged that "physicians' prescriptions would be particularly attended to," and that all medicines would be carefully labeled. Long also carried the "most approved patent medicine."[23] Dr. William M. Rivers in July of 1826 advertised that he was resuming "the practice of Medicine, Surgery, and Midwifery, and hopes by industry, attention, and assiduity to merit the confidence of those who may feel disposed to employ him."[24] Natchitoches also had lawyers. Sibley, writing in 1828, noted that a number of lawyers had settled in Natchitoches, and he felt there were already too many. A variety of men practiced their trades in Natchitoches in the 1820s, including H. Hafmier, a paperhanger and painter; Matthias Wright, a carpenter; Pierre Bertin, a gold and silversmith; Fred Langenbery, a tailor; N. Mellville, a blacksmith; and for a while Henry Jaccard, a watchmaker.[25]

The town had a newspaper in the mid-1820s, the *Natchitoches Courier*, published by Milton Slocum. The *Courier*, printed in both English and French, provided its readership with articles of national and international interest. It listed recent actions of the federal government, including legislation and the opening of public lands for purchase. It also announced local sheriff sales and probate matters. The newspaper printed prices offered for various grades of cotton in New Orleans, along with poetry and short jokes. In addition, it served as a vehicle for the police jury to publish ordinances and the outcome of their meetings. For example, the *Courier* announced a new parish tax for schools and printed the results of the June 1825 session of the police jury, which divided the parish into six districts: Cloutierville, Natchitoches, Kisatchie, Hickory Woods, Bayou Pierre, and the Allen Settlement.[26]

The board of trustees for the town of Natchitoches also printed its ordinances in the newspaper. In July 1825, it announced that slaves were "not allowed to have balls, except on Sundays and festivals, and not after sunset." If a ball was discovered, the person giving a slave ball would be fined twenty dollars and the slaves would receive twenty lashes for attending. Due of the cost of flour (seven dollars per barrel), the board of trustees required that bakers must give thirty-one ounces of bread for one bit (12.5¢). The board passed an ordinance that established an inspector who, when asked by any person in the town, would check and measure carpenters' work, hewed timbers, and lumber of all descriptions. For his service, the inspector would receive 2 percent of the value of the carpenter's work or lumber. The trustees also provided regulations concerning the ferry crossing in town.[27]

The *Natchitoches Courier,* in addition to advertising slaves for sale, listed runaways. During the mid-1820s, P. Bossier reported that his slave Anderson, about five feet eight or nine inches tall, had run away and was believed to be going downriver. Bossier noted that Anderson spoke English well but very little French. In April 1826, Antoine Cotonmais announced that his very dark slave Robin had absconded. Standing five feet two or three inches, Robin spoke both English and French. When a runaway slave from outside the Natchitoches area was found, he was put in the parish jail and the newspaper included an announcement of his apprehension. In December 1825, Jim, who belonged to Mr. H. Munson of Rapides Parish, was captured. In April 1826, Lewis, said to belong to Mr. Ashford of Mississippi, was jailed. Another man, Manuel, a twenty-two-year-old who claimed he belonged to John McGrew of Alabama, had been taken from the plantation by a Mr. James Callier and brought to the Sabine River, where he left Callier and "gave himself up to a company of regulators, for the purpose of getting to his master." During the mid-1820s, the *Courier* also ran nine announcements listing twelve slaves that their owners or, in two cases, the executor of wills were planning to emancipate (see figures 8–9).[28]

Other announcements that appeared in the newspaper included a request for proposals for work to be done on the Catholic church and the announcement that the military at Cantonment Jesup would be constructing a military road between Natchitoches and Fort Towson. Mr. Muscarelli advertised his intentions of opening a music school and a dance school in Natchitoches.[29] The August 23, 1827, issue contained a statement from Firmin Poissot: "Notice. Mr. Jerome Rachal, having refused to give me satisfaction as a gentleman ought to have done after having basely insulted me, I pronounce him to be *a coward, a liar and a poltroon.*"[30] The *Natchitoches Courier* was published for four years. Eventually two lawyers, Davenport and Ragland, purchased the newspaper and a short time later it ceased publication. John Sibley blamed Davenport and Ragland for want of "industry, temperance & steady habits" for its demise.[31]

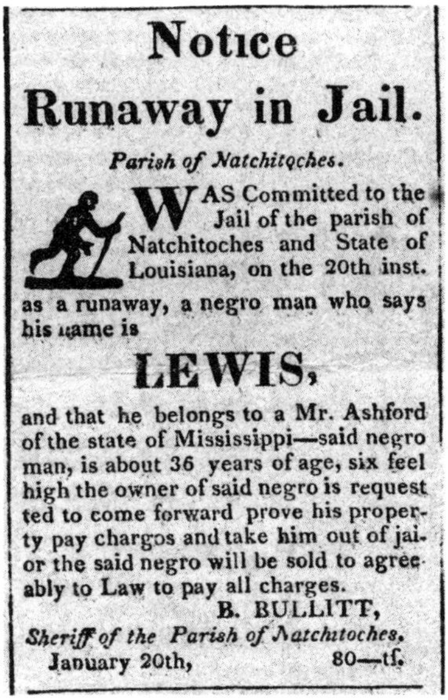

Notice

Runaway in Jail.

Parish of Natchitoches.

WAS Committed to the Jail of the parish of Natchitoches and State of Louisiana, on the 20th inst. as a runaway, a negro man who says his name is

LEWIS,

and that he belongs to a Mr. Ashford of the state of Mississippi—said negro man, is about 36 years of age, six feel high the owner of said negro is requested to come forward prove his property pay charges and take him out of jail or the said negro will be sold to agreeably to Law to pay all charges.

B. BULLITT,
Sheriff of the Parish of Natchitoches.
January 20th, 80—tf.

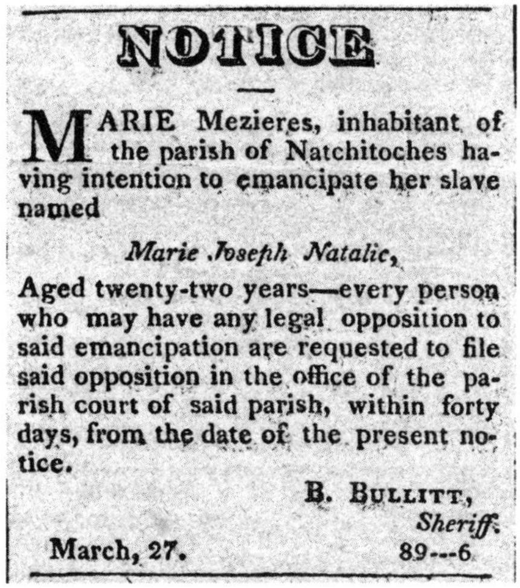

NOTICE

MARIE Mezieres, inhabitant of the parish of Natchitoches having intention to emancipate her slave named

Marie Joseph Natalie,

Aged twenty-two years—every person who may have any legal opposition to said emancipation are requested to file said opposition in the office of the parish court of said parish, within forty days, from the date of the present notice.

B. BULLITT,
Sheriff.
March, 27. 89---6

Figs. 8–9. Runaway and emancipation notices in the *Natchitoches Courier*, April 17, 1826. Northwestern State University of Louisiana, Watson Memorial Library, Cammie G. Henry Research Center.

The Rio Hondo District

West of the town of Natchitoches was the Rio Hondo District, primarily the old Neutral Ground and including the long-established Bayou Pierre community. In 1810, both the United States and Spain claimed ownership of this area and, in 1812, most of the houses in this disputed area had been burned by the American military to stop the outlaws who infested the region. Since then, families had settled in the old Neutral Ground.[32] By 1820 the people in the Rio Hondo District, totaling 2,582, lived in 309 households (see appendix table 2). Most of the population was white (89.7 percent), but there were 250 slaves and 14 "free colored persons." The slaves lived in 61 of the households. The larger slaveholders were Pierre Doulet (Dollet) with 23 and Frans Rouquier with 21. The district was culturally diverse, with people of many different ethnic and national origins. Many were descendants of the early French and Spanish settlers. Americans from the northern and eastern parts of the United States were arriving in ever-increasing numbers, but almost a quarter of the people had been born outside of the United States and were non-nationalized foreigners. Although some, like Jean Baptiste Trezzini, hailed from Europe, in his case Milan, many had Spanish surnames with large families and appear to be recent arrivals. For example, all 14 in the Alexander Sumino family were foreign-born, all 13 in the Pedro Gonzales family, and 9 of the 10 in the Jose Santos family. Many of these may have been refugees from Spanish Texas, the results of the failed filibuster effort in 1813.[33]

Most of the households in the district relied on agriculture as their main occupation (see appendix table 3). Jean Baptiste Trezzini and J. P. Harrison, however, were involved in commercial activities, possibly as rural storekeepers. Trezzini lived at the time in the old Bayou Pierre community, and J. P. Harrison appears to have managed a store at Brown's Mill, also known as Hickory Woods (south of present-day Many). By 1827, S. Wiley was operating a store at Sabine Crossing, where he sold dry goods, groceries, and hardware.[34]

Fifty-one people in the Rio Hondo District engaged in some form of manufacturing. Most were small operations where only one person in the household was involved in production with others in the families farming. The exception was Robin Brown, who, with his large household of nineteen white people and six slaves, had four people occupied in manufacturing with eight growing crops. Benjamin Biles lived near Brown and listed two people involved in manufacturing. He owned four slaves but grew no commercial crops. These households, along with that of J. P. Harrison, formed part of the Brown's Mill–Hickory Woods community. In 1827, Nathaniel Jones advertised his plan to open an English school near Mr. Brown's Hickory Woods for orphan children or children of indigent persons at no charge.[35]

Another community in the Rio Hondo District was the village of Adayes, occupied by the descendants of the people of the old settlement around the long-gone Spanish presidio and mission located along the old Camino Real, now the road to Fort Jesup. As described by one traveler in the 1820s, the village was

> a curious collection of great, upright log houses, plastered with mud, and having an appearance very different from a French village of the same character. The church was a mean log-building, with four bells, some of them

> cracked. . . . The people had a distinct physiognomy. . . . They do not speak so rapidly as the French, have a kind of listlessness of manner, and a great deal of guttural sound in their speech. . . . These people are poor, and addicted to theft, but otherwise simple and amiable in their manners, and carry their hospitality to the greatest lengths.[36]

Although the area was not as crime prone as it had been during Neutral Ground days and even after the establishment of Fort Jesup, those living on the Louisiana-Texas frontier still faced peril. Indians such as the Kickapoo, who felt "ill used by the Americans," informed an officer at Nacogdoches that they "intended to have satisfaction . . . and that the Shawnees and Delawares would join them."[37] According to reports, an armed dozen or more Shawnee and Delaware were forcing their way into homes, terrifying the families. The Indians took what they wanted from the house, killed cattle and hogs, and stole the crops in the fields. Unfortunately, the Indian agent, George Grey, who was in poor health, could do little to stop the pilfering.[38]

Indians were not the only problem. In 1827, a man named Renshaw, believed to be a Frenchman, and a woman, said to be the daughter of Doctor Valentin and presumably a woman of color, lived in the district with their children. A Captain Grosvenor, who at the time ran a tavern in Natchitoches, and three or four other men developed a scheme to kidnap the Renshaw family, take them to the Rio Grande, and sell them as slaves in exchange for horses and mules. As planned, the slavers went to the Renshaw home, seized the family, took them across the Sabine River, and hid them in a canebrake. The seventeen- or eighteen-year-old son managed to escape, found his way to a house nearby, and alerted the residents to the kidnapping. Armed men accompanied the boy back to the camp, where they captured Grosvenor and two other men and freed the family. The prisoners were taken to Nacogdoches to stand trial. At the trial, members of the Renshaw family served as witnesses. It seems the slavers had taken Renshaw, the father, away from the rest of the group and presumably killed him. The woman testified that her daughter was thought to be too white to sell as a slave and that Grosvenor had planned to kill the two-year-old. The jury found the men guilty, and they were jailed in Nacogdoches awaiting orders from San Antonio on whether the men would be hanged, shot, or "sent to the mines."[39]

Fort Jesup

With the signing of the Adams-Onís Treaty in 1819, the United States established a new boundary with Spain, about forty-three miles west of Natchitoches and the old, dilapidated Fort Claiborne and the partially constructed Fort Selden. The military, needing to move closer to the new border, selected a site near Shield's Springs along the Natchitoches-Nacogdoches Road. The site stood on a ridge that divided the Sabine and the Red River drainages, about twenty-five miles from Natchitoches. First known as Cantonment Jesup and eventually Fort Jesup (located near present-day Many), this post would guard the border for the next twenty-three years.[40]

In April 1822, Lieutenant Colonel Zachary Taylor with officers and men from the Seventh Infantry undertook the construction of the new post. Charles M. Gray, a private stationed at the post at the time, describes the process:

> The building of the Fort progressed more rapidly every day, under the systematic arrangements and intelligent control and supervision of the commanding officer. The command was divided into working parties—some designed to hew out the timbers—some to get the boards and shingles—some to prepare the brick and mortar,—some to burn the brick, and some to raise the edifice itself. I was of the party detailed to make the brick. This was the most difficult task to perform, as the men had to tread the mortar with their own feet. . . . In the course of six or seven weeks the brick-yard party was enabled to report to Colonel Taylor that the bricks for the Fort were all completed, and in readiness to be placed in the works.[41]

Fort Jesup would be an open, unpalisaded post and would eventually have buildings on both sides of the Natchitoches-Nacogdoches Road. By December of 1822, the military had completed the initial construction. The soldiers built additional structures when, in 1831, more troops arrived in the area. The fort would be enlarged again in 1837. In addition to the quarters for the officers and enlisted men, the fort had a hospital, commissary, stores, offices, kitchens, stables, blacksmith shops, a magazine, guardhouse, and quarters for the band. Extensive gardens between one hundred and two hundred acres supplied the fort with food.[42] Timothy Flint, who visited the post in the 1820s, wrote "We were most hospitably welcomed at 'Cantonment Jessup,' . . . They have very comfortable quarters, two companies of soldiers, and a number of very gentlemanly officers, the whole under the command of Col. Many. . . . It produced singular sensations, to see all the pomp and circumstance of military parade, and to hear the notes of the drum and fife, breaking the solitude of the wilderness of the Sabine."[43]

The army shipped supplies to Fort Jesup by Red River and maintained warehouses and a quartermaster in Natchitoches. The army also contracted with local people to provide some of the dry goods as well as pork, flour, whiskey, beans, soap, candles, salt, vinegar, books, and clothing for the fort. The quartermaster supervised the transport of supplies from Grand Ecore and Natchitoches to Fort Jesup at the rate of one or two dollars per one hundred pounds. After the establishment of Cantonment Towson (in present-day Oklahoma), the quartermaster coordinated the shipment of supplies to there as well.[44]

The primary duties for those stationed at Fort Jesup were to protect the frontier from the encroachment of Mexico and from Indian raids, but they performed other tasks. When the Comanches threatened Fort Towson and the settlers in that area in 1829, the army dispatched a detachment of forty men from Fort Jesup as reinforcements. At the request of the Indian agent, Jeheil Brooks, a detachment from Fort Jesup attended the signing of the treaty between the Caddo Nation and the United States in 1835 at the Caddo Indian Agency. Other duties included building Military Road No. 11 during the winter of 1827–28. This road ran from the Arkansas border across the uplands on the east side of the Red River Valley, through Campti, and crossed the river at Grand Ecore. Officers occasionally sent soldiers from Fort Jesup to apprehend escaped slaves and to discourage slave insurrections.[45]

The number of troops assigned to Fort Jesup varied over the years, but Jesup was deemed a major post because of its location on the border with Mexico. In 1831, Brigadier General Henry Leavenworth arrived in Natchitoches bound for Fort Jesup with six companies of men and "two doctors, three settlers [sutlers], clerks etc. & more than a dozen officers wives & daughters, & 40 or 50 soldiers wives & children. They came in one large steam boat & two keelboats. They had abt. fifty wagon loads of baggage, settlers [sutler's] stores etc. General Leavenworth . . . [had] with him a band of Music & a handsome regimental library."[46]

For over a decade, Americans had been settling in Texas. Late in 1835, news reached Natchitoches that people in Texas had revolted against Mexico. The U.S.

secretary of war instructed Major General Edmund P. Gaines, the commander of the Western Department of the Army, to proceed to Fort Jesup and take command of the forces on the frontier. Gaines was told that the United States was to remain neutral in the conflict but, if any combatants cross the boundary line, force could be used. He was also instructed to guard against Indian uprisings.[47]

Gaines, a man with political aspirations, recognized the advantage to his career of a successful military campaign. However, by the time Gaines arrived in Natchitoches in April 1836, the Alamo had fallen, Texas forces had been captured, and all of South Texas was under the control of the Mexican president, General Antonio López de Santa Anna. Sam Houston, who commanded the main Texas force, was retreating. Americans who had settled in Texas were streaming back across the Sabine.[48] As reported in a newspaper,

> Hundreds of families were returning from Texas, and there was more misery among them than could well be imagined. All throughout the woods were living under sheds, those going to Texas who had been stopped by the accounts which they heard, and others who were returning to their old homes. Under the same sheds were to be seen blacks and whites, who had sickened with the measles, some of whom were actually dying, and the whole destitute of the means of relief. It made one's heart sick to witness these spectacles.[49]

Gaines, who had for a long time been arguing for an invasion of Texas, established Camp Sabine only a few miles from the Sabine River. At Camp Sabine, Gaines waited for an excuse to invade Texas. Then on April 21, Sam Houston's Texas troops defeated Santa Anna at the Battle of San Jacinto and Mexico acknowledged Texas's independence. The crisis was over. Gaines's hope for military glory did not come to pass. Meanwhile the United States continued to maintain a considerable force in the area with 360 troops at Fort Jesup and 124 at Camp Sabine in 1836.[50]

Fort Jesup provided an economic market for the Natchitoches area. The army shipped most of its supplies through Grand Ecore, often using local teamsters to transport the provisions to Fort Jesup. It also purchased food and supplies in Natchitoches. The merchant Alexandre Louis DeBlieux, for one, engaged in a thriving business with the officers from Fort Jesup. Natchitoches served as post office and as a recreational venue for many at the fort.[51]

The 1840s was the decade of "Manifest Destiny," a belief that the United States of America was ordained to extend westward to the Pacific Ocean. The election of James K. Polk as president in 1844, who had campaigned on a pro-expansionist platform, led to the annexation of Texas in December 1845. But the western border of Texas was in dispute. The Americans felt that Texas extended to the Rio Grande while the Mexicans claimed that Texas stopped at the Nueces River. President Polk at first offered to purchase the area between the two rivers as well as California, but Mexico was unwilling to sell.[52]

With a conflict imminent between Mexico and the United States, the army appointed General Zachary Taylor as commander of the South Department of the Army with his headquarters at Fort Jesup. Prior to this, Fort Jesup had seven companies of the Second Regiment of Dragoons stationed at the fort. In May of 1844, eight companies of the Third Regiment of Infantry from Missouri transferred to Fort Jesup, pitching their tents at Camp Wilkins, a short distance from the fort. Also, in May almost four hundred officers and men of the Fourth Regiment of Infantry arrived at the new Camp Salubrity, situated just one and a half miles northwest of Natchitoches. The soldiers anticipated a quick deployment, but their time at Camp Salubrity and Fort Jesup stretched on for fourteen months.[53] Among the men stationed at Camp Salubrity was a young, recent West Point graduate, Second Lieutenant Ulysses S. Grant. Grant seemed to have enjoyed his stay in the area. As he relates, the "summer was whiled away in social enjoyments among the officers, in visiting those stationed at, and near Fort Jesup, twenty-five miles away, visiting the planters on Red river, and the citizens of Natchitoches and Grand Ecore. There was much pleasant intercourse between the inhabitants and the officers of the Army." Grant found the winter "more agreeably than the summer had been. There were occasional parties given by the planters along the 'coast'—as the bottom lands on the Red River were called."[54] Reportedly, the twenty-two-year-old Grant was particularly fond of the young ladies of the community.[55]

The presence of the army and so many soldiers created an economic boom for the town of Natchitoches but, on July 2, 1845, the soldiers of the Fourth Infantry Regiment marched off to Grand Ecore to take passage on steamboats to New Orleans and eventually to war. The Third Infantry Regiment followed on July 7, while the dragoons traveled cross-country. This left Fort Jesup nearly deserted. Taylor's troops would occupy the disputed land between the Nueces River and the Rio Grande and precipitate the Mexican-American War (1846–48). In 1846, the governor of Louisiana called for volunteers to serve for six months in the war with Mexico. S. M. Hyams of Natchitoches raised a company of volunteers and served as its captain. It became part of the Fifth Louisiana Volunteers. At war's end in 1848, Mexico relinquished its claims to all of Texas and the United States purchased California and much of what is now the southwestern United States for fifteen million dollars. With the conclusion of the war, Fort Jesup's role as a frontier post came to an end. The frontier was now at the Rio Grande and the army no longer needed Fort Jesup. The old fort property was divided, the lots and buildings offered at auction in Natchitoches in April of 1850. With Fort Jesup's closure, Natchitoches lost a valuable economic outlet for its goods and services.[56]

The Natchitoches Proper and River aux Cannes Districts

East of the Rio Hondo were the Natchitoches Proper and River aux Cannes districts. These two districts covered the Red River Valley and the adjacent upland areas mainly to the east. The Natchitoches Proper District extended from the present-day Arkansas border south to and including the plantation of Emanuel Prudhomme, located about twelve miles below the town of Natchitoches. The River aux Cannes District extended south from Emanuel Prudhomme's plantation to the confluence of the Rigolette de Bon Dieu with the Red River, the boundary of Rapides Parish. In 1820, there were relatively fewer non-nationalized foreigners in either of these two districts, with 128 (5.8 percent) in the Natchitoches Proper District and only 89 (5.2 percent) in the River aux Cannes (see appendix table 2).[57]

The Natchitoches Proper District

In 1820, excluding the town of Natchitoches, the Natchitoches Proper District had 171 households with a total population of 2,212. Of these almost half were whites, almost the same number slaves, and 120 listed as "free colored persons." This included 36 living in the household of François Grappe. These may have been members of the Natchitoches Indian tribe. Louis C. DeBlanc, who was commandant of the Post of Natchitoches in 1790, had recorded, "In consequence of the death of Tomoc, chief of the Natchitoches nation of Indians, and finding that the said Indians are now inhabiting land not belonging to them, in the settled parts of this post, I grant to them, subject to the will of the Governor, Don Estaven Miro, twenty arpents of land on each side of Red river, at a place called Lac De Meures, about ten leagues above the post of Natchitoches. October 3, 1790."[58] Less than 6 percent of the free population had been born outside the United States. Almost all the households engaged in agriculture with over half having slaves (see appendix tables 2 and 3). More than half of the enslaved people lived on plantations with 20 or more slaves. Plantation owners with 20 slaves or more, included J. B. Fontaineau (42 slaves), Ant. Demeziere (21), S. Davenport (27), Louis Rachel Sr. (27), Frans. Vienne (30), Wd. Murphy (24), Placide Bossier (21), Jno Baptiste Buard (37), W. Murry (23), and Nerville Prudhomme (45), Ant. Poisot (60) Ant. Prudhommes (50), J. B. Prudhomme (58), and Emanuel Prudhomme (73).

Almost a quarter of the slaves lived on large plantations with more than 50 slaves. Six slaves lived in households where they were the only bondsmen. The rest lived in households with 2 to 19 slaves. This district included the farmers and planters in the Red River Valley but also those living in the uplands east of the river. Many in the uplands relied more on herding than farming. The soil was not as productive as that in the river valley, but the forest provided ample food for the free-ranging livestock.[59]

Not all those living in the district were full-time farmers. Some (thirty-two) engaged in manufacturing; however, all but one of these lived in households that also farmed (see appendix table 3). Most listed only one person in the household involved in manufacturing, but two households listed two people, one the household of the planter Jean Baptiste Prudhomme and the other that of Louis Quallette. Some of those involved in manufacturing could have been sawmill or gristmill workers, salt makers, or blacksmiths.[60]

One of the men who lived in the uplands was Simon Manning. Born in Georgia, Manning arrived in the area in 1820. Although not without funds, Manning never became a planter, choosing instead a career as an entrepreneur. At various times, he farmed, traded in land and slaves, kept two taverns, operated a ferry across Red River, and ran a sawmill. Manning utilized some bottomland but selected the uplands for his original homestead in the Social Springs area (about ten miles south of today's Ringgold). After the army built the military road through the region in 1827–28, Manning moved at least part of his family to the junction of the military road and a road connecting Lake Bistineau to Black Lake (present-day Ringgold). The later road became a busy route for farmers taking their cotton to Lake Bistineau for shipment to New Orleans. At the junction of these two roads, Manning established a sawmill. With Philip Purser Brinson, Manning also maintained a tavern to take advantage of the stagecoach and mail routes that now followed the military road to Washington, Arkansas. Stops occurred every ten miles along the road to rest and/or change the horses and to offer food to the travelers. In 1837, when the federal government opened this area for sale, Simon Manning purchased the property.[61]

In the district, only five people listed commerce as their primary occupation. Three of these lived in the Felix Estrader household. Four people in this household farmed. The old settlement of Campti served as a commercial center and as a jumping-off point for those heading north toward Arkansas. After its construction, the military road passed though the settlement as well.[62]

The River aux Cannes District

The southern portion of the parish, the River aux Cannes District, included 155 households with a total population of 1,721 with almost equal numbers of whites and slaves (see appendix table 2). The rest (8 percent) were listed as "free colored persons." Almost all the households in this district engaged in agriculture, almost two-thirds having slaves. More than half of the enslaved people lived on plantations with 20 or more slaves while of these over a quarter of the total enslaved population lived on the plantations of the large French Creole planters Ambrose LeComte (96 slaves), Alexis Cloutier (70), and Benjamin Metoyer (57).[63]

Nineteen of the households were involved in manufacturing. All but two of these also farmed. The exceptions were the households of Manuel Lorens and George Sneed, which did no commercial farming. The household of Osgood Witcher had seven people working in manufacturing and one farming. There were seven people involved in commerce with all but one also farming. In time, Cloutierville would serve as the principal commercial center for the district (see appendix tables 2 and 3).[64]

The people of the River aux Cannes were predominately French Creole Catholics and, in the early years, a priest came to the area from Avoyelles or Natchitoches about once a year to bless the marriages and baptize the children who had been born since the last visit. But the people wanted a church and priest of their own, and the planter Alexis Cloutier helped them reach this goal.

Cloutier, the man who would give Cloutierville its name, was born in Pointe Coupee Parish on July 10, 1769, the son of a Canadian father and a mother from the Poste des Natchitoches. Cloutier, a talented individual and a good businessman, acquired considerable land and became a successful planter in the River aux Cannes area. In 1816 Cloutier appeared before P. D. Gailleau La Fontaine, then the judge of Natchitoches Parish, to donate a piece of his land for the establishment of a church for the people of River aux Cannes. As a condition of Cloutier's donation, the pastor of St. Francis Church in Natchitoches agreed to send a priest to say mass at least every three months until the congregation could support a priest of its own. In the donation documents, the judge described Cloutier as a man whose "only ambition is to exercise honorably the privileges of a free and independent man and receive the esteem of individuals. He does not desire that his name be handed down to posterity, but only that the remembrance of a modest good remain in the memories of families of his fellow citizens for as long as they enjoy the benefits thereof. He exacts no gratitude."[65] The church was constructed and dedicated as St. John the Baptist. Cloutier's purpose might have been altruistic, but he saw an opportunity and quickly divided more of his land into streets and lots, which he sold to create the town of Cloutierville (figs. 10–11). In 1822, he moved to have the town incorporated.[66]

In 1826, working with the Creole Placide Bossier, who at the time was a state senator, Cloutier attempted to have a new parish created out of the southern part of Natchitoches Parish with Cloutierville as the new parish seat. This was not an unreasonable request. Natchitoches was a huge area, covering most of northwest Louisiana. As the population grew, the parish would be subdivided. The Cloutierville-Bossier's petition argued that some of the citizens who lived in the southern part of the parish had to travel over eighty miles to reach the parish seat at Natchitoches to conduct their legal business. The Isle Brevelle area north of Cloutierville was to be part of the new parish, but some of the residents in this area were only about twelve miles from the parish seat at Natchitoches. When they learned of the petition, many of the farmers and planters north of Cloutierville objected, and within three weeks of Bossier submitting his request, the legislature received a protest from some of the residents. In the end, Bossier's

Figs. 10–11. Alexis Cloutier's townhouse (now Kate Chopin House) in Cloutierville, built ca. 1809, burned 2008. To the right is a drawing of the east elevation. Library of Congress, Prints and Photographs Division.

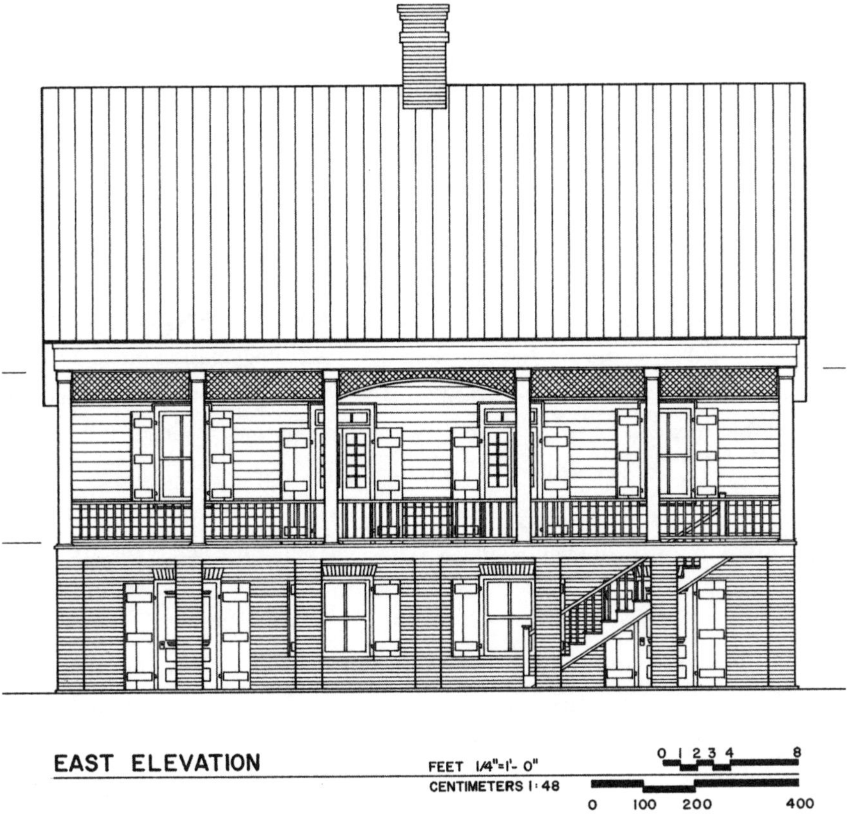

petition was defeated. Cloutier, sure that the petition would succeed, had donated additional land to the town for a civic building, and a large structure had already been erected on the property. This building became a store and saloon with a dance hall on the second floor.[67] Timothy Flint, traveling through the area in the 1820s, spent a night at the Cloutier plantation. As described by Flint, the Cloutier plantation house was surrounded by cabins for about eighty slaves and pens for numerous hogs, cattle, goats, and geese. Flint noted some Indians living on the property as well. He wrote, "Every thing in and about the house was in perfect keeping. We had for supper duck-pies, coffee, and claret. In the morning duck-pies, milk, custards, coffee, and claret. The owner accompanied us some miles to where he was laying off a new town. . . . He showed us, apparently with no little pride, a dancing hall, ornamented in ancient French style, with dragons, coarse paintings, hangings of different colours, rendered more gay with the beautiful plumage of some of their birds."[68]

The River

The Red River and the Great Raft that blocked the Red River above the old Natchitoches Indian settlement were instrumental in the location and development of the early French settlement of Natchitoches. In 1713 the French located their first two huts at what was then the head of navigation on Red River. During the early years, the river was the major means for settlers and supplies to reach Natchitoches and for the peltry and later indigo, tobacco, and cotton to be transported downstream to New Orleans. The river made Natchitoches in the eighteenth and early nineteenth centuries an important commercial center. The shifting of the main channel of the river, starting in the late 1820s, from the Cane River course which flowed past Natchitoches to the Bon Dieu to the east was to be its undoing.

For the eighteenth and most of the nineteenth centuries, the people of Natchitoches relied primarily on river transport to move their crops and other commodities to market and to obtain supplies and merchandise. To keep transportation costs down, most farmers and merchants attempted to ship their goods and acquire supplies during the high-water periods, which usually extended from about January to July or August, but this could vary. As the winter rains increased and the snow melted in the mountains, the water flowing into the Red River tributaries resulted in a rise of the Red River. As the summer progressed, however, the river fell, making navigation on some of the smaller bayous and streams that fed into the river increasingly difficult even for shallow draft vessels. Inland farmers and even some of the planters along Cane River had to load their cotton bales onto oxcarts and make their way, sometimes over muddy roads, other times over rutted and dusty tracts, to steamboat landings on Red River or one of its still open tributaries. At times farmers from as far away as East Texas hauled their cotton to Grand Ecore on the Red River to ship it south.[69]

During the late winter and spring, the Red River carried enough water to provide easy passage over the two sets of rapids upstream from the town of Alexandria. But as the water fell siltstone ledges appeared in the riverbed and it became increasingly difficult to navigate the shoals until, in dry years, crossing them became impossible. Although some boats, such as keelboats, could be poled or towed over the rapids, this was not feasible for steamboats with their paddlewheels. During dry years, the rapids cut off direct steamboat transportation between Natchitoches and the world below the falls for several months. Any merchandise or people coming upriver had to be off-loaded below the lower rapids and transported by land around the falls and reloaded onto small steamers or keelboats, or the people could continue on horseback to Natchitoches. The owners of some steamboats, such as the *Dolphin,* kept a keelboat for the delivery of freight above the falls when the river was low. Most years, Natchitoches planters could not ship their cotton until late winter or spring and could miss the higher prices often offered for early cotton in the New Orleans market.[70]

The ubiquitous dugout canoe served as a major type of river transport from prehistoric times well into the twentieth century. The early French explorers made extensive use of the dugout or, as they called it, the *pirogue.* By the late eighteenth and first two decades of the nineteenth century, keelboats transported most of the goods between Natchitoches and New Orleans, although pirogues continued to be used by both planters and farmers for local transportation. There may have been the occasional use of flatboats, although these would have been difficult to navigate in the twisting and snag-infested river north of Alexandria.[71]

Flatboats were essentially boxes built with boards, rectangular in shape, flat-bottomed, and partially or fully decked, providing covered storage and a sleeping area. Designed to carry cargo and people downstream, they floated with the current, being steered with a sweep at the stern. The flatboats were equipped with oars and sometimes with a mast and sail. To cross sandbars and shoals, the crews employed cordelling or towing, the practice of using a rope extending from the boat to a tree or to men on the riverbank to pull the boat. Flatboats on the Mississippi could be large, some reaching one hundred feet long and twenty feet wide, but those on the Red River were undoubtedly smaller to facilitate steering in the narrow, meandering channels. Most often, when the flatboats reached their destination and their cargo was delivered, they would be broken up and sold for lumber.[72]

The keelboats were designed for upriver as well as downriver travel. Keelboats involved in the Red River trade were usually about ninety feet long and eleven to fifteen feet wide with a draft of two to four feet when loaded. They generally carried between twenty-two and thirty-seven tons. Tonnage was a measure of volume, not weight, with a ton representing about one hundred cubic feet of storage. The boats had shallow keels, were pointed on both ends, with a cabin in the center of the boat, and a twelve- to eighteen-inch cleated walkway running down each side. Some had seats for rowers in the bow and/or were equipped with a mast and sail. A boatman steered the keelboat, using a large sweep at the stern. Depending on their size, keelboats could carry between fifteen and fifty tons of cargo. Like the flatboats, the keelboats floated with the current downriver, but for the upriver trip required considerable effort, especially when the current was strong. The boatmen used sails when possible but usually traveled upstream by "setting poles." Men on each side of the vessel carried twenty-foot-long poles to the bow of the boat. There the men would position their poles on the river bottom and, while pushing against the pole with their shoulders, walked to the stern, thereby propelling the boat forward. When they reached the stern, the men would raise the poles, walk to the bow of the boat, and reset the poles. When the bottom was too deep, the men could row the keelboat, or the captain would send out men with a towline or cordelle, sometimes up to several hundred feet long, and the men would tow the boat upstream. If the bank was too dense with vegetation, a skiff would take the towrope and tie it to a tree or snag upstream. The other end would be fastened to a hand-cranked winch, or the crew would pull the rope hand over hand, moving the boat forward. This was the hardest method, and six miles' progress a day was considered a good rate. The crew could also use "bushwhacking" if the river was high and trees extended over the water. The crew members would grab branches at the bow of the boat and walk toward the stern, most often in conjunction with setting poles and/or rowing on the river side.[73]

During the 1820s, Natchitoches served as the home port for five or six keelboats owned by Antoine Cornu. His keelboats ran from the large 33-ton *Eliza* to the small 21-ton *Messenger* (table 8). Cornu listed himself as a trader and was living in New Orleans when he enrolled a keelboat, the *Saucy Eagle,* for the New Orleans trade. He sold the *Saucy Eagle* and in March 1819 purchased the larger *Little Tom.* By this time, he had moved to Natchitoches with his family. In 1820, he purchased two more keelboats, the *Eliza* in May and the *Buffalo* in November, and would sell the *Little Tom* in 1821. In May of 1826, he enrolled the *Messenger* and in May 1827 the *General Brown* in New Orleans. Within the year the *Mes-*

senger sank. The *General Brown* was the last keelboat entered at New Orleans for the Red River–New Orleans trade. By this time the steamboats were taking over much of the New Orleans transportation, but not all the keelboats on the Red River were involved in the New Orleans trade.[74] During the 1820s and 1830s, several keelboats also operated between Natchitoches and settlements upriver, including after its establishment in 1824 Cantonment Towson. Until the Great Raft was cleared in the mid-1830s, keelboats used a series of bayous and lakes to navigate around the raft. It would be 1831 before the first steamboat ascended the river through the raft.[75]

Table 8. Keelboats owned by Antoine Cornu of Natchitoches

Name	*Tonnage*	*Dimensions of Hull (ft.)*	*Year Built*	*Year Registered in New Orleans*	*Where Built*	*Home Port*
Little Tom	31	96 × 13 × 2	1818	1819	Ohio River	Red River (Natchitoches?)
Saucy Eagle	25	87 × 11 × 2	1815	1819	Ohio River	?
Buffalo	26	93 × 15 × 2	1819	1820	Pittsburgh	Natchitoches
Eliza	33	91 × 13 × 10	1819	1820	Ohio River	Natchitoches
General Brown	23	?	?	1827	?	Natchitoches?
Messenger	21	90 × 12 × 2	1825	1827	Kentucky River	Natchitoches

Note: All these boats were registered at New Orleans.

Source: Pearson and Wells, *Steamboats on Red River,* 48.

Robert Fulton is often credited with the development of the first steamboat, but there were other men involved. Many of the early experimenters recognized the opportunities and challenges presented by navigation on the Ohio and Mississippi rivers. It was relatively easy to float crops and other commodities in flatboats downstream from the Ohio and Tennessee valleys to New Orleans but much more difficult to ship merchandise upriver against the strong currents. Many believed a steam-powered boat was the answer. Among them was Robert Fulton. To protect their investment in their western steamboat efforts, Fulton and Robert Livingston, Fulton's partner, attempted to obtain exclusive steam navigation rights for the Ohio and Mississippi. Most of the states and territories along the rivers denied Fulton and Livingston's request except for Orleans Territory which, through the influence of Edward Livingston, a well-established lawyer in New Orleans and Robert Livingston's brother, granted the monopoly. In late October 1811, the steamboat *New Orleans,* built in Pittsburgh and owned by Fulton, made her maiden voyage down the Ohio and Mississippi to New Orleans, arriving in the second week of January 1812. She would be used in the trade between Natchez and New Orleans.[76]

Meanwhile, a group of mechanics and inventors about fifty miles upstream from Pittsburgh were also experimenting with steam transportation. Among these were Daniel French and Henry Shreve. In 1814, French and Shreve built the seventy-five-ton *Enterprise* and, late that year, Shreve with the *Enterprise* ventured down the Mississippi River to New Orleans, loaded with munitions for General Andrew Jackson, who was preparing for an attack by the British in the War of 1812. Shreve arrived just days before the Battle of New Orleans. Fulton's only steamboat in the area, the *Vesuvius,* was mired in the mud on the batture side of the levee, and Shreve with the *Enterprise* was pressed into service for several critical missions for Jackson prior to the battle. Shreve's trip down the Mississippi with the *Enterprise* had been in violation of Fulton's monopoly. Henry Shreve and others would become involved in several legal contests with the Fulton monopolists. In 1816, the court ruled that the territorial legislature had no authority to establish the monopoly, and the Mississippi River was opened to all in the steamboat trade.[77]

After the Battle of New Orleans, Jackson tasked Shreve and his *Enterprise* with returning the soldiers to Fort Claiborne. The *Enterprise* was the first steamboat to ascend the Red River, but it is unclear whether she crossed the rapids at Alexandria. The steamboat *Beaver,* under the command of Captain Jacob Black, did reach Natchitoches in March of 1820. She had made the trip from New Orleans in six days and three hours. On her return, she carried 350 bales of cotton. However, the *Beaver* took the Little River channel of the Red River with its sharp bends, rapid current, and obstacles for the return trip. She lost most of her railing during this journey and damaged her wheelhouse and rudder. Still, she made ten or eleven more trips that same year. The *Beaver* with Jacob Black as captain would claim Natchitoches as her home port (see table 9 for other steamboats that listed Natchitoches as their home port). In 1821, both the *Beaver* and the smaller steamboat *Arkansas* were making regular trips between Natchitoches and New Orleans. By 1822, four steamboats operated between Natchitoches and New Orleans, the *Beaver, Arkansas, Yankee,* and *Neptune.* Seven steamboats made thirty-six voyages during 1825. Other boats involved in the Natchitoches–New Orleans trade in the 1820s included the *Hornet, Teche, Kiamichi, Alexandria, Superior, Car of Commerce, Eliza, Governor Shelby, Grecian, Miami,* and the *Planter.* With the coming of the steamboat, the freight rates between Natchitoches and New Orleans fell from three dollars per barrel in 1820 to one and a half dollars by 1825. Not all steamboats were involved in the Natchitoches–New Orleans trade. For example, the *Highland Laddie* with D. McCallum as master ran between Natchitoches and Natchez, and the *Pilot* from Maysville, Kentucky, delivered flour, whiskey, and apples to Natchitoches merchants.[78]

Table 9. Steamboats with Natchitoches as home port

Name	*Tonnage*	*Year Built*	*Where Built*	*Master*	*Year(s) Registered at New Orleans*
Beaver	135	1819	New Albany, IN	Jacob Black	1821
Planter	116	1831	Pittsburgh	Blanchard	
Privateer	146	1832	Pittsburgh	Mather	1834–37
Brian Boroihme	187	1836	Louisville, KY	Ruth Edwards	1836–40
John Linton	309	1834	Cincinnati	McGuire Shreiver Kimball	1841
*Cote Joyeuse**	142	1842	Unknown	P. F. Kimball	1842–46
Cora	179	1845	New Albany, IN	P. F. Kimball	1845

*Natchitoches to New Orleans trade by Cane and Little rivers (Norman, "The Red River of the South," 435).

Source: Norman, "The Red River of the South," 397–535; Pearson and Wells, *Steamboats on Red River,* 68.

The builders of the early steamboats followed the design of those of the Eastern Seaboard, that is with deep, rounded hulls and powered by a single, low-pressure engine. But as early as 1816 Henry Shreve and Daniel French placed high-pressure engines and boilers horizontally on the main deck rather than in the hold with each engine powering one of the side paddlewheels. They also built a second deck, known as the boiler deck, over the engines and boilers and constructed a pilothouse above the boiler deck. Most of these characteristics had become standard features of the steamboat by the 1830s. In fact, it was largely the ingenuity and inventiveness of Henry Shreve that resulted in the form of the western steamboat. By the 1830s, the hulls of the western steamers were rectangular with little or no keel. Most of the early steamboats were side-wheelers.[79]

The Red River steamers were generally between 90 and 150 feet long, 12 to 24 feet wide with holds 2 to 4 feet deep and burdens ranging between 80 and 190 tons. The early Red River steamers were workboats designed to transport commodities to the New Orleans market. In 1834, those making regular trips included the steamboat *Caspian, Daniel O'Connell,* and *Chesapeake.* The *Lady Washington* and the *Ouachita* made occasional trips. These boats stopped at different landings and plantations on their downriver voyage, picking up cargo, and upon reaching New Orleans, they delivered it to different commission merchants or the planter's agent. For example, on April 9, 1837, among the two towboats, four ships, one schooner, eight flatboats, and five other steamboats arriving in New Orleans was the *Levant* from Natchitoches. The *Levant* carried 686 bales of cotton with 192 bales to be delivered to J. Plauche and 195 bales to Lambeth and Thompson with the other bales sent to eight other agents. Also on board were twenty-nine packs of peltries, one bundle of deerskins, eighty-eight beef hides for Peroux Arceuil and Co., as well as other cargo. The *Levant* also had over thirty-five passengers, including some from Natchitoches, among them L. Durbanne (Derbanne), C. Pavie, P. S. Compere, F. Prudhomme, J. Cohen, J. E. Suggett, A. Metoyer, W. Wakefield, and N. Prudhomme and his family. Although cotton bales by volume were the most common cargo on steamboats, other freight was shipped as well (see table 10). Some steamboats specialized in the transportation of livestock, particularly cattle, to the New Orleans markets.[80]

On their trips upstream, the steamboats brought a wide variety of goods for the various merchants to sell. Planters often asked their factors to send specialty items. In December 1849, for instance, J. Lestan Prudhomme received on the *Hecla:* "leather, a box of codfish, one box of glassware, a box of snuff, a keg of powder, a bunch of bananas, a keg of nails, some French blankets, some silk fabric and a cotton umbrella." At other times he received sardines, cinnamon, raisins, reboiled molasses, Duffield's hams, sweet oil, a keg of pickled oysters, a jar of prunes, a jug of lime juice, and a box of cheese.[81]

Table 10. Sample of commodities shipped by steamboat from Natchitoches to New Orleans in 1834

Date	Steamer	No. of Commission Merchants	Commodities*
Feb. 7	*Caspian*	12	573 bales cotton, 46 hides, 14 packs skins
Feb. 12	*Daniel O'Connell*	10	366 bales cotton, skins (1 pack otter, 24 packs deer, 8 packs, 7 bales), 123 hides, 2 bales hide
	Chesapeake	7	261 bales cotton, 243 hides, 32 packs peltries, 5 packs skins, 108 carrots tobacco
Feb. 21	?	20	689 bales cotton, skins (25 packs, 32 packs deer, 5 bear), 1 barrel wax, 1,526 hides
Feb. 26	*Chesapeake*	15	857 bales cotton, 4 boxes tobacco, 139 bags cotton seed, skins (27 packs, 1 pack otter, 11 packs deer), 59 hides, 1 barrel wax
Feb. 27	*Daniel O'Connell*	17	884 bales cotton, 763 hides, skins (14 bales deer, 4 packs, 1 bale), 1 barrel horn tips, 1 barrel wax
Mar. 11	*Caspian*	16	868 bales cotton, 333 carrots tobacco, skins (20 packs deer, 6 packs coon, 3 packs, 2 bales bear, 28 bales beaver, 1 pack otter, 78 bales), hides (432 cow, 378), 2 boxes merchandise, 2 bags wax
Mar. 17	*Chesapeake*	12	669 bales cotton, 420 hides, skins (63 packs deer, 26 packs otter, 6 bales deer, 20 packs), 1 lot horn, 2 rolls leather, sundries
Mar 25	*Caspian*		500 bales cotton, 14 bales tobacco, oil, skins, etc.
Apr. 1	?	11	228 bales cotton, 18 hogsheads sugar, peltries (194 bales, 42 packs), 3 barrels merchandise, 607 hides, sundries
Apr. 3	*Daniel O'Connell*	11	655 bales cotton, 30 packs skins, 520 hides
Apr. 8	*Caspian*	20	448 bales cotton, 433 hides, 7 rolls leather, 196 packs deer skin
Apr. 16	?	18	458 bales cotton, 269 hides, 116 packs peltries, skins (1 pack coon, 6 packs beaver, 4 beaver, 4 otter, 1 bale), 2 bags horn, 10 rolls leather, 3 boxes merchandise

(*continued*)

Table 10. *(continued)*

Date	*Steamer*	*No. of Commission Merchants*	*Commodities**
Apr. 21	*Caspian*	12	286 bales cotton, hides (2 packs, 17 loose, 21), skins (45 packs, 3 bales bear, 24 packs deer), 2 boxes sundries, 239 carrots tobacco, 84 barrels pork, 16 barrels lard
	Daniel O'Connell	11	471 bales cotton, 470 hides, 67 carrots, 2 boxes tobacco
Apr. 30	*Chesapeake*	10	1,012 bales cotton, 4 packs peltries, 1 pack otter skin
May 2	*Caspian*	4	36 bales cotton, 200 hides, 10 packs skins
June 5	*Daniel O'Connell*	6	114 bales cotton, sundries
June 9	*Vermillion, Hogan*	4	20 bales cotton, 8 rolls leather
June 11	*Caspian*	7	76 bales cotton, trunk
July 7	*Lady Washington*	5	13 bales cotton, 2 packs skins
Aug. 2	*Lady Washington*		19 barrels brandy, 6 dozen chickens
Dec. 20	*Ouachita*	10	925 bales cotton
Dec. 30	*Daniel O'Connell*	6	1,200 bales cotton, 44 barrels of apples, etc.

*Some of the amounts in this column do not indicate the type of commodity (e.g., 8 packs). These are how the quantities were listed in the original. The abbreviations "b," "p," "c," and "bl" in the original have been replaced in this table with "bales," "packs," "carrots," and "barrels" for clarity.

Source: Merchants' Daily News, February 7–December 30, 1834, in Hong, "The Evolution of the Red River Settlement Pattern," 431.

The hold on most boats stored "wet items" such as mess pork, whiskey, and molasses. In addition to accommodating the engines with their boilers and the piles of wood used as fuel, the main deck provided the primary storage area for most of the cargo. On the cotton boats, "guards" extended from the hull, providing extra areas to pile rows upon rows of cotton bales, stacked in some cases almost to the pilothouse (figs. 12–13). Above the main deck, the boiler deck provided staterooms for passengers, a dining hall also used as a social hall, clerk's office, and bar. Prior to the 1840s, accommodations for passengers were anything but lavish. The staterooms were small with little room except for bunk beds and a washstand. Additional cargo could be stored on the boiler deck. On larger boats, there was often a hurricane deck which provided quarters for the captain and some of the crew. The pilothouse stood on the Texas deck.[82]

Figs. 12–13. Loading and loaded steamboats. Northwestern State University of Louisiana, Watson Memorial Library, Cammie G. Henry Research Center, Dellmon Collection.

A western steamboat of about 154 tons had an average crew of twenty-one. The minimum number of officers on a steamboat included the captain, two pilots, a clerk, two engineers, and a mate. The pilots were generally the most highly skilled members of the crew and were responsible for navigation and steering. The clerk served as business manager for the boat. He acted as the freight as well as passenger agent, bargained with those shipping materials on the boat, made out bills of lading, checked the cargo, and maintained the accounts. The engineers tended the engines and boilers, keeping the machinery well oiled, cleaning and, when necessary, repairing the equipment. The mate directed the deck crew with the loading and unloading of the cargo and, when the boats stopped at woodyards along the river, with the loading of wood. Wood fueled most of the steamboats, smaller boats burning twelve to twenty cords of wood every twenty-four hours and the larger boats fifty to seventy-five cords. The cabin crew included the cooks, stewards, waiters, cabin boys, and chambermaids. Working and living conditions for the cabin crew were somewhat better than for the deck crew. The deck crew was generally half or more of the total number of personnel. They lived and worked on the main deck, sleeping among the freight. The early deck crews consisted of former flatboat and keelboat men but, in later years, more and more unskilled laborers from river towns, surplus slaves, or occasional agricultural laborers made up the deck crews. During the early years, most were native-born Americans but, with the influx of immigrants during the 1840s and 1850s, Irish and German laborers became increasingly common.[83]

The construction of most steamboats was flimsy. Few lasted more than a few years. Most fell prey to snags in the river or explosions of boilers but, on occasion, other factors were involved. One of the worst steamboat disasters on Red River was that of the *Lioness.* It was Sunday, a calm and beautiful spring morning on May 19, 1833. Many of the passengers were not yet up. The ship's mate and several of the crew members had gone below deck to rearrange the cargo in the hold. The hold carried, among other things, crates containing a quantity of dry straw, several cases of oil, and barrels of gunpowder. It was dark in the hold, and it is assumed that one of the workers lite a candle. An explosion blew the forecabin and boiler deck to pieces. The hull, burning from bow to stern, quickly sank. The hurricane deck and a portion of the ladies' cabin became detached by the explosion and floated away. Some of the people swam to shore; others, including the women who had been in the ladies' cabin, drifted to shore on pieces of the wreck. Fifteen people were either killed by the explosion or drowned, including Josiah S. Johnson, a member of Congress. Thirteen were wounded, among them Michael Colgen, J. V. Bossier, and M. Rupen, all from Natchitoches.[84]

Entertainment on the Frontier

The expansion of river navigation not only improved the shipment of commodities but also opened the area to the larger world, including new forms of entertainment which, on the frontier, took many forms. One Natchitoches native described a game that took place about 1825 on the "common" in Natchitoches. The game was stickball, and about fifty members each of the Caddo and Choctaw tribes participated. The tribes selected the common at Natchitoches because of its large, flat area and its location near the town. Gambling was a significant part of the event for tribal members, and Natchitoches residents were known for their "generosity, charity and wealth, so that the losing party might soon make up its losses by begging." The participants arrived two or three days before the event to prepare the two-hundred-yard-long field by setting goalposts ten feet apart at each end.

> The town was excited beyond precedent. Old men and young freedmen and slaves flocked from every quarter. . . . On the day of the game . . . the "common" was filled with the populace of the town and the surrounding country. Negroes and whites and Indians, commingled in a motley throng of eager and excited spectators, awaiting with impatient expectancy the hour for the commencement of the game. At length the champions on either side were marshaled to the arena by the chiefs of the respective tribes. Yells of defiance issued from the throats of the athletes, as they stood grouped fronting each other, every muscle and sinew of their frames taut to the utmost tension of expectant activity.

The participants held rackets made of hickory with one end bent and enclosed with a net of buckskin. The chiefs of the tribes, standing between the two groups of men, tossed the ball into the air and the game began.

> The eager competitors rush forward to catch the ball in their rackets as it descends, and give it the first send-off in the direction of the opposite goal, and here occur the most remarkable feats of strength and agility. The sinewy arms of the outsiders grasp their opponents, and hurl them like infants from the eddying mass of contestants, when lo! One more lucky than the rest seizes the ball from the ground, or in its flight and sends it spinning through the air to the opposite goal. Watchful and ready skirmishers are on the alert to intercept it, and send it flying in the opposite direction, and so the struggle goes on, ebbing and flowing from one goal to the other, in alternate contests of skill and endurance.

Meanwhile, the women of the tribes stood on the sidelines "with brush and switches, to urge on the competitors to greater exertion." The townspeople, both white and Black, cheered and "vent to their sentiments in violent clamors and gesticulations." The game was played in three heats and continued for several hours, the victor winning two of three rounds.[85] John Sibley in 1807 provides another description of a stickball game. The players were Choctaws and Pascagolas. Sibley describes a rough game with blows and falls and breaks and dislocations and notes that on occasion players were killed. Betting was a significant component of the game, with the men betting their horses, guns, and other items and the women betting among themselves as well.[86]

People on the frontier also enjoyed dancing, especially the French. In December 1825, Renoy and Gagnon announced they would host a ball in the new Washington Ballroom at Mr. Renoy's at Isle Brevelle, giving a ball each Saturday until the end of Carnival. They invited the people of the town and parish of Natchitoches to attend. The Carnival season began January 6 and continued until the beginning of Lent, forty days before Easter. Antoine B. Rachal advertised that he would be giving a ball every Saturday at Cloutierville, starting December 23, for the season. Admission would be six bits for adults and half-price for children. In the multiethnic community of Natchitoches, in addition to the French balls, the Spanish had their "fandangos" and the Americans their "frolics." There were "Musical Olios" at the Lascal Ballroom on St. Denis Street as well as musical soirees.[87]

As the town grew and transportation to and from Natchitoches became easier, harbingers of "civilization" began to appear. These included thespian performances. The first company of comedians arrived by steamboat in January 1831. The touring group set up a theater in the town's old ballroom. Their first two nights, they performed to full houses, and they were to stay for three or four weeks. Touring groups apparently were not always so well received. The young lawyer William S. Tomney in 1839 attended a performance of "Warlock of the Elm" at a theater on Trudeaux Street and described it as "horribly mutilated; miserable performers." At least as early as 1837, a theater boat or showboat was making regular visits to Natchitoches.[88]

Showboats began appearing on the Mississippi River in 1831. These early floating theaters purported to bring "culture" and entertainment to those along the rivers on the frontier. The performers, often members of an extended family, presented melodramas, comedies, and primitive olios with an occasional offering from Shakespeare. The olios with their variety acts kept the audience entertained while the sets were being changed. The showboats were barges, most with three decks, the first two enclosed to serve as a long narrow auditorium with the stage at the stern. The smaller showboats had seating for about two hundred. The living quarters for the theater company were also included in the enclosed decks. The third deck was open but often had a cupola. A steamboat at the stern propelled the boat forward. The showboats would dock at a town's landing and send a person into town to advertise the upcoming performances. The most expensive seats generally cost fifty cents. The repertory "remained conservative" and in time came to appear absurd to the more sophisticated audiences in the urban areas, but showboats continued to serve the entertainment needs of the rural populace up to and then after the Civil War.[89]

Theatrical performances were not the only entertainment that made its way to the Red River. In 1826, the *Natchitoches Courier* announced performances by Mr. Mathis, "well known, for his extraordinary talents, having performed in France, London, and in the United States, with the greatest encouragement, and lastly at New Orleans . . . with splendid success." Mathis was to provide three presentations in Natchitoches of "his exercise of strength and agility." He was also to perform at Isle Brevelle at Mr. Renoy's. His act included "rope dancing on a tight rope," "grand equilibrium with chairs," and ending with a stilt dance. Such performances became common elements of circuses. Early circuses, prior to 1825, took place inside buildings, but after the adoption of the tent in 1825 most were held under the "Big Top." Performing in a ring forty-two feet in diameter, the early nineteenth-century circus acts included feats of horsemanship and gymnastics and "herculean powers." Most had at least one clown and a band. Many of the rural circuses of the day in Louisiana traveled by steamboat. Some included menageries with exotic animals. Circuses stopping at Natchitoches included in 1838 the Waterman's circus.[90]

The Changing Course of the Red River and Removal of the Great Raft

The Red River was the major conduit of commerce for the Natchitoches area. For years, the Cane River channel carried most of the flow of the Red River past the town of Natchitoches. This provided ready access to water transportation for the town and for the plantations downriver. However, a sandbar began to form below the Rouquier Plantation just south of Grand Ecore. By 1828, this sandbar was diverting much of the flow of the Red River to the Rigolette de Bon Dieu and away from Natchitoches. In time, many of the planters along the Cane River channel found themselves without any steamboat navigation during certain times of the year, especially along the lower part of the river. Even as the river level began to fall, navigation to the town of Natchitoches was still possible. Boats could come up the Bon Dieu channel of the Red River, enter Cane River south of Grand Ecore, and continue down to the town. Here the boats would turn around in the narrow, shallow channel and steam north before reentering the Red River. However, with the diversion of the Red River down the Bon Dieu, Grand Ecore just five miles to the north became Natchitoches' port, at least during part of the year.[91]

In the 1830s the federal government attempted to remove the Great Raft. When first settled in 1713, Natchitoches had been the head of navigation on the Red River. An accumulation of tree stubs, logs, driftwood, and other debris choked the river channel above this point. By 1806, the lowest raft was just above the Campti settlement. Timothy Flint described the raft in the 1820s: "The river is blocked up by this immense mass of timber for a length, on its meanders, of between sixty and seventy miles. There are places where the water can be seen in motion under the logs. In other places, the whole width of the river may be crossed on horseback. . . . Weeds, flowering shrubs, and small willows have taken root upon the surface of this timber, and flourish above the waters."[92] By 1833, the foot of the Great Raft was just above Loggy Bayou, about thirty miles upriver from Campti and about twenty miles south of current-day Shreveport. Above the foot of the raft, tree trunks and brush clogged the channel, hampering transportation. Pirogues, keelboats, and on rare occasions steamboats could work their way around by taking routes through certain bayous and lakes, but these routes were unpredictable. The raft impeded boat traffic on the upper Red River, often closing transport off entirely.[93]

In 1824, the U.S. Army built Cantonment Towson on the Red River near its junction with the Kiamichi River in what is today Oklahoma. The purpose of the fort was to reduce conflicts between white settlers and the Indian tribes. But the difficulty of supplying the post by boat was one of the reasons for its abandonment in 1829. The military argued that, if the Great Raft could be removed, the fort could be supplied by steamboat at least four months of the year.[94]

The Arkansas farmers also lobbied for removal of the raft. The raft impounded water, flooding much of the very fertile Red River Valley above the raft, making it impractical to grow crops. In October of 1825, General Winfield Scott, unaware of the raft's magnitude, directed Captain Birch at Fort Jesup to take twenty-five men to clean out the raft. Birch reported back that he and his men had traveled ninety-six miles above the foot of the raft and had counted 168 log jams, ranging from one hundred yards to one mile in length with logs tightly packed into a jumbled mass. Removing the raft would prove to be a formable and costly endeavor. The relocation of the Choctaw Indians from their ancestral homes to Indian Territory along the Red and Arkansas rivers in the 1830s was the catalysis for building a permanent fort, Fort Towson, and for the removing the Great Raft. River transportation was needed to provision both the tribal members and the military stationed in the area.[95]

Several early attempts to remove the raft met with little success. Finally, the U.S. Army Corps of Engineers selected Captain Henry M. Shreve to undertake this effort. On April 1, 1833, Shreve, now the superintendent for the improvement of the Missouri, Arkansas, and Red rivers, attacked the lower end of the Great Raft with four specially designed snag boats and 150 men. By the end of the season, Shreve and his men had cleared seventy-five miles of the river and navigation by steamboat was possible as far as the Caddo Indian Agency, which had been moved to the area near current-day Shreveport. But during the ensuing months the raft reformed. Shreve worked on raft removal for the next six years. In 1838, the secretary of war announced that the Great Raft had been removed, but in 1841 it began to reform. It would be the 1880s before the raft was removed for the last time. With the removal of the raft, an estimated million and a half acres of prime alluvial farmland became available for settlement. In time, Shreveport became a major commercial hub for farmers who settled in the surrounding areas as well as those from East Texas, who could now ship their cotton from Jefferson, Texas, through Caddo Lake to the Red River.[96]

Removal of the Caddo

Federal policies forced Indian peoples from the eastern United States to migrate across the Mississippi River. Some stayed in Louisiana, but others continued into Texas with some eventually settling on lands allotted them in Indian Territory (present-day Oklahoma). By 1827, some estimated that 550 lodges of Shawnee, 500 of Delaware, and 200 of Kickapoo and many Cherokee had settled in Texas. Mexican officials complained to the American government about the numbers of Indians tribes from the United States entering Texas.[97]

The Caddo, who still maintained a village on the Louisiana-Texas border, were troubled by the encroachment of both Indian and white settlers onto their traditional tribal lands and felt the influence of their chief Dehahuit eroding. Before, when the United States needed the assistance of the great Caddo chief to maintain peace on the frontier, Governor Claiborne referred to Dehahuit as "a man of great merit . . . brave, sensible and . . . the most influential Indian on this side of the River Grande."[98] But now, John Fowler, the factor at the government trading house, described Dehahuit as "a mischievous Indian" who showed no appreciation for the gifts given him, who claimed all the land on both sides of the river, and said that he would drive out all Whites who settled on his lands above the raft.[99] Fowler wanted Dehahuit replaced as chief or a second chief appointed who could work with the Americans. By 1825, so many Americans had entered the area that Dehahuit asked Indian agent George Grey to designate the boundaries of the Caddo lands using natural features that would be easily recognized by all. Grey, who was having trouble keeping settlers off Caddo lands, saw this request as a possible solution and used various rivers to establish the borders. In an 1818 treaty, the Quapaw gave up their lands in Arkansas, believing the U.S. government had purchased land for them among the Caddo. When the Quapaw arrived in Caddo territory in 1826, they learned this was not the case, but the Caddo agreed to allow the Quapaw to stay. In the same year, the agent Grey informed Dehahuit that the government wanted to settle several small Louisiana tribes among the Caddo. Dehahuit agreed but, due to the increasing scarcity of game and other resources, asked for a small annuity, and the government allocated fifty dollars. By 1828, Choctaw, Coushatta, Cherokee, Quapaw, Shawnee, Delaware, and Kickapoo had villages in the old Caddo-Hasinai territory of northwest Louisiana and East Texas. At a meeting held in May 1828 and attended by many tribes, Mexican officials asked Dehahuit whether the Caddo land was in Mexico or the United States. He replied that "he was neither on Mexican nor United States Territory, but on his own land which belonged to nobody but him." Grey, the Indian agent, had at least attempted to keep white settlers off Caddo land. When Grey died in 1828, the government appointed a new agent.[100]

Jeheil Brooks, a recently arrived lawyer in Natchitoches, was interested in the position of Indian agent and solicited signatures of support from many in Natchitoches before traveling to Washington to plead his case. John Sibley, who had maintained his interest in the Caddo Indians even after his removal as Indian agent in 1815, opposed Brooks's appointment and was greatly concerned when he learned that Brooks had been selected as agent for the Caddo.[101] As Sibley wrote "I Scarsely [*sic*] ever heard of an act of any government more exceptionable. . . . An Indian Agent has been appointed here, who was tried in New Orleans before the Criminal Court. . . . He was regarded as an Acquitted felon. He is Accused of Swindling & Cheating at Cards, & he is here Buying Goods . . . giving dinners [etc.] . . . all at the Expence of the United States, for he has not a dollar of his own funds."[102]

Sibley had cause for concern. So did Dehahuit. The Caddo chief had a letter sent to the president of the United States expressing the lack of trust the tribe had in Brooks and requesting a new agent and interpreter of their choice be appointed. He asked that the president respond through John Sibley rather than Brooks. Sibley's and Dehahuit's distrust in Brooks proved well founded. But Brooks remained and in 1831 moved the agency away from the tribe and toward the future site of Shreveport.[103]

For years, the Great Raft had protected the Caddo lands, at least to some extent, from the encroachment of cotton plantations. The seasonal flooding of the bottomlands and the lack of river access for shipping cotton made developing the area impractical. By 1830, the new Indian agent Brooks knew that Congress had authorized the removal of the raft and that Henry Shreve had been appointed to undertake the task. With the removal of the raft, acres and acres of prime bottomlands would become available for cotton cultivation. The only obstacle was that much of the land belonged to the Caddo.[104] In 1834, Brooks wrote the commissioner of Indian affairs that, "Since the practicability of removing the obstructions to the navigation of Red river has been established, much excitement has been manifested respecting the *river lands* throughout the region of the raft." The problem, Brooks noted, was that most of the land belonged to the Caddo. Brooks went on to write that this "state of things was anticipated by me from the first, and was the occasion of my suggesting to the President, when last at Washington, the necessity of extinguishing the Indian title to all such land prior to the removal of the raft." Brooks argued that it would be best "to negotiate for these lands at once, before the further progress of the work shall open the eyes of the tribe, as to their importance to the whites, or before their interest shall be surrendered to the cupidity of evil advisors who surround them."[105] In other words, before the Caddo recognized the real value of their land. Dehahuit had died in 1833 and so did not live to see the loss of the Caddo homeland. In March 1835, Brooks received instruction to negotiate a treaty with the Caddo for their lands.[106]

By 1835, the Caddo's hunting grounds had been depleted, white settlers were moving onto Caddo lands, and Brooks told the Caddo he was no longer their agent and the agency would no longer provide a gunsmith or blacksmith for the Caddo. After holding a Great Council to discuss the matter, the Caddo reluctantly concluded that their only option was to sell their lands to the U.S. government. The Caddo chiefs, with the assistance of Brooks, sent a memorial to the President of the United States. The head chief, Tarshar, and twenty-three other chiefs signed the document with the former Caddo interpreter Larkin Edwards, the former Quapaw interpreter John W. Edwards, J. C. Mcleod, and J. Brooks serving as witnesses. In January of 1835, President Andrew Jackson endorsed the Caddo's memorial.[107]

In June, Brooks sent for the Caddo, telling them he had been authorized to arrange for the purchase of their lands on behalf of the United States. The Caddo were having second thoughts. On June 25, about five hundred members of the Caddo tribe arrived at the agency and asked that three men, Manuel Flores, Francis Bark, and Joseph Valentine, attend the treaty negotiations with them. Brooks refused to allow these men to participate and, using the troops from Fort Jesup who were at the agency for the treaty negotiations, removed the men. The Caddo formed a council to deal with the negotiations.[108]

Brooks addressed the council. He told them the president of the United States had designated him to meet with the Caddo to negotiate a price that would be agreeable to both parties. Brooks believed the amount offered would make the Caddo independent when compared to their present situation but, if they finalized a treaty, the Caddo would have to vacate their homeland. He stated that he had never deceived them and had been sent as their friend to negotiate for the land that was of no use to the Caddo and which the white settlers would soon take from them anyway.[109]

Tsauninot, under chief of the Caddo, responded: "We salute you, and through you, our great father, who has sent you again with words of comfort to us. We are in great want, and have been expecting you to bring us relief; for you told us, before you departed last fall, that you had no doubt our great father would treat with us for our country, and would supply us with things of much more value to us than these lands, which yield no game." He admitted the Caddo had been advised by several men not to attend the council or sign any treaty and that the Caddo would be cheated out of their land and "then driven away like dogs," but that the Caddo placed no reliance on the advice of these men. He added: "[W]e have warned our people, from time to time, not to heed such tales, but wait and see what our great father would do for us. We now know his wishes, and believe he will deal justly with us. We will therefore go and consult together, and let you know tomorrow morning what we are willing to do."[110] At the end of the meeting, Brooks distributed presents to the tribal council and then showed the Caddo samples of the goods that the tribe would be receiving if they signed the treaty.

The council returned to the rest of the Caddo and related Brooks's offer. Tarshar, the chief, spoke to the sorrowful tribal members: "My Children: For what do you mourn? Are you not starving in the midst of this land? And do you not travel far from it in quest of food? The game we live on is going further off, and the white man is coming near to us; and is not our condition getting worse daily? Then why lament for the loss of that which yields us nothing but misery? Let us be wise then, and get all we can for it [the land], and not wait till the white man steals it away, little by little, and then gives us nothing."[111]

At the negotiations that followed with Brooks, the Caddo said they had been advised to ask two hundred dollars per mile to be paid with one hundred in currency and one hundred in goods for their land. Brooks argued that, since the boundary with Texas had yet to be settled, it was impossible to determine the size of the Caddo lands. When the Caddo asked Brooks for his advice, he suggested eighty thousand dollars for the land. On July 1, 1835, twenty-five Caddo chiefs signed the "Treaty Between the United States of America and The Caddo Nation of Indians," relinquishing all their lands in Louisiana. The U.S. Senate ratified the treaty on January 26, 1836, and President Jackson signed it on February 2. The Caddo sold approximately one million acres of land for thirty thousand dollars in goods and horses to be paid immediately and ten thousand dollars a year for each of the next five years. The Caddo had sold their land for eight cents an acre. At the time, prime bottomland was worth twenty dollars an acre with the uplands selling between fifty cents and ten dollars per acre. Unfortunately, the Caddo did not even receive the agreed-upon amount. According to Larkin Edwards, rather than the ten thousand dollars promised, the second payment was not made in cash but rather ten boxes labeled as one hundred dollars each. Brooks required the Caddo to sign a receipt before opening the boxes. The Caddo initially refused but eventually signed. When they opened the boxes, they were very dissatisfied. Larkin Edwards, who was there at the time, estimated that the contents of the boxes were worth only between fifteen hundred and two thousand dollars rather than ten thousand dollars. The Caddo asked that a Mr. John G. Green act on their behalf for the third installment. The third shipment proved even more unsatisfactory. Brooks had not represented well the interests of his former charges, but there were no repercussions relating to his treatment of the Caddo. However, Brooks was accused of fraud in another matter.[112]

Henry Shreve, who was at the time under contract with the federal government to remove the Great Raft, wrote President Jackson in April 1836, stating that "an extensive fraud has been practiced on the United States by the agent of the Government making a treaty with the Caddo Indians."[113] This related to property Brooks included as a supplement to the Caddo treaty. According to Brooks, the Caddo requested that an area they had given to François Grappe and his heirs be included in a supplement to the treaty. The supplementary articles reserved four leagues of land for François Grappe, known to the Caddo as Touline, the son of the French trader Alexis Grappe, and for François's heirs and a small piece of property for the old Caddo interpreter, Larkin Edwards. As soon as the treaty was approved in Washington, Brooks went to the Grappes and offered $6,000 for the property. Shreve in his letter contented that the land was worth "upward to $150,000, if not double that amount."[114] Others were also concerned. About eighteen months later, in September 1837, the Caddo chiefs, head men, and warriors sent the U.S. Senate a document stipulating they had a white man who spoke their language read the treaty to them and, at the time of the treaty, the Caddo never reserved any land for any individual except for Larkin Edwards.

> Jehiel Brooks told one of the chiefs that one Jacques Grappe requested him to ask the Indians for a piece of land on Red river, in the bottom, and on the east side of the bayou Pierre, (the western water of Red River;) that the said chief told Mr. Brooks that was not their land, and Mr. Brooks told him that it was their land. The chief then told Mr. Brooks that, if it was their land, he was willing to give Jacques Grappe a little piece; but that they never made any reserve to Francois Grappe, or any of his heirs or representatives, by the treaty, within the limits of land they claimed or sold to the United States.[115]

Tarshar, Tsauninot, and nineteen other Caddo and four white men including the interpreter Cesair Lafitte signed the statement. The statement was certified by twenty-six men in the parish of Natchitoches as a true interpretation of what the chiefs had said. The Congressional Committee on Indian Affairs in Washington upon investigating the case resolved that the land in question had never been part of the Caddo territory ceded in the tribe's treaty and referred the question of fraud to the courts for judgement. The Circuit Court of the United States for the District of Louisiana ruled the charges of fraud against Brooks unwarranted and confirmed Brooks title to the land. The U.S. government appealed the case to the Supreme Court, which, in 1851, upheld the lower court ruling. During this time, Brooks faced financial difficulties on several fronts. In addition to the fraud allegation, Brooks engaged in several lawsuits over land in the former Caddo territory most of which he lost.[116]

Natchitoches in the 1830s

By 1830, Natchitoches Parish had a population of 7,905 with whites making up 48.1 percent, slaves 45.2 percent, and "free colored persons" 6.7 percent (see appendix table 4). This compares to 7,372 people listed in the 1820 census. Such a small increase in population is deceptive. In fact, the parish had grown so large that a new parish had been carved out of the old Natchitoches Parish, creating Claiborne Parish in 1828. In 1830, Claiborne Parish had a population of 1,764.[117]

Edward Russell, a forty-three-year-old man from Maine who traveled through the town on his way to Texas, provides a description of Natchitoches in 1834. Arriving by steamboat in early February, Russell received a generally positive impression of Natchitoches. He viewed the town as larger and better than Alexandria. Russell describes it as what "would be called in Maine a homely village," yet he acknowledged that the town was "a place of much business" with a bank, two printing offices, and courthouse and jail. The former jail had been repurposed as a tavern. The stores were "well filled" and the merchants "gentlemanly & active young men." He estimated that the town contained about two thousand people, but many of the buildings were "very mean indeed" and "half the population French. No public house." The Catholic congregation had rebuilt the church, which had burned in 1823.[118]

On March 17, 1838, another fire broke out in Natchitoches, this time starting in the kitchen of Mr. Crossman on Second Street. The blaze spread rapidly, burning the "splendid Roman Catholic Church" a second time, as well as several other properties. Although the people of the town worked to remove the furniture from the burning buildings, the estimate of damage from the fire was over $100,000. Of the church, only the walls remained standing. Repairs would cost $7,000. Ambrose Lecomte offered the use of his new townhouse on Front Street for services while the church was being repaired, and the pews and items saved from the fire were moved to Lecomte's home. When fully repaired, the church measured eighty-five by forty-eight feet with a thirty-foot-high bell tower.[119]

The early and mid-1830s were prosperous times for Natchitoches and the South. Cotton was king. In the autumn of 1836, cotton was selling for an average of twenty-one cents a pound and the South was expecting to produce 1.5 million bales. At the same time, the Jackson administration was becoming increasingly concerned about the rampant speculation in tracts of public land. To curtail this,

Jackson issued the "Species Circular" in July of 1836, requiring that all future purchases of most governmental land be made in silver and gold. The sale of governmental land plummeted. President Jackson vetoed the rechartering of the (Second) Bank of the United States and distributed the federal funds to a number of local banks in the various states. These policies forced the banks on the East Coast to scale back their loans. At the same time, Congress passed legislation to eliminate regulations on banks. In the South, state banks maintained unsafe reserve ratios, printed paper currency, and made loans and then printed more currency and made more loans—all based on the expected continuation of the high price paid for cotton.[120]

Meanwhile, Britain was facing its own financial difficulties. The textile mills had a considerable inventory of raw cotton, and the demand for cotton cloth was dropping. Factories began to lay off workers. Officials at the Bank of England, the source of much of the credit for the cotton buyers in Liverpool, England's major port for cotton imports, became worried about the overproduction of cotton cloth and therefore restricted credit. As a result, the top cotton dealers in Liverpool began closing their doors. Suddenly there was little demand for the South's cotton, and prices fell precipitously. While in 1836 cotton sold for twenty-one cents, a year later the average price was thirteen cents. Fearing the planters would soon be unable to pay their debts, banks in the United States began to refuse further loans. The Panic of 1837, which would have a devastating effect on Natchitoches and the South as a whole, had begun.[121]

CONCLUSION

Natchitoches in 1840 was a very different place than it had been just forty years earlier. In 1800, Natchitoches was an inland settlement of the Spanish Empire with many free people of French descent. It had begun almost ninety years earlier as a fur-trading center and outpost of French presence on the French-Spanish frontier. In 1762, with the Treaty of Fontainebleau, Natchitoches became Spanish, although the people remained culturally French. By the late 1700s, in addition to having a commercial fur trade, Natchitoches had become an agricultural area with plantations and farms growing indigo and a particularly fine grade of tobacco in the rich alluvial valleys. By 1800, commercial cotton production was becoming increasingly important. Despite forty years of Spanish rule and the arrival of some Americans in the area, Natchitoches remained primarily a French community.

With the Louisiana Purchase, Natchitoches once again found itself on an international frontier, this time between the competing nations of the United States and Imperial Spain. Recognizing Natchitoches' strategic importance, the U.S. government quickly sent a military force to occupy the area to guarantee that Spain respected the new international boundary. The United States also established a government-run Indian trading post and an Indian agency to shore up its developing relationship with the Native peoples and to ensure the loyalties of the tribal groups against any encroachments by the Spanish. These three governmental entities dominated Natchitoches for most of the next twenty years. Activities in the area and the dispute over the international boundary brought the United States and Imperial Spain to the brink of war. The Spanish and American military leaders avoided a war by negotiating the Neutral Ground

Agreement. The Neutral Ground, under the jurisdiction of neither country, became a refuge for outlaws and served as a staging ground for filibuster ventures into Texas. The Adams-Onís Treaty finally settled the land dispute. By the 1820s Natchitoches, now largely freed of the federal presence, had become a growing commercial center with the Red River the major highway of commerce. People were flooding into the area, with some staying and others continuing their way west to settle in Texas. Although the fur trade declined, cotton production increased and with it the wealth of the planters. The early and mid-1830s were prosperous times for Natchitoches and the South. Cotton was king. Unfortunately, new monetary directives from the Jackson administration and financial problems facing Great Britain contributed to the Panic of 1837. The price offered for cotton plummeted. Hard times were ahead.

By 1840, many of the old markers of Natchitoches were gone. Gone were Fort Claiborne and its soldiers who had guarded the American-Spanish frontier. Gone were the government trading post and Indian agency and the constant stream of Indians coming to town to trade and meet with the Indian agent. Gone was the use of Natchitoches as the staging ground for armed incursions into Mexico and the major gateway for many immigrants going west. And gone was the Red River, which had redirected its course away from the town. With the river gone, so was Natchitoches' role as a commercial center on the Red River. After two fires, gone were many of the older buildings in the town. With the Panic of 1837, gone was much of the area's prosperity, which had largely depended upon cotton. But, after adjustments in the late 1830s and early 1840s, King Cotton would reign again, and prosperity would return to Natchitoches—at least for a time.

Through it all, the French Creole influence endured. Catholicism, a hallmark of the Creole community, remained a strong influence in Natchitoches, where the first resident priest had arrived in 1728. Despite the flood of Americans into the area, it would be 1839 before another denomination built a church in the town—an Episcopal church. Natchitoches would become the base for a new Catholic diocese in 1853, which continued to serve the Catholics of north Louisiana until 1910.[1] In 1847, the Religious of the Sacred Heart would open the Academy of the Sacred Heart, a girls' boarding school, where many Creole planters sent their daughters. The College of St. Joseph, founded in 1856, provided educational opportunities for French Creole boys in the Natchitoches area. As late as 1878, the nuns in Natchitoches Parish were still teaching their students in the French language.[2]

Frederick Law Olmsted, a newspaper reporter who traveled through Natchitoches in the early 1850s, noted the ethnic mix of the town even after almost fifty years of American rule. "French blood rather predominates in the population in the vicinity of Natchitoches, but there is also a considerable amount of the Spanish and Indian mongrel breed. . . . [They] are very regular in their attendance on divine worship, at the cathedral. . . . The Children in the streets speak Spanish, and French, and English, with the negro dialect, indifferently; and a schoolhouse exposes a sign, 'Ecole Primaire Anglais et Français.' . . . The slaves are, some French and Spanish Creole negroes, and many from 'Old Virginny.'"[3]

Although many of the early town officials were Americans, the Natchitoches Police Jury, the parish governing authority on which many Creoles served, continued to keep its official records in French as late as 1855.[4] The Natchitoches newspapers that served the community published in both English and French through the Civil War. Aaron Walker, a Freedmen's Bureau official who visited Natchitoches in 1865, noted that Natchitoches was "the oldest town in the state &, almost of course, the people speak French." He continued, "Whoever goes here will not only have to teach the rudiments of language, but teach the children to speak *English*."[5] Many of these children were probably from the Creole plantations. There would be people who spoke some Creole French into the early twenty-first century. Even today, the legacy of the French influence is still evident in the large number of people in the area with French surnames.

APPENDIX

Table 1. Population Summary, Natchitoches Parish, 1810

Population	*Total*	%
Whites	1,313	44.2
Slaves	1,476	49.7
All others	181	6.1
Total	2,970	100.0

Source: U.S. Census, 1810. Population Census, Natchitoches Parish, Louisiana, microfilm, CGHRC.

Table 2. **Population by District in 1820, Natchitoches Parish**

	Rio Hondo		*Natchitoches Proper*		*River aux Cannes*		*Town*		*Total*	
Population	*No.*	*%*	*No.*	*%*	*No.*	*%*	*No.*	*%*	*No.*	*%*
White males	1,240	48.0	601	27.2	437	25.4	355	41.4	2,633	35.7
White females	1,078	41.7	441	19.9	359	20.9	234	27.3	2,112	28.6
Total whites	**2,318**	**89.7**	**1,042**	**47.1**	**796**	**46.3**	**589**	**68.7**	**4,745**	**64.3**
Free males of color	10	0.4	53	2.4	71	4.1	15	1.8	149	2.0
Free females of color	4	0.2	67	3.0	68	3.9	13	1.6	152	2.0
Total free people of color	**14**	**0.6**	**120**	**5.4**	**139**	**8.0**	**28**	**3.4**	**301**	**4.0**
Male slaves	136	5.3	511	23.1	399	23.2	108	12.6	1,154	15.7
Female slaves	114	4.4	539	24.4	387	22.5	132	15.4	1,172	15.9
Total slaves	**250**	**9.7**	**1,050**	**47.5**	**786**	**45.7**	**240**	**28.0**	**2,326**	**31.6**
Total people	**2,582**	**100**	**2,212**	**100**	**1,721**	**100**	**857**	**100.1**	**7,372**	**99.9**
Non-nationalized foreigners	638		128		89		180		1,035	
					Households					
No. households	309		171		155		104		739	
Number of slave-owning households	61	19.7	92	53.8	97	62.6	48	44.9	298	40.2
Avg. no. slaves per slave-owning household	4.1		11.4		8.1		5.0		7.8	

Source: U.S. Census, 1820, Natchitoches Parish, Louisiana, microfilm, CGHRC.

Table 3. Economic Activities by Household in 1820, Natchitoches Parish

	Rio Hondo		*Natchitoches Proper*		*River aux Cannes*		*Town*		*Total*	
	No.	*%*	*No.*	*%*	*No.*	*%*	*No.*	*%*	*No.*	*%*
Households	309	41.8	171	23.1	155	21.0	104	14.1	739	100
Households engaged										
in agriculture	300	86.5	166	83.4	152	85.4	56	51.8	674	81.0
in commerce	2	0.6	3	1.8	7	4.5	21	20.2	33	4.0
in manufacturing	45	13.0	30	15.1	19	10.7	31	28.7	125	15.0
Total number of people (ages 14/16 and up)	1,383		1,281		1,184		559		4,407	
	No.	*%*	*No.*	*%*	*No.*	*%*	*No.*	*%*	*No.*	*%*
People engaged										
in agriculture	866	94.1	911	96.0	756	95.5	168*	70	2,701	93.1
in commerce	3	0.3	5	0.5	7	0.9	22	9.2	37	1.3
in manufacturing	51	5.5	32	3.4	29	3.7	50	20.8	162	5.6
Total	**920**	**99.9**	**948**	**99.9**	**792**	**100.1**	**240**	**100**	**2,900**	**100**

*Several of the large planters lived in the town of Natchitoches. The slaves engaged in agriculture are listed under these owners. These agricultural workers undoubtedly lived on the plantations.

Note: Some households and individuals engaged in more than one economic activity.

Source: U.S. Census, 1820, Natchitoches Parish, Louisiana, microfilm, CGHRC.

Table 4. Population Summary, Natchitoches Parish, 1830

Population	*Males*	*%*	*Females*	*%*	*Total*	*%*
Free white persons	2,154	50.9	1,648	44.9	3,802	48.1
"Free colored persons"	261	6.2	270	7.4	531	6.7
Slaves	1,818	42.9	1,754	47.8	3,572	45.2
Total	4,233	100.0	3,672	100.1	7,905	100.0

Source: U.S. Census, 1830, Natchitoches Parish, Louisiana, microfilm, CGHRC.

NOTES

Introduction

1. Cerami, *Jefferson's Great Gamble,* 11, 41, 69, 201–5, 245; Peterson, "Louisiana!" 22; Smith, "Napoleon and Louisiana," 55, 58.

2. Davis, *Louisiana,* 163.

3. Peterson, *Thomas Jefferson and the New Nation,* 778–80; Hatfield, *William Claiborne,* 44; Ellis, "Jefferson and the Purchase," 10. Also see Beauchamp, *Instruments of Empire.*

1. What the Americans Found

1. Miller, "History of Fort Claiborne," 4–5; Lytle, "Public Life of Edward Dumaresque Turner," 148.

2. Turner to Claiborne, May 1, 1804, in Carter, comp. and ed., *The Territorial Papers of the United States* 9: *The Territory of Orleans 1803–1812,* 238. Hereafter cited as *TP.*

3. Isaac Joslin Cox, "The Louisiana-Texas Frontier, Part II," 14.

4. Martin, *History of Louisiana,* 300.

5. John Sibley to Henry Dearborn, Natchitoches, April 10, 1805, in Sibley, "An Account of the Red River," 727.

6. Sibley to Governor Claiborne, Natchitoches, October 10, 1803, *TP* 9: 75.

7. Sibley, "An Account of the Red River," 727. This might have been something of an exaggeration on Sibley's part. There had been a number of men who engaged in the trades during the colonial period. See Byrd, *Colonial Natchitoches.*

8. Darby, *Emigrant's Guide,* 101–2.

9. Stoddard, *Sketches,* 184–92; Sibley to Dearborn, Natchitoches, April 10, 1805, in *American State Papers, Indian Affairs* (hereafter *ASP, IA*), vol. 1: 726. For a description of the ecology of the Red River in the early 1800s see Flores, "The Ecology of the Red River," 1–42.

10. Flores, *Jefferson & Southwestern Exploration,* 110–11; Stoddard, *Sketches,* 186.

11. Stoddard, *Sketches,* 188, 187; Flores, *Jefferson & Southwestern Exploration,* 114–15.

12. Darby, *Geographical Description of the State of Louisiana,* 249; Sibley to Dearborn, Natchitoches, April 10, 1805, *ASP, IA* 1: 727; Flores, *Jefferson & Southwestern Exploration,* 221–22; Sibley to Dearborn, Natchitoches, April 10, 1805, *ASP, IA* 1: 727.

13. Flores, *Jefferson & Southwestern Exploration,* 127–31.

14. Darby, *Emigrant's Guide,* 85.

15. Bridges and Reames, "The Bayou Pierre Settlement," 134, 140; Stoddard, *Sketches,* 189; Burton and Smith, *Colonial Natchitoches,* 146–67; Sibley, "An Account of the Red River," 721–23, 728. Los Adaes, located about twelve miles west of Natchitoches, served as the capital of the Spanish province of Texas from 1729 to 1770. It was abandoned by the Spanish in 1773. Martin, *History of Louisiana,* 20.

16. Darby, *Emigrant's Guide,* 87.

17. Burton and Smith, *Colonial Natchitoches,* 146–67.

18. Darby, *Emigrant's Guide,* 87; Burton and Smith, *Colonial Natchitoches,* 146–67; Sibley, "An Account of the Red River," 723, 727; Mayer, "Drake's Salt Dome."

19. The term *Creole* has had different meanings at different times. In the 1820s and 1830s, it referred to those born in Louisiana irrespective of race or national origins, excluding the Indians. The term *ancienne population* identified those of French or Spanish descent who could trace their families back to colonial times in Louisiana. In this work, *French Creole* will be used in place of the more cumbersome *ancienne population* generally to differentiate the native population from the recently arrived Anglo-Americans. For more information on the term *Creole,* see Tregle, *Louisiana in the Age of Jackson,* 23–41, 337–43.

20. Stoddard, *Sketches,* 324, 325, 327.

21. Stoddard, *Sketches,* 324, 327, 323, 322.

22. Stoddard, *Sketches,* 323, 324, 327, 322.

23. Stoddard, *Sketches,* 307, 314, 320.

24. Stoddard, *Sketches,* 320, 307, 314, 320, 321.

25. Stoddard, *Sketches,* 310.

26. Stoddard, *Sketches,* 324, 325, 305–6.

27. Stoddard, *Sketches,* 321, 316.

28. These numbers include the slaves in West Florida. Hall, *Africans in Colonial Louisiana,* 278–79, fig. 2, 35, 10, 35–42; Davidson, *West Africa Before the Colonial Era,* 187–205.

29. Taylor, *Negro Slavery in Louisiana;* Dumont de Montigny, *Memoires sur la Louisiane,* qtd. in Taylor, *Negro Slavery in Louisiana,* 15–16; Brasseaux, "Administration of Slave Regulations in French Louisiana," 210–11; Hall, *Africans in Colonial Louisiana,* 10.

30. Hall, *Africans in Colonial Louisiana,* 276–315.

31. See Mills, *Forgotten People,* for an extensive discussion of this topic and the Creoles of color on Cane River. Burton and Smith, *Colonial Natchitoches,* 85–86, 98–99.

32. Coutts, "Boom and Bust," 240–42; Hall, *Africans in Colonial Louisiana,* 318.

33. Hall, *Africans in Colonial Louisiana,* 378, 352.

34. Hall, *Africans in Colonial Louisiana,* 317–74; Carondelet to Las Cases, New Orleans, July 30, 1795, qtd. in Hall, *Africans in Colonial Louisiana,* 370.

35. Hall, *Africans in Colonial Louisiana,* 344–45.

36. For additional information on the history and prehistory of the Caddo, see Carter, *Caddo Indians;* Le Vere, *Caddo Chiefdoms;* Neuman, *Introduction to Louisiana Archaeology;* Neuman, "Historical Locations of Certain Caddoan Tribes"; Pertulla, *"The Caddo Nation";* Smith, *Caddo Indians;* Smith, *From Dominance to Disappearance;* Swanton, *Source Material;* Webb and Gregory, *The Caddo Indians of Louisiana.*

37. Ewers, "Influence of Epidemics on the Indian Populations," 104–15; La Vere, *Caddo Chiefdoms,* 33.

38. Swanton, *Source Material,* 7–25.

39. Swanton, *Source Material,* 37.

40. Chipman and Joseph, *Notable Men and Women of Spanish Texas,* 112–14.

41. Smith, *Caddo Indians,* 86; Sibley, "Historical Sketches," 721. Most of Sibley's knowledge about the various tribes was based on secondhand reports and should be viewed as estimates. The numbers for the various groups could have been and probably were higher.

42. Sibley, "Historical Sketches," 721.

43. Sibley, "Historical Sketches," 722. The Adai are Sibley's "Adaize."

44. Sibley, "Historical Sketches," 724; Smith, *Caddo Indians,* 85–86.

45. Smith, *Caddo Indians,* 86; Sibley, "Historical Sketches," 722.

46. Kniffen, Gregory, and Stokes, *The Historic Indian Tribes of Louisiana,* 84; McEwan, "Apalachee and Neighboring Groups," 669–76; Lankford, "Chacato, Pensacola, Tohomé, Naniaba, and Mobila," 664–68; Flores, *Jefferson & Southwestern Exploration,* 112–13; Sibley, "Historical Sketches," 724–25; Flores, "Red River Branch of the Alabama-Coushatta Indians," 65; Martin, *History of Louisiana,* 301.

47. Walker, "Creek Confederacy," 373–75; Flores, "Red River Branch of the Alabama-Coushatta Indians," 56–57; Usner, *American Indians,* 99; Sibley, "Historical Sketches," 724; Smith, *Caddo Indians,* 87. Anthropologists use the term "*Koasati*" for this Creek group. In the early historic records of the Natchitoches area the term used is "*Coushatta.*" The Indians today use "*Coushatta.*" The term "*Coushatta*" will be used in this work for the tribe anthropologists refer to as the Koasati.

48. Kniffen, Gregory, and Stokes, *Historic Indian Tribes of Louisiana,* 84; Kinnaird and Kinnaird, "Choctaws West of the Mississippi," 349–70; Usner, *American Indians,* 99.

49. Usner, *American Indians,* 97–98.

50. Usner, *American Indians,* 98.

2. Fort Claiborne and the Military on the Frontier

1. Lytle, "Public Life of Edward Dumaresque Turner," 148; Miller, "History of Fort Claiborne," 4; Lafon, *Carte Générale du Territoire D'Orleans comprenant.* See also Old Plat Map District Northwestern, T9N, R7W.

2. Lytle, "Public Life of Edward Dumaresque Turner," 155–57; Miller, "History of Fort Claiborne," 6, 8–14; Seale, "From French Village to American Town," 59–61. For a discussion of the location of Fort Claiborne and archaeological investigations at the site, see Smith, ed., *Military Heritage,* 68–93. The Natchitoches Event Center now sits on the site of the former fort.

3. Miller, "History of Fort Claiborne," 6–7; Seale, "From French Village to American Town," 62–66.

4. Turner to Governor Claiborne, Natchitoches, July 30, 1804, in *TP* 9: 272.

5. Turner to Claiborne, April 5, 1805, Claiborne (William C. C.) Letters and Depositions (1799–1846), MSS 5018, Louisiana and Lower Mississippi Valley Collections, LSU Libraries, Baton Rouge.

6. Turner to Claiborne, May 5, 1805, Claiborne (William C. C.) Letters and Depositions (1799–1846), MSS 5018.

7. Turner to Claiborne, April 3, 1805, Claiborne (William C. C.) Letters and Depositions (1799–1846), MSS 5018; Baudier, *Catholic Church in North Louisiana,* 12.

8. Robin, *Voyage to Louisiana,* 263.

9. Lytle, "Public Life of Edward Dumaresque Turner," 156, 160.

10. B. Lafon, a well-known New Orleans architect, builder, engineer, surveyor, cartographer, town planner, planter, land speculator, publisher, and in later years pirate, drew a "Plan of the Fort Claiborne Natchitoches" dated ca. 1813–14. This map shows a rectangular palisade with a blockhouse toward the north end of the enclosure and two barracks and several other buildings. It also depicts the geography and a number of other buildings in the town. Unfortunately this beautifully drawn and colored map appears to be more representative than factual and, although some researchers have attempted to explain the differences between this map and better documented maps as possibly an earlier rendition of the fort, there are so many inconsistences between the Lafon map and the known locations of buildings, roads, and geographical features and the history of Fort Claiborne that the map is of little value in understanding Fort Claiborne and the location of structures in the town. This is very surprising considering the reputation of Lafon as a mapmaker. For information on Lafon, see Ann Masson, "Barthélémy Lafon," *64 Parishes,* 64 parishes.org/entry/barthlmy-lafon.

11. Miller, "History of Fort Claiborne," 9–10. A soldier named Nowland had been serving under Lieutenant Bowmar at Fort Miro (current-day Monroe) and was carried to Fort Claiborne in August, critically ill. Dr. Sibley treated him until his death. Lytle, "Public Life of Edward Dumaresque Turner," 165–66.

12. United States, Louisiana Purchase: Treaty between the United States of America and the French Republic, April 30, 1803.

13. Hatfield, *William Claiborne,* 117; Byrd, *Colonial Natchitoches,* 46–47; Bolton, *Texas in the Middle Eighteenth Century,* 1, 33. For a fuller discussion of the Louisiana/Texas border issue, see Cox, "Louisiana-Texas Frontier, Part II," and Pichardo, *Pichardo's Treatise on the Limits of Louisiana and Texas.*

14. Turner to Claiborne, July 30, 1804, *TP* 9: 272.

15. Turner to Claiborne, July 30, 1804, *TP* 9: 271–73, 238.

16. Turner to Claiborne, Natchitoches, May 1, 1804, *TP* 9: 238–39.

17. Turner to Wilkinson, Natchitoches, August 1, 1804, *American State Papers, Foreign Relations* 2: 690 (hereafter *ASP, FR*).

18. Turner to Claiborne, Natchitoches, July 30, 1804, *TP* 9: 272.

19. Turner to Wilkinson, Natchitoches, August 1, 1804, *ASP, FR* 2: 690.

20. Cox, "Louisiana-Texas Frontier, Part II," 37.

21. Claiborne to Casa Calvo, New Orleans, September 1, 1804, in Rowland, ed., *Official Letter Books of W. C. C. Claiborne, 1801–1816,* 315 (hereafter Rowland, ed., *CLB*).

22. Petition to Edward Turner, July 29, 1804, *TP* 9: 273–74.

23. Turner to Claiborne, July 30, 1804, *TP* 9: 271–72.

24. Cox, "Louisiana-Texas Frontier, Part II," 38.

25. Turner to Claiborne, Natchitoches, October 17, 1804, Rowland, ed., *CLB* 2: 386.

26. Casa Calvo to Claiborne, November 6, 1804, *TP* 9: 324.

27. Governor of Texas to Commandant General, San Antonio, November 7, 1804, Bexar Archives Translations, Microfilm reel 19 (hereafter BAT).

28. Sibley to Claiborne, March 8, 1805, Natchitoches, William C.C. Claiborne Letters and Depositions, MSS 5018.

29. Sibley to Claiborne, March 8, 1805, Natchitoches, William C.C. Claiborne Letters and Depositions, MSS 5018.

30. Turner to Claiborne, Natchitoches, November 21, 1804, *TP* 9: 335; Claiborne to Secretary of State, New Orleans, April 5, 1805, *TP* 9: 432–33.

31. *American State Papers, Military Affairs* 1: 177; Miller, "History of Fort Claiborne," 53n4; *American State Papers, Miscellaneous* 1: 320.

32. Pike, *Exploratory Travels,* 288.

33. Haggard, "Neutral Ground," 1029.

34. Dearborn to Commanding Officer at Natchitoches, War Dept., November 5, 1805, *TP* 9: 534–35.

35. Haggard, "Neutral Ground," 1028–31. Translation of Major Porter's letter by Don Sebastián Rodríguez, January 30, 1806, MS, Bexar Archives, qtd. in Haggard, "Neutral Ground," 1031.

36. Turner to Porter, Adies, February 6, 1806, *ASP, FR* 2: 799; Haggard, "Neutral Ground," 1031–32.

37. Haggard, "Neutral Ground," 1032–34; Cordero to Salcedo, February 18, 1806, MS, Bexar Archives, quoted in Haggard, "Neutral Ground," 1033.

38. Pike, *Exploratory Travels,* 288–89.

39. Salcedo to Cordero, June 16, 1806, qtd. in Haggard, "Neutral Ground," 1035.

40. Isaac Joslin Cox, "The Louisiana-Texas Frontier during the Burr Conspiracy," 281; Haggard, "Neutral Ground," 1035.

41. Linklater, *An Artist in Treason,* 236.

42. Wilkinson to Cushing, St. Louis, May 6, 1806, *American State Papers, Miscellaneous* 1: 562.

43. Flores, *Jefferson & Southwestern Exploration,* 68, 100, 103.

44. Anonymous to Viana, Natchitoches, June 2, 1806, Bexar Archives, qtd. in Flores, *Jefferson & Southwestern Exploration,* 124. Flores, *Jefferson & Southwestern Exploration,* 122–23, 131, 134. Philip Nolan was a horse trader who entered Texas first with and then without a permit to capture wild horses to sell in the United States. He is considered the first of a series of filibusters or armed forces to enter Texas to remove it from Spanish control. He was killed north of Nacogdoches in March 1801 by the Spanish. Jack Jackson, "Nolan, Philip."

45. Flores, *Jefferson & Southwestern Exploration,* 127.

46. Flores, *Jefferson & Southwestern Exploration,* 131.

47. Flores, *Jefferson & Southwestern Exploration,* 132, 143.

48. This approximately 230-man force was commanded by Juan Ignacio Ramón. They had left Camp Miguel del Santo on the Neches and arrived at the Caddo village "quite by accident" about June 20. Flores, *Jefferson & Southwestern Exploration,* 146n37, 145–46, 149.

49. Flores, *Jefferson & Southwestern Exploration,* 157, 161.

50. Flores, *Jefferson & Southwestern Exploration,* 162, 161–63.

51. Flores, *Jefferson & Southwestern Exploration,* 164, 165, 163. The Spanish commander who had entered the Caddo village was Juan Ignacio Ramón.

52. Flores, *Jefferson & Southwestern Exploration,* 165–66.

53. Flores, *Jefferson & Southwestern Exploration,* 167, 174–75.

54. Flores, *Jefferson & Southwestern Exploration,* 173.

55. Flores, *Jefferson & Southwestern Exploration,* 193–94, 196, 198n34.

56. Flores, *Jefferson & Southwestern Exploration,* 198–99.

57. Flores, *Jefferson & Southwestern Exploration,* 203, 199–204, 204n39. Bernard d'Ortolan was a Frenchman and brother-in-law of Touline (François Grappe) and had moved to Nacogdoches in about 1796.

58. Flores, *Jefferson & Southwestern Exploration,* 204–7.

59. Turner to Claiborne, Natchitoches, August 8, 1806, Rowland, ed., *CLB* 3: 382; Flores, *Jefferson & Southwestern Exploration,* 207; Abernethy, *Burr Conspiracy,* 51.

60. Cushing to Herrera, Natchitoches, August 5, 1806, *ASP, FR* 2: 801.

61. Herrera to Cushing, Plantation of Mr. Prudhomme, August 6, 1806, *ASP, FR* 2: 801.

62. Turner to Claiborne, Natchitoches, August 8, 1806, Rowland, ed., *CLB* 3: 382.

63. Claiborne to Dearborn, Natchitoches, August 28, 1806, Rowland, ed., *CLB* 3: 388; Claiborne to Dearborn, Natchitoches, September 4, 1806, Rowland, ed., *CLB* 3: 397.

64. Claiborne to Dearborn, Natchitoches, August 28, 1806, Rowland, ed., *CLB* 3: 387.

65. Claiborne to Herrera, Natchitoches, August 26, 1806, *ASP, FR* 2: 801–2.

66. Herrera to Claiborne, Spanish Camp, August 28, 1806, *ASP, FR* 2: 802.

67. Claiborne to Dearborn, Natchitoches, September 4, 1806, Rowland, ed., *CLB* 3: 396–99; Claiborne to Mead, Natchitoches, September 5, 1806, Rowland, ed., *CLB* 4: 2.

68. Wilkerson to Claiborne, Near Rapide of Red River, September 19, 1806, Rowland, ed., *CLB* 4: 8–9.

69. LeBreton, "History of the Territory of Orleans," 377.

70. John H. Sibley to Samuel H. Sibley, Natchitoches, September 26, 1806, in Whittington, "Dr. John Sibley of Natchitoches," 500–501.

71. There have been several books about Wilkinson, including Shreve, *Finished Scoundrel;* Jacobs, *Tarnished Warrior;* Hay and Werner, *Admirable Trumpeter;* and Linklater, *An Artist in Treason.* Wilkinson wrote his own biography, a three-volume, two-thousand-page *Memoirs of My Own Times.*

72. Linklater, *An Artist in Treason,* 2–4.

73. Cox, "Louisiana-Texas Frontier, Part II," 29–30.

74. Cox, "Louisiana-Texas Frontier, Part II," 30–32.

75. Wilkinson to Cordero, Natchitoches, September 24, 1806, *ASP, FR* 2: 803–4.

76. Cordero to Wilkinson, Nacogdoches, September 29, 1806, *ASP, FR* 2: 804; Cox, "The Louisiana-Texas Frontier during the Burr Conspiracy," 284.

77. Wilkinson to Cordero, Natchitoches, October 4, 1806, *ASP, FR* 2: 804; Haggard, "Neutral Ground," 1038.

78. Salcedo to Cordero, October 24, 1806, BAT, reel 22, typewritten copy: 57; Haggard, "Neutral Ground," 1039.

79. Dargo, *Jefferson's Louisiana,* 51–73.

80. LeBreton, "History of the Territory of Orleans," 407.

81. Wilkinson to Secretary of War, November 4, 1806, qtd. in LeBreton, "History of the Territory of Orleans," 408; Wilkinson to Claiborne, November 12, 1806, Rowland, ed., *CLB* 4: 55–56.

82. Wilkinson to Secretary of War, Natchitoches, October 21, 1806, *ASP, FR* 2: 804.

83. Wilkinson to Cordero, Sabine River, November 4, 1806, BAT, reel 22: 73.

84. Herrera to Cordero, Camp on the Sabine, November 6, 1806, BAT, reel 22: 83.

85. Herrera to Cordero, Camp on the Sabine, November 6, 1806, BAT, reel 22: 89.

86. Herrera to Cordero, Camp on the Sabine, November 6, 1806, BAT, reel 22: 87–88.

87. Cordero to N. Salcedo, no date, BAT, reel 22: 96.

88. Haggard, "Neutral Ground," 1041.

89. Abernathy, *Burr Conspiracy,* 199–226.

90. Transcript of the Burr Conspiracy trial, *American State Papers, Miscellaneous* 1: 544.

91. Shepherd, trans., "James Wilkinson to José de Iturrigaray," 533–37.

92. Shepherd, trans., "Wilkinson to Iturrigaray," 537; Haggard, "Neutral Ground," 1042–43.

93. Linkletter, *Wilkerson,* 312–28.

94. Miller, "History of Fort Claiborne," 53n4, 54, 175–76; *American State Papers: Military Affairs* 1: 673 (hereafter *ASP, MA*).

95. Prucha, *Sword of the Republic,* 331.

96. *Army and Navy Chronicle* 6 (May 17, 1838): 314–15 qtd. in Prucha, *Sword of the Republic,* 169–70.

97. Adjutant General to Congress, Washington, DC, January 11, 1826, *ASP, MA* 3: 228.

98. Miller, "History of Fort Claiborne," 129–30.

99. Prucha, *Sword of the Republic,* 197–99. See Wesley, *Guarding the Frontier.*

100. Miller, "History of Fort Claiborne," 76; Fowler to McKenny, Natchitoches, March 4, 1817, "Letter Book of the Natchitoches–Sulphur Fork Factory," 102 (hereafter cited as NSFLB).

101. Miller, "History of Fort Claiborne," 58–60.

102. Miller, "History of Fort Claiborne," 61–64. The spring was located at the head of what is now Rowena Street, Natchitoches. An old man was still selling water from the spring into the 1950s (Hiram "Pete" Gregory, personal communication, September 2020).

103. Miller, "History of Fort Claiborne," 71.

104. Miller, "History of Fort Claiborne," 65–66.

105. Miller, "History of Fort Claiborne," 68, 72n57.

106. Miller, "History of Fort Claiborne," 77–78, 83.

107. Miller, "History of Fort Claiborne," 77, 79, 83; Sibley to Dearborn, Natchitoches, September 7, 1808, in Garrett, ed., "Letters and Documents," vol. 46: 276; West, ed., "Diary of Jose Bernardo Gutiérrez de Lara, Part II," 293.

108. Miller, "History of Fort Claiborne," 80–81; Lytle, "Public Life of Edward Dumaresque Turner," 179.

109. With every one hundred rations, the post received two quarts of salt, four quarts of vinegar, four pounds of soap, and one and a half pounds of candles. Miller, "History of Fort Claiborne," 108, 111, 117; Wesley, *Guarding the Frontier*, 80–81.

110. Miller, "History of Fort Claiborne," 118n82, 119.

111. Miller, "History of Fort Claiborne," 92, 86–88, 91, 99.

112. *ASP, MA* 1: 225; Miller, "History of Fort Claiborne," 124, 126.

113. Miller, "History of Fort Claiborne," 128–29.

114. Miller, "History of Fort Claiborne," 126–27.

115. Miller, "History of Fort Claiborne," 134, 140.

116. Miller, "History of Fort Claiborne," 134–35.

117. Mills, *Biographical and Historical Memoirs of Northwest Louisiana*, 299.

118. Lytle, "Public Life of Edward Dumaresque Turner," 183n10; Miller, "History of Fort Claiborne," 135–36.

119. *ASP, MA* 1: 672; Miller, "History of Fort Claiborne," 175–76.

3. Relations with the Native Peoples

1. Prucha, *American Indian Policy*, 1–4; Prucha, *Sword of the Republic*, 320, 193; Usner, *American Indians*, 75. See also Wesley, *Guarding the Frontier.*

2. Usner, *American Indians*, 77.

3. Lipscomb and Bergh, eds., *Writings of Thomas Jefferson* 17: 373–74.

4. See Usner, *American Indians*, 78–80, for a fuller discussion of this approach to obtaining tribal lands.

5. Usner, *American Indians*, 97–98.

6. Sibley to Secretary of War, Natchitoches, May 1, 1805, *ASP, FR* 2: 690; Turner to Wilkinson, Natchitoches, October 15, 1804, *ASP, FR* 2: 690; Haggard, "Neutral Ground," 1085; Usner, *American Indians*, 98.

7. Smith, *Caddo Indians*, 89; Smith, *From Dominance to Disappearance*, 75, 79.

8. The Indian factory system was originally organized under the Treasury Department, but in 1811 the system was transferred to the War Department (see Wesley, *Guarding the Frontier*, 37). The president appointed the early factors but, beginning in 1818, the president nominated and the Congress elected the new factors (see Peake, *History of the United States Indian Factory System*, 40).

9. Wesley, *Guarding the Frontier*, 31–46.

10. *ASP, IA* 2: 520–21.

11. Peake, *History of the United States Indian Factory System,* 96; Wesley, *Guarding the Frontier,* 44; Usner, *American Indians,* 77.

12. Peake, *History of the United States Indian Factory System,* 38–39, 53, 57, 89; LeBreton, "History of the Factory System," 28. Wesley, *Guarding the Frontier,* 41, 43.

13. Peake, *History of the United States Indian Factory System,* 56, 57, 270. The three-point blankets measured about six feet, six inches, by five feet, six inches, and weighed about eight and a half pounds. The two-and-a-half-point blankets were six feet, three inches, by five feet, two inches, and when dressed weighed seven and a half pounds.

14. Peake, *History of the United States Indian Factory System,* 60, 63–64.

15. Peake, *History of the United States Indian Factory System,* 58–60, 64–68.

16. Byrd, *Colonial Natchitoches,* 53; Peake, *History of the United States Indian Factory System,* 132–33; quote from Indian Department Letter Book, D, 285, qtd. in Peake, *History of the United States Indian Factory System,* 133.

17. Peake, *History of the United States Indian Factory System,* 6, 42, 135, 138, 158, 236.

18. Claiborne to Jefferson, August 30, 1804, *TP* 9: 287.

19. Wesley, *Guarding the Frontier,* 40; *ASP, IA* 1: 768; LeBreton, "History of the Factory System," 4–6, 11, 15; Linnard to Mason, July 8, 1810, NSFLB, 13; *American State Papers, Commerce and Navigation* 1: 596.

20. Baudier, *Catholic Church in Louisiana,* 149.

21. Baudier, *Catholic Church in Louisiana,* 281.

22. Seale, "From French Village to American Town," 77, 82–84; LeBreton, "History of the Factory System," 13–14; Sibley to Dearborn, Natchitoches, April 3, 1807, in Garrett, ed., "Letters and Documents," vol. 45: 300. Richard Seale believes that the site selected for the factory was the area between current-day Third and Fourth streets and between St. Denis and Church streets. For his reasoning, see Seale, "From French Village to American Town" 82–84. John Fowler described the main building at the Natchitoches trading house (see John Fowler to McKenney, March 4, 1817, NSFLB, 100–101). John Fowler in his letter to Thomas McKenney described the trading house he planned to build near Fort Seldon. It was to include a one-story, square pine log buildings with as many buildings as possible under one roof. Fowler lists a house for the interpreter, a skin house, and a store house (eighteen by twenty feet). Presumably, there would also be a store and dwelling for the factor (Fowler to McKenney, Natchitoches, March 4, 1817, NSFLB, 101–3).

23. Linnard to Mason, Natchitoches, August 26, 1809, NSFLB, 2–3; Linnard to Mason, Natchitoches, February 14, 1811, NSFLB, 22–23. Blankets were sold as pairs. These blankets could be cut down the center and made into two blankets or left as one and folded with half used as a top and the other part used as a bottom blanket (Kapoun with Lohrmann, *Language of the Robe,* 27).

24. Peake, *History of the United States Indian Factory System,* 267, 131.

25. Peake, *History of the United States Indian Factory System,* 154, 272, 276.

26. LeBreton, "History of the Factory System," 20–25, 27–30; Linnard to Mason, February 14, 1811, NSFLB, 23–24; Sibley to Eustis, November 28, 1812, in Garrett, ed., "Letters and Documents," vol. 49: 418.

27. LeBreton, "History of the Factory System," 11–12; Wesley, *Guarding the Frontier,* 46.

28. LeBreton, "History of the Factory System," 32–34; Peake, *History of the United States Indian Factory System,* 228; Linnard to Mason, Natchitoches, March 25, 1812, NSFLB, 38–39.

29. Mason to Linnard, September 15, 1810, qtd. in LeBreton, "History of the Factory System," 35.

30. Mason to Linnard, June 12, 1811, qtd. in LeBreton, "History of the Factory System," 36; Linnard to Mason, Natchitoches, August 6, 1811, NSFLB, 30; LeBreton, "History of the Factory System," 36.

31. Peake, *History of the United States Indian Factory System,* 155–56.

32. Peake, *History of the United States Indian Factory System,* 158–62.

33. Governor Claiborne to the President, September 29, 1803, *TP* 9: 16.

34. Secretary of War Dearborn to John Sibley, December 13, 1804, *TP* 9: 352–53.

35. Secretary of War to John Sibley, October 17, 1805, *TP* 9: 352–53, 514–15; Miller, "Dr. John Sibley," 14–47, 103; Seale, "From French Village to American Town," 74; Whittington, "Dr. John Sibley of Natchitoches," 467–73; Malone, ed, "John Sibley," in *Dictionary of American Biography* 17: 147–48. See also Purser, "Administration of Indian Affairs in Louisiana."

36. Miller, "Dr. John Sibley," 14–47. See also Garrett, ed., "Letters and Documents," vol. 45: 286–92; Whittington, "Dr. John Sibley of Natchitoches," 467–73.

37. Claiborne to President, January 29, 1805, *TP* 9: 385–86.

38. Rouquier to Prudhomme, April 22, 1805, document 3267, Conveyance Book 32, Bound Conveyances, Natchitoches Parish Courthouse.

39. François Rouquier Jr. to Manuel Prudhomme, April 22, 1805, document 3267, Conveyance Book 32, Bound Conveyances, Natchitoches Parish Courthouse. John Sibley answered the complaint, but the result of this matter is missing from courthouse records.

40. Sibley, *Report from Natchitoches,* 52. The current author has edited the passages in Sibley's report to improve readability.

41. Sibley, *Report from Natchitoches,* 11, 13, 15.

42. Sibley, *Report from Natchitoches,* 17.

43. Sibley, *Report from Natchitoches,* 40–42. The men left in the Wichita village were Alexander, Litton, Lusk, and Lucas.

44. Sibley, *Report from Natchitoches,* 68–69, 82–84.

45. Sibley, *Report from Natchitoches,* 17–19.

46. Sibley, *Report from Natchitoches,* 12–15.

47. Sibley, *Report from Natchitoches,* 14–15.

48. Sibley, *Report from Natchitoches,* 14–15.

49. Sibley, *Report from Natchitoches,* 19–20.

50. Sibley, *Report from Natchitoches,* 36.

51. Sibley, *Report from Natchitoches,* 30–39. The six-person jury consisted of Edmund Teal, James Teal, William Rollings, Allen W. Berry, Piere Suricks, and Joseph Eastep.

52. Sibley, *Report from Natchitoches,* 46–47.

53. Sibley, *Report from Natchitoches,* 67–68.

54. Smith, *Dominance to Disappearance,* 76. Sibley, *Report from Natchitoches,* 22–26.

55. Sibley, *Report from Natchitoches,* 26–28; Garrett, ed., "Letters and Documents," vol. 45: 381.

56. Sibley, *Report from Natchitoches,* 39–40.

57. Smith, *From Dominance to Disappearance,* 65.

58. Sibley to Claiborne, Natchitoches, October 10, 1803, *TP* 9: 75; Sibley to Eustis, January 30, 1810, in Garrett, ed., "Letters and Documents," vol. 47: 389.

59. A Talk from William Charles Cole Claiborne, Governor of Louisiana, and Commander in Chief of the Militia thereof, to the great Chief of the Caddo Nation," October 18, 1813, in Rowland, ed., *CLB* 6: 277.

60. Claiborne to Jackson, New Orleans, October 28, 1814, in Rowland, ed., *CLB* 6: 293.

61. Smith, "The Kadohadacho Indians," 95: 198; Sibley to Dearborn, Natchitoches, April 5, 1805, "Historical Sketches," 721.

62. Carter, *Caddo Indians,* 265.

63. Sibley, *Report from Natchitoches,* 31.

64. Sibley, *Report from Natchitoches,* 40–41, 48–51; Smith, *From Dominance to Disappearance,* 89; Kavangh, "Comanche," 887.

65. Sibley, *Report from Natchitoches,* 48–51.

66. Sibley, *Report from Natchitoches,* 52–53.

67. Sibley, *Report from Natchitoches,* 54–55.

68. Sibley, *Report from Natchitoches,* 56–60.

69. Sibley, *Report from Natchitoches,* 60–61. Smith identifies the Tawakoni chief as Daguariscara (see Smith, *From Dominance to Disappearance,* 90).

70. Sibley, *Report from Natchitoches,* 61–62. Smith identifies the Comanche chief as Pisinampe of the Kotsoteka band of the Comanche (see Smith, *From Dominance to Disappearance,* 90).

71. Sibley, *Report from Natchitoches,* 63–64. Smith identifies the Kichai chief as Castor (see Smith, *From Dominance to Disappearance,* 90).

72. Sibley, *Report from Natchitoches,* 63–64.

73. Garrett, ed., "Letters and Documents," vol. 46: 89.

74. Sibley, *Report from Natchitoches,* 64–65.

75. Sibley, *Report from Natchitoches,* 64–65. On September 26, Tuscatoga, the Choctaw chief, informed Sibley that, since his brother Chechemastubby had been sick, he had sent another messenger to the Mississippi Choctaw in an attempt to get them to give up the man who led the party that killed the Nadaco women (Sibley, *Report from Natchitoches,* 69).

76. Sibley, *Report from Natchitoches,* 65–66.

77. Sibley, *Report from Natchitoches,* 66–67.

78. Sibley, *Report from Natchitoches,* 69–72. Smith identifies the Comanche as the Yamparika band, the chief as Quilvalparica, and the Wichita chiefs as Awahakei, Eriascoc, and Ecani (see Smith, *From Dominance to Disappearance,* 90–91).

79. Sibley, *Report from Natchitoches,* 74, 76; Flores, *Journal of an Indian Trader,* 107n48.

80. Sibley to Dearborn, November 20, 1808, Garrett, ed., "Letters and Documents," vol. 47: 50; Flores, *Journal of an Indian Trader,* 28; Claiborne to Secretary of State, August 8, 1808, *TP* 9: 799. It seems likely that Sibley requested that Glass keep a journal of his trip, which was not a common

practice of traders. From this journal, anthropologists have learned many ethnographic facts about the Wichita and Comanche tribes during this period.

81. Flores, *Journal of an Indian Trader,* 28–29.

82. Flores, *Journal of an Indian Trader,* 85, 47. In addition to Glass, the men on the trip included George Schamp, Stephen Holmes, Ezra McCall, W. Alexander, Jacob Low, John Davis, James Davis, Peter Young, and Joseph White. The eleventh member was Joseph Lucas, a *metis* or man of both Indian and European ancestry, who acted as interpreter (Flores, *Journal of an Indian Trader,* 37, 109n1). Several of these men had traded with the Wichita and Comanche for horses in the past.

83. Sibley to Eustis, Natchitoches, May 10, 1809, in Garrett, ed., "Letters and Documents," vol. 47: 321–23.

84. Sibley to Eustis, Natchitoches, May 10, 1809, in Garrett, ed., "Letters and Documents," vol. 47: 321–23.

85. Flores, *Journal of an Indian Trader,* 88–89.

86. Flores, *Journal of an Indian Trader,* 88–90.

87. Flores, *Journal of an Indian Trader,* 69.

88. Flores, "John Maley Journal," 48–49.

89. The meteorite, known today as "Red River," is currently housed in the Peabody Museum at Yale University (Flores, *Journal of an Indian Trader,* 88–89).

90. Purser, "Administration of Indian Affairs in Louisiana," 78; Claiborne to Macarty, Natchitoches, October 16, 1813, Rowland, ed., *CLB* 6: 274. Claiborne reports that "War Talks" were sent to the Caddo, Coushatta, and other tribes by the Creek.

91. Sibley to Armstrong, October 6, 1813, in Garrett, ed., "Letters and Documents," vol. 49: 602–3.

92. Sibley to Armstrong, October 6, 1813, in Garrett, ed., "Letters and Documents," vol. 49: 601–3.

93. Claiborne to Macarty, Natchitoches, October 18, 1813, in Rowland, ed., *CLB* 6: 275–76.

94. Linnard to Mason, Natchitoches, October 14, 1813, NSFLB, 62.

95. Sibley to Secretary of War, Natchitoches, February 12, 1813, in Garrett, ed., "Letters and Documents," vol. 49: 421.

96. Purser, "Administration of Indian Affairs in Louisiana," 85.

97. Jackson to Armstrong, August 5, 1814 in Bassett, ed., *Correspondence of Andrew Jackson,* 31.

98. Claiborne to John Perkins, New Orleans, October 21, 1814, Rowland, ed., *CLB* 6: 283.

99. Jackson to Secretary Monroe, Pearch's Stockade, October 26, 1814, in Bassett, ed., *Correspondence of Andrew Jackson,* 83; Purser, "Administration of Indian Affairs in Louisiana," 84.

100. Sibley to Monroe, Natchitoches, January 10, 1815, in Garrett, ed., "Letters and Documents," vol. 49: 611.

101. Purser, "Administration of Indian Affairs in Louisiana," 85.

102. Miller, "Dr. John Sibley," 110, 8–13; Whittington, "Dr. John Sibley of Natchitoches," 467–73. Throughout his years in Natchitoches, Sibley maintained an extensive correspondence with his older children as well as others, providing first-person accounts of many of the historical events as well as day-to-day happenings in Natchitoches.

103. Purser, "Administration of Indian Affairs in Louisiana," 94–97.

104. Purser, "Administration of Indian Affairs in Louisiana," 99.

105. Jamison to Calhoun, Indian Agency, Natchitoches, March 31, 1817, *TP* 15: 257.

106. Fowler to McKenney, April 8, 1817, in Magnaghi, ed., "Red River Valley North of Natchitoches," 288.

107. Smith, *From Dominance to Disappearance,* 114; Purser, "Administration of Indian Affairs in Louisiana," 100.

108. Jamison to Calhoun, Indian Agency, Natchitoches, March 31, 1817, *TP* 15: 257; Jamison to Secretary of War, Natchitoches, May 10, 1817, *TP* 15: 302; Purser, "Administration of Indian Affairs in Louisiana," 100–102.

109. Smith, *From Dominance to Disappearance,* 114.

110. Smith, *From Dominance to Disappearance,* 106; Purser, "Administration of Indian Affairs in Louisiana," 105–7.

111. Purser, "Administration of Indian Affairs in Louisiana," 121, 103–4.

4. A Town on the Frontier

1. Mills, *Natchitoches Colonials,* 124; Broutin, *Carte Particuliere Des Natchitoches* (map); Seale, "From French Village to American Town," 55, 60.

2. Haggard, "House of Barr and Davenport," 71, 75; LaVere, "Barr, Davenport, Murphy and Smith," 20, 28–29, 51.

3. Byrd, *Colonial Natchitoches,* 50–58, 118–26, 137; LaVere, "Barr, Davenport, Murphy and Smith," 1, 11–12, 14n48, 62, 66; Haggard, "House of Barr and Davenport," 83.

4. LaVere, "Barr, Davenport, Murphy and Smith," 13, 19; Haggard, "House of Barr and Davenport," 73.

5. Haggard, "House of Barr and Davenport," 77.

6. LaVere, "Barr, Davenport, Murphy and Smith," 13, 19; Haggard, "House of Barr and Davenport," 72–73, 77–78, 86–87. Although the partnership was officially dissolved in 1806, the partners continued to work together for several years (LaVere, "Barr, Davenport, Murphy and Smith," 100). Davenport died in 1824 and is buried in the DeRussey Cemetery at Grand Ecore.

7. Kinnaird and Kinnaird, "Red River Valley in 1796," 190.

8. De Laussat, *Memoirs of My Life,* 23.

9. Stoddard, *Sketches,* 188.

10. For a discussion of the arpent and other survey systems used in Louisiana see Hall, "Louisiana Survey Systems."

11. Coles, "Confirmation of Foreign Land Titles," 2; Gates, *History of Public Land Law Development,* 87, 93; Coles, "Applicability of the Public Land System," 41; Gates, "Private Land Claims," 188.

12. Gates, *History of Public Land Law Development,* 94–95; Poret, "History of Land Titles," 27–29; Coles, "Confirmation of Foreign Land Titles," 4; Gates, "Private Land Claims," 186, 204; Coles, "Applicability of the Public Land System," 54; Hatfield, *William Claiborne,* 196.

13. Gayarré, *History of Louisiana,* 7, 116; Hatfield, *William Claiborne,* 196–200; Peterson, *Thomas Jefferson and the New Nation,* 779; Tregle, *Louisiana in the Age of Jackson,* 139–41.

14. Monthly return of certificates issued by the Commissioners of the Western District of Orleans Territory, for December 1811, *American State Papers, Public Lands* 2: 711.

15. Claim no. 510.00079, Claim Papers NWD T9N R6&7W, vol. 8, wwwslodms.doa.gov. Others who had their claims approved on the same day included Jean François Levasseur, François Rouquier Sr., Pierre Badin, Jean Bte Trichel, Emanuel Lavesseur, Emanual Prudhomme, John Sibley, J. B. Buard, James Bludworth, Manuel Rachel, J. B. Ailhaud St. Anne, and Pierre Derbanne. (538.13922; 538.13923; 538.13924: US Tract Book vol. 58: 34, 35, 36, wwwslodms.doa.la.gov).

16. Claim no. 538.13920, US Tract Book vol. 58: 32, wwwslodms.doa.la.gov. Partain, *Tool Pushed by Providence,* 47. Monthly return of certificates issued by the Commissioners of the Western District of Orleans Territory, for December 1811, *American State Papers, Public Lands* 2: 711.

17. Gayarré, *History of Louisiana,* 7, 116; Hatfield, *William Claiborne,* 196–200; Peterson, *Thomas Jefferson and the New Nation,* 779; Tregle, *Louisiana in the Age of Jackson,* 139–41.

18. Haggard, "Neutral Ground," 1046–49. The boundaries of the Neutral Ground as described by Haggard ("Neutral Ground," 1046) started at Calcasieu Pass and continued on the west bank of the Calcasieu River to its source, then in a straight line north to Kisatchie Creek, along the creek to 93 degrees 7 minutes latitude, where Arroyo Hondo fades into Sibley's march, then along Arroyo Hondo to its source, then north to the Bayou Pierre Lake at the Bayou Pierre Settlement. (See Darby, *Map of Louisiana.*)

19. Haggard, "Neutral Ground," 1050–53, 1104–9; LaVere, "Barr, Davenport, Murphy and Smith," 14–16.

20. Haggard, "Neutral Ground," 1071.

21. Chipman and Joseph, *Notable Men and Women of Spanish Texas,* 243; Sibley to Dearborn, Natchitoches, September 7, 1808, in Garrett, ed., "Letters and Documents," vol. 46, no. 3: 276; Haggard, "Neutral Ground," 1072.

22. Haggard, "Neutral Ground," 1071–73; Claiborne to Salcedo, New Orleans, November 22, 1808, in Rowland, ed., *CLB* 4: 254–56, 319. Slaves from Louis Derbanne's plantation had also been involved in the 1804 escape.

23. Commanding officer at Nacogdoches to Cordero, Nacogdoches, June 15, 1807, BAT, microfilm reel 23, vol. 26, ser. 2: 92.

24. Sibley to Claiborne, Natchitoches, August 6, 1807, in Brandt, "Unpublished Letter of Doctor John Sibley," 24.

25. Haggard, "Neutral Ground," 1061–63. The Crow ranch was spared under orders of Governor Salcedo. Haggard, "Neutral Ground," 1062.

26. Haggard, "Neutral Ground," 1063–65, 1100; Memorial of Natchitoches Merchants to Governor Claiborne, Natchitoches, January 4, 1812, *TP* 9: 976–77.

27. Memorial of Natchitoches Merchants to Governor Claiborne, Natchitoches, January 4, 1812, *TP* 9: 976–77.

28. Sibley to Eustis, Natchitoches, April 27, 1812, in Garrett, ed., "Letters and Documents," vol. 59, no. 3 (1946): 406.

29. Hampton to Claiborne, Headquarters, January 23, 1812, *TP* 9: 989–90; Hampton to Pike, Baton Rouge, February 6, 1812, *TP* 9: 998–1000; Haggard, "Neutral Ground," 1067–68.

30. U.S. Census, 1810.

31. U.S. Census, 1810.

32. U.S. Census, 1810; Sibley, "Historical Sketches," 724.

33. Haggard, "House of Barr and Davenport," 75; Coxe, *Statement of the Arts and Manufactures of the United States of America, for the Year 1810*, 154–57.

34. Filibusters were groups of armed men who invaded a foreign country with the hope of obtaining financial gains, for ideological reasons, or simply for adventure. Their efforts were not formally sanctioned by governments that maintained neutrality treaties with their neighbors. But this did not mean that the governments were uninterested or unsupportive behind the scenes. See Owsley and Smith, *Filibusters and Expansionists: Jeffersonian Manifest Destiny*, for a fuller discussion.

35. Nemesio to the Viceroy, Chihuahua, September 28, 1808, BAT, reel 26, vol. 38: 250–51, Cammie G. Henry Research Center (hereafter CGHRC).

36. Garrett, *Green Flag*, 16, 20, 32.

37. Chipman and Joseph, *Notable Men and Women of Spanish Texas*, 233.

38. Garrett, *Green Flag*, 34, 84–85; Chipman and Joseph, *Notable Men and Women of Spanish Texas*, 234–35; Warren, *The Sword Was Their Passport*, 4–5; Sibley to Edmond Randolph, in Garrett, ed., "Letters and Documents," vol. 49, no. 3: 399–400. Gutiérrez was often referred to by Sibley and others as "Bernard" or "Bernardo."

39. Garrett, *Green Flag*, 87–88.

40. Warren, *The Sword Was Their Passport*, 6; Garrett, *Green Flag*, 87; Chipman and Joseph, *Notable Men and Women of Spanish Texas*, 235.

41. Warren, *The Sword Was Their Passport*, 7, 9–10; Garrett, *Green Flag*, 90–91, 102.

42. "Gutiérrez de Lara"; Warren, *The Sword Was Their Passport*, 21; Chipman and Joseph, *Notable Men and Women of Spanish Texas*, 236.

43. West, ed., "Diary of Jose Bernardo Gutiérrez de Lara, Part II," 293.

44. West, ed., "Diary of Jose Bernardo Gutiérrez de Lara, Part II," 293; Sibley to Eustis, July 14, 1812, in Garrett, ed., "Letters and Documents," vol. 49, no. 3: 410–12; Chipman and Joseph, *Notable Men and Women of Spanish Texas*, 237.

45. Sibley to Eustis, June 24, 1812, in Garrett, ed., "Letters and Documents," vol. 49, no. 3: 407–10.

46. Sibley to Eustis, August 5, 1812, in Garrett, ed., "Letters and Documents," vol. 49, no. 3: 413–15; Warren, *The Sword Was Their Passport*, 24; Chipman and Joseph, *Notable Men and Women of Spanish Texas*, 226; Garrett, *Green Flag*, 142.

47. Warren, *The Sword Was Their Passport*, 29, 31–32; Claiborne to Carr, August 7, 1812, Rowland, ed., *CLB* 6: 149–50; Claiborne to Wilkinson August 9, 1812, Rowland, ed., *CLB* 6: 151–52; "A Proclamation" by William Charles Cole Claiborne, Rowland, ed., *CLB* 4: 229–30. For more on the American government's views of the filibuster movement, see "Madison and the Problem of Mexican Independence: The Gutiérrez-Magee Raid of 1812."

48. Garrett, *Green Flag*, 150, 152–56; Warren, *The Sword Was Their Passport*, 33–35; Sibley to Eustis, August 18, 1812, in Garrett, ed., "Letters and Documents," vol. 49, no. 3: 415–17; M'Caleb, "First Period of the Gutiérrez-Magee Expedition," 222.

49. Warren, *The Sword Was Their Passport*, 35–36, quoting Shaler to Monroe, October 1, 1812.

50. Garrett, *Green Flag,* 156–57; Pratt, *Expansionists of 1812,* 249–51.

51. Warren, *The Sword Was Their Passport,* 36–37, 44–45; Garrett, *Green Flag,* 162, 206; Chipman and Joseph, *Notable Men and Women of Spanish Texas,* 237; Yoakum, *History of Texas* 1: 166. Chipman and Joseph list the Lipan and Tonkawa as the tribes who supported the revolutionaries (*Notable Men and Women of Spanish Texas,* 237). Garrett indicates that it was the Lipan and Comanche (*Green Flag,* 206). According to Warren rumors suggested that the Alabama, Conchatta, and Choctaw might join (*The Sword Was Their Passport,* 44). After the defeat of the revolutionaries, people, including tribal people, fled to Louisiana for protection. There are descendants of the Lipan Apache living in Sabine parish today and are recognized by the state as the Choctaw-Apache tribe.

52. Chipman and Joseph, *Notable Men and Women of Spanish Texas,* 237–39; Warren, *The Sword Was Their Passport,* 49–50; Yoakum, *History of Texas* 1: 172; Garrett, *Green Flag,* 196.

53. *El Mexicano,* Natchitoches, June 19, 1813.

54. *El Mexicano,* Natchitoches, June 19, 1813.

55. Sibley to Johnston, Natchitoches, September 14, 1824, in Miller, "Dr. John Sibley," 204.

56. "Gutiérrez de Lara."

57. Warren, *The Sword Was Their Passport,* 66–68; Garrett, *Green Flag,* 224–26; Sibley to Armstrong, in Garrett, ed., "Letters and Documents," vol. 49, no. 4: 601.

58. Sibley to Armstrong, September 4, 1813, in Garrett, ed., "Letters and Documents," vol. 49, no. 4: 599–600.

59. Sibley to Armstrong, September 4, 1813, in Garrett, ed., "Letters and Documents," vol. 49, no. 4: 599–601; Claiborne to Macarty, October 16, 1813, in Rowland, ed., *CLB* 4: 273–74.

60. Claiborne to L. B. Macarty, Natchitoches, October 16, 1813, in Rowland, ed., *CLB* 6: 273.

61. Warren, *The Sword Was Their Passport,* 68–69; Garrett, *Green Flag,* 230–31. According to Sibley, over two thousand inhabitants and Indians fled across the Sabine and either wandered in the Neutral Ground or sought refuge in Natchitoches (Sibley to Armstrong, October 3, 1813, in Garrett, ed., "Letters and Documents," vol. 49, no. 4 [April 1946]: 601). It would be August 24, 1821, before Mexico won independence from Spain. Gutiérrez after leaving San Antonio resettled for a time in the Natchitoches area but continued participating in revolutionary efforts, including the Long filibuster. (*Natchitoches Courier,* July 26, 1825, ad of Cortes & Huppe, CGHRC). After independence, Gutiérrez returned to Mexico and was elected governor of Tamaulipas in 1824. In September, he sent about a hundred horses and mules and a squadron of cavalry to escort his family from Grand Ecore to their new home in Tamaulipas (Sibley to Johnston, September 14, 1824, in Miller, "Dr. John Sibley," 204). By May 1813, promises had been made between the volunteers and the Junto at St. Fernando de Bexar concerning pay for volunteers' services. The April 24, 1826, issue of the *Natchitoches Courier* included an announcement that the Mexican Congress had decreed on June 13, 1823, that the volunteers who had fought in 1812 and 1813 for independence from Spain would receive their pay. The volunteers were to come themselves or send someone with their power of attorney and proof of their service within six months to receive their pay (*Natchitoches Courier,* Monday April 24, 1826).

62. Warren, *The Sword Was Their Passport,* 89–95.

63. Claiborne to Gales, September 10, 1815, in Rowland, ed., *CLB* 6: 364–65.

64. Chipman and Joseph, *Notable Men and Women of Spanish Texas,* 237; Haggard, "Neutral Ground," 1050–53, 1104–9; LaVere, "Barr, Davenport, Murphy and Smith," 14–16. Los Adaes and Bayou Pierre were under the jurisdiction of Nacogdoches.

65. Warren, *The Sword Was Their Passport,* 234–35, 239.

66. Warren, *The Sword Was Their Passport,* 234–35, 242–46.

67. De Blanc to Carondolet, February 18, 1792, in Kinnaird, ed., *Spain in the Mississippi Valley* 4: 9–11.

68. Seale, "From French Village to American Town," 53.

69. Miller, "History of Fort Claiborne," 70.

70. Walter Overton to Zebulon M. Pike, Fort Claiborne, March 6, 1812. *TP* 9: 1003–4.

71. Miller, "History of Fort Claiborne, 70.

72. Miller, "History of Fort Claiborne," 161–68.

73. Miller, "History of Fort Claiborne," 169–75.

74. Middleton, "Outpost"; Smith, ed., *Military Heritage,* 109–40; Hardin, "Fort Jesup—Fort Selden—Camp Sabine—Camp Salubrity," 10–78. For a full description of the border between Spain and the United States, see Brooks, *Diplomacy and the Borderlands.*

75. Conveyance Book 31, co. 3157, Bound Conveyances; Seale, "From French Village to American Town," 62–63, 65–66; Miller, "History of Fort Claiborne," 7; U.S. Tract Book, vol. 58: 32; Nancarrow to Pike, Natchitoches, February 25, 1812, in *TP* 9: 1001. Others receiving payment included Henry Burgher, David Case, James Bludworth, Pierre Joseph Maes, Antoine Prudhomme, and John Sibley (Miller, "History of Fort Claiborne," 7n18).

76. *American State Papers: Public Lands* 3: 171, claim 260 (hereafter *ASP, PL*); see also Dollar, "Black, White, or Indifferent."

77. Linnard to Mason, Natchitoches, December 8, 1813, NSFLB, 65–66.

78. Linnard to Mason, Natchitoches, December 15, 1813, NSFLB, 70.

79. Linnard to Mason, Natchitoches, December 15, 1813, NSFLB, 70.

80. Linnard to Mason, Natchitoches, December 15, 1813, NSFLB, 70–71.

81. Linnard to Mason, Natchitoches, December 15, 1813, NSFLB, 71.

82. Petition of P. S. Cailleau Lafontaine, December 1813, Records of the Secretary of War, Letters Received, cited by Seale, "From French Village to American Town," 79.

83. Linnard to Mason, December 15, 1813, NSFLB, 68; see also Seale, "From French Village to American Town," 76–80, and LeBreton, "History of the Factory System," 50–58.

84. Compere to the President of the United States, September 10, 1816, Records of the Secretary of War, cited in LeBreton, "History of the Factory System," 67–70.

85. Claiborne to Jamison, May 18, 1816, in Rowland, ed., *CLB* 6: 401. For the background to this move, see LeBreton, "History of the Factory System," 63–72.

86. Fowler to McKenney, Natchitoches, March 4, 1817, NSFLB, 101–2; see also Magnaghi, ed., "Red River North of Natchitoches," 287–94; LeBreton, "History of the Factory System," 76, 80.

87. Fowler to McKenney, Natchitoches, April 8, 1817, NSFLB, 108–10; Fowler to McKenney, April 14, 1817, NSFLB, 110–12; Fowler to McKenney, May 9, 1817, NSFLB, 113–17; LeBreton, "History of the Factory System," 82, 84.

88. LeBreton, "History of the Factory System," 108–16, 130, 134, 137; Fowler to Jamison, Sulphur Fork, April 16, 1819, *TP* 19: 70–71; Purser, "Administration of Indian Affairs in Louisiana," 110.

89. Peake, *History of the United States Indian Factory System,* 184; Wesley, *Guarding the Frontier,* 49; LeBreton, "History of the Factory System," 140.

90. Peake, *History of the United States Indian Factory System,* 215; *ASP, IA* 1: 784; 2: 60; LeBreton, "History of the Factory System," 150–51.

91. Memorial to Turner, April 13, 1805, Document 3266, Conveyance Book 32, Bound Conveyances, Natchitoches Parish Courthouse, Natchitoches; Seale, "From French Village to American Town," 68–69. Unfortunately, the outcome of this incident is unknown. The relevant documents are missing from courthouse records.

92. Deposition of Daniel Eams, May 5, 1814, qtd. in Purser, "Administration of Indian Affairs in Louisiana," 89.

93. Purser, "Administration of Indian Affairs in Louisiana," 87. Members of the Louisiana Legislature to the President James Monroe, n.d., in Garrett, ed., "Letters and Documents," vol. 49, no. 4: 611–12.

94. Sibley to Monroe, January 18, 1815, qtd. in Purser, "Administration of Indian Affairs in Louisiana," 90.

95. Claiborne to Jackson, New Orleans, October 28, 1814, in Rowland, ed., *CLB* 6: 294.

96. Purser, "Administration of Indian Affairs in Louisiana," 90; Claiborne to Jackson, October 28, 1814, in Rowland, ed., *CLB* 6: 294. There was considerable confusion surrounding the Gales appointment. Following the instructions of then secretary of war Armstrong, Governor Claiborne appointed Thomas Gales as Indian agent. But in September 1814 James Monroe replaced Armstrong as secretary of war and directed Claiborne to appoint Michael A. Garvain to be Indian agent. Claiborne asked Monroe to honor the appointment Claiborne had already made to Gales, which Monroe did. Purser, "Administration of Indian Affairs in Louisiana," 91–93.

97. Purser, "Administration of Indian Affairs in Louisiana," 121, 103–4, 132–33.

5. The Development of a Regional Center

1. U.S. Census, 1810, and U.S. Census, 1820. The census taker in 1820 divided the parish into three districts: the district west of the Rio Hondo; the district east of the Rio Hondo, or Natchitoches Proper, which extended south from the Arkansas border and included Emanuel Prudhomme's plantation south of the town of Natchitoches; and the area south of Emanuel Prudhomme's plantation to the border with Rapides Parish listed as the Lower Division, or the River aux Cannes District. The district east of the Rio Hondo included the town of Natchitoches, which was enumerated separately and is treated separately here (see appendix table 2 for summaries of the 1820 census data). On the 1820 summary sheet, the total population of Natchitoches is listed as 7,476. However, if the raw data are used, the total comes to 7,372. This is the number used in this study.

2. Sibley to Josiah S. Johnston, Natchitoches, June 26, 1821, in Miller, "Dr. John Sibley," 178.

3. U.S. Census, 1820.

4. John Sibley to Josiah S. Johnston, Natchitoches, June 26, 1821, in Miller, "Dr. John Sibley," 178.

5. Gates, *Economic History* 3: 55–56, 63–64.

6. Gracy, *Moses Austin*, 200–201, 215; Gracy, "AUSTIN, MOSES."

7. Austin, "Journal," 286; Cantrell, *Stephen F. Austin*, 89, 95, 98; Barker, "AUSTIN, STEPHEN FULLER."

8. Sibley to Johnston, October 11, 1825, in Miller, "Dr. John Sibley," 214; McDonald, "EDWARDS, HADEN;" Gates, *Public Land Policies*, 80.

9. Sibley to Johnston, January 3, 1826, in Miller, "Dr. John Sibley," 217.

10. Deposition of R. Vaughn, April 17, 1827, Sixth District Court, bundle 39, no. 649, Clerk of Court, Natchitoches Parish Courthouse; Partain, *Tool Pushed by Providence*, 61; Portré-Bobinski and Smith, *Natchitoches*, 87. On April 21, 1823, B. Leonard, the parish and town surveyor, at the request of trustees of the town, surveyed the boundaries for a forty-foot-wide road on Front or River Street in Natchitoches. He showed only seven properties on the map, all toward the north end of the street: Charles Pavie's house, David Case's house, market house, Joseph Tauzin's cake shop and store—and Landriane's house and A. Coe's house (Map 931, CGHRC). The rest may have been destroyed by the fire.

11. Ruling of Sixth District Court, May term 1826, bundle 39, no. 649, Clerk of Court, Natchitoches Parish Courthouse. Father Maynes had left the parish in August 1822, and there was no resident priest at the time of the fire. The congregation argued the church was incorporated by an act of the legislature on February 10, 1813, for a period of ten years, and that the corporation had expired on February 10, 1823. The corporation was revised by an act passed March 17, 1823, twelve days before the fire, but the officers had not yet been elected at the time of the fire. On March 29, 1823, the Supreme Court found that the Congregation of St. Francis was not guilty of negligence regarding the fire. The church was under the direction of a member of the congregation on March 29, 1823, but no officer was legally authorized to take charge of the church. And the plaintiff was "as well situated by his proximity to the church as any other individual to see if the church was properly guarded." Case filed June 2, 1825, bundle 39, no. 649, Clerk of Court, Natchitoches Parish Courthouse.

12. Sibley to Johnston, May 15, 1826, in Miller, "Dr. John Sibley," 221.

13. Sibley to Austin, Natchitoches, July 30, 1828, *Austin Papers* 2: 83.

14. Map by B. Leonard, 1823; *Natchitoches Courier*, September 13, 1825, and June 12, 1826. A. L. DeBlieux and J. B. Trezzini entered into a partnership in July of 1825 (*Natchitoches Courier*, July 26, 1825).

15. Atherton, "Itinerant Merchandising in the Ante-bellum South," 48.

16. *Natchitoches Courier*, September 13, 1825.

17. *Natchitoches Courier*, December 26, 1825, and December 19, 1826.

18. *Natchitoches Courier*, April 17, 1826; July 3, April 24 and 17, 1826; July 3, 1827.

19. *Natchitoches Courier*, January 2, April 17 and 24, December 19, 1826; July 3, 1827; and September 13, 1825. Sibley to Josiah S. Johnston, May 6, 1832, in Miller, "Dr. John Sibley," 243.

20. *Natchitoches Courier*, January 2, April 24, 1826; July 26 and 19, 1825. On April 1, 1827, Cortes & Huppe dissolved their partnership and asked that "those that are indebted to them to call and settle their accounts, without delay" (*Natchitoches Courier*, May 29, 1827). One of the properties for sale belonged to Bernardo Gutiérrez of filibuster fame. He had been living in the Natchitoches area since his failed attempt at the revolution.

21. *Natchitoches Courier,* February 20, July 10, May 29, 1827.

22. *Natchitoches Courier,* April 24, 1826; July 3, 1827.

23. *Natchitoches Courier,* April 17 and 27, 1826.

24. *Natchitoches Courier,* July 26, 1825.

25. *Natchitoches Courier,* April 17, 1826; July 26, December 26, 1825; February 27, 1827. *Courrier des Natchitoches,* Mai 22, 1826. Sibley to Josiah S. Johnston, December 29, 1828, in Miller, "Dr. John Sibley," 241.

26. *Natchitoches Courier,* April 24, July 3, 1827; July 26, 1825.

27. *Natchitoches Courier,* July 26, 1825; January 2, 1826.

28. *Natchitoches Courier,* July 26, December 26, 1825; April 17, 1826; *Courrier des Natchitoches,* Avril 17, 1826.

29. *Natchitoches Courier,* July 3, 24, 1827; *Courrier des Natchitoches,* Mai 8, 1826.

30. *Natchitoches Courier,* August 23, 1827.

31. Sibley to Johnston, Natchitoches, December 29, 1828, in Miller, "Dr. John Sibley," 241. This Davenport is the son of Stephen Davenport, who died in 1824.

32. The Rio Hondo had been recognized as the international boundary between French and Spain during colonial times.

33. U.S. Census, 1820. This is based on the Spanish surnames in the 1820 census, the number of children under ten who were foreign-born, and marriages recorded by the Catholic priest in the late 1810s and early 1820s. Many of those getting married had been born in San Antonio de Bexar or Nacogdoches (see Mills, *Natchitoches Church Marriages,* entries 1–3, 14–16, 20, 25–26, 30–34, 37, 39). For Jean Baptiste Trezzini, see *Natchitoches Church Marriages,* entry 13.

34. U.S. Census, 1820. Trezzini presence in the Bayou Pierre are based on the people who lived around him, many of them old families known to live in that area. A notice in the *Natchitoches Courier* (July 26, 1825) announced that Trezzini was running a store with A. DeBlieux in Natchitoches. For Wiley, see *Natchitoches Courier,* Tuesday, July 10, 1827.

35. U.S. Census, 1820; *Natchitoches Courier,* July 24, 1827.

36. Flint, *Recollections,* 268.

37. Sibley to Johnston, July 10, 1827, in Miller, "Dr. John Sibley," 223.

38. Sibley to Johnston, November 8, 1828, in Miller, "Dr. John Sibley," 236.

39. Sibley to Ann Eliza Sibley Johnston, November 12, 1827, in Miller, "Dr. John Sibley," 254–55.

40. Hardin, "Fort Jesup—Fort Selden—Camp Sabine—Camp Salubrity," 14–26.

41. Gray, *The Old Soldier's Story,* 41–42.

42. Smith, ed., *Military Heritage,* 111–12, 115; Middleton, "Outpost," 61, 79.

43. Flint, *Recollections,* 268.

44. Smith, ed., *Military Heritage,* 115; Middleton, "Outpost," 62–64; Hardin, "Fort Jesup—Fort Selden—Camp Sabine—Camp Salubrity," 17.

45. Hardin, *Northwestern Louisiana* 1: 316–17; Gray, *The Old Soldier's Story,* 50; Hardin, "Fort Jesup—Fort Selden—Camp Sabine—Camp Salubrity," 55–56. See Gray, *The Old Soldier's Story,* 52–54, for a discussion of the confrontation at Fort Towson.

46. Sibley to Ann Eliza Johnston, October 23, 1831, in Miller "Dr. John Sibley," 258–59.

47. Hardin, *Northwestern Louisiana* 1: 166.

48. Hardin, "Fort Jesup—Fort Selden—Camp Sabine—Camp Salubrity," 32; Marshall, *History of the Western Boundary of the Louisiana Purchase,* 142–49.

49. *Niles' Register* 50 (August 6, 1836): 385–86.

50. Marshall, *History of the Western Boundary of the Louisiana Purchase,* 168–69; Hardin, "Fort Jesup—Fort Selden—Camp Sabine—Camp Salubrity," 53, 58.

51. Guardia and Willard, "A Guide to Historic Natchitoches," Historic Natchitoches Scrapbook, no. 44; Hardin, "Fort Jesup—Fort Selden—Camp Sabine—Camp Salubrity," 17. Guardia and Willard based their guide on old diaries, courthouse and church records, and conversations with old residents.

52. K. Jack Bauer, "Mexican War," Texas State Historical Association, www.tshaonline.org/handbook/entries/mexican-war.

53. Hardin, *Northwestern Louisiana* 1: 197; Henry, *Campaign Sketches of the War with Mexico,* 8–10; Smith, ed., *Military Heritage,* 141, 145.

54. Grant, *Personal Memoirs,* 38–40.

55. Guardia and Willard, "A Guide to Historic Natchitoches," no. 12.

56. Henry, *Campaign Sketches of the War with Mexico,* 10; Hardin, *Northwestern Louisiana* 1: 211–12; Mills, *Biographical and Historical Memoirs of Natchitoches Parish,* 15.

57. U.S. Census, 1820. The town of Natchitoches, although part of the Natchitoches Proper District, was enumerated separately.

58. For land grant to the Natchitoches Indians in October 3, 1790, see *ASP, PL* 3: 74, no. 6. Descendants of the Natchitoches Indians have received state recognition as a tribe (ntl-tribe.org).

59. U.S. Census, 1820. Also see appendix tables 2 and 3.

60. U.S. Census, 1820.

61. Sherrod, *Plain Folk, Planters, and the Complexities of Southern Society,* 32–33, 119, 121; Cook, "Ante-bellum Bienville Parish," 68–69. This area became part of Claiborne Parish when it was created from its parent parish, Natchitoches, in 1828.

62. U.S. Census, 1820.

63. U.S. Census, 1820. Plantation owners, those with 20 slaves or more but fewer than 50, included T. F. Hertzog (21 slaves), Augustine Metoyer (25), Louis Metoyer (22), Louis Derbanne (20), Gasparte Lacour (20), Wm Owens (20), Sylvetters Rachall (20), and —— Metoyer (38).

64. U.S. Census, 1820.

65. Deed of Donation of Alexis Cloutier qtd. in Portré-Bobinski and Smith, *Natchitoches,* 205–6.

66. Portré-Bobinski and Smith, *Natchitoches,* 205–6; Mills, *The Forgotten People,* 232.

67. Mills, *Forgotten People,* 232–36; Portré-Bobinski and Smith, *Natchitoches,* 206. As the population of the area grew, Claiborne Parish was created out of Natchitoches in 1828, Caddo Parish in 1838, Sabine in 1843, DeSoto Parish from parts of Natchitoches and Caddo in 1843, Winn Parish from portions of Natchitoches, Rapides, Catahoula parishes in 1852, and Red River Parish from portions of Bienville, Bossier, Caddo, DeSoto and Natchitoches in 1871 (Hardin, *Northwestern Louisiana* 2: 1, 95, 160, 151, 172, 204).

68. Flint, *Recollections,* 264.

69. Pearson and Wells, *Steamboats on Red River,* 12; Olmsted, *A Journey through Texas,* 60–65.

70. *Natchitoches Courier,* July 10, 1827, and November 8, 1851; *New Orleans Daily Crescent,* June 13, 1860; Pearson and Wells, *Steamboats on Red River,* 13. In the 1850s, E. H. Flint acted as forwarding and commission agent at the rapids with warehouses both above and below the falls. By 1860, there was a horse railroad two miles long which ran from above the upper rapids to below the lower rapids.

71. Pearson and Wells, *Steamboats on Red River,* 44–45. The earliest documented dugout canoe used on the Red River is a thirty-one-foot-long, twenty-two-inch-wide vessel made from a single cypress log and dated to about A.D. 1000 (Pearson and Wells, *Steamboats on Red River,* 43; Van Osdell, "A Bygone Era Resurrected through Wood," 18–21).

72. Pearson and Wells, *Steamboats on Red River,* 44–45.

73. Pearson and Wells, *Steamboats on Red River,* 45–46, 48, 49n4; Baldwin, *The Keelboat Age,* 62, 64–65.

74. Pearson and Wells, *Steamboats on Red River,* 48–50; U.S. Census, 1820. Antoine Cornu is listed as "Free Color Person" in the 1820 census.

75. Wright, "Early Navigation and Commerce," 77–78.

76. Hunter, *Steamboats on the Western Rivers,* 5, 9–12; Pearson and Wells, *Steamboats on Red River,* 52.

77. Hunter, *Steamboats on Western Rivers,* 13–14; McCall, *Conquering the Rivers,* 116–27.

78. Norman, "The Red River of the South," 401. Norman claims the *Enterprise* made two trips up the Red River. In December 1814, Shreve had ascended the Red River as far as the rapids. In 1815, on his second trip, he reached Natchitoches. Norman says the *Beaver* was the second boat to reach Natchitoches in 1820. Hyams ("History of Navigation on Red River," 65) claims the *Beaver* was the first boat to reach Natchitoches. See also Hardin, *Northwestern Louisiana* 1: 323; Henry C. Dethloff, "Paddlewheels and Pioneers on Red River," 91; Hyams, "History of Navigation on Red River," 65; Foreman, "River Navigation in the Early Southwest," 47; Pearson and Wells, *Steamboats on Red River,* 66, 68; Sibley to Johnston, June 26, 1821, and February 26, 1822, in Miller, "Dr. John Sibley," 178, 190; *Natchitoches Courier,* April 21, 1827; December 19, April 24, 1826.

79. Pearson and Wells, *Steamboats on Red River,* 53; Hunter, *Steamboats on Western Rivers,* 15, 170. Stern-wheelers did not become popular until after the Civil War (Hunter, *Steamboats on the Western Rivers,* 172). See also Bates, *The Western Rivers Steamboat Cyclopoedium.*

80. Pearson and Wells, *Steamboats on Red River,* 57; Dethloff, "Paddlewheels and Pioneers on Red River," 101; *True American,* April 10, 1837, morning ed.; Hong, "Evolution of the Red River Settlement Pattern," 431.

81. DeBlieux Collection, folders 24, 27, CGHRC; Lott, "Natchitoches and the Red River Steamboat Trade," 93–94.

82. Somdal, "A Century of Steamboating on Red River," 845–63; Norman, "The Red River of the South," 325.

83. Hunter, *Steamboats on Western Rivers,* 239–44, 259–62, 342–43, 382–84, 442–43, 446–48.

84. Lloyd, *Lloyd's Steamboat Directory,* 83–87. Josiah S. Johnson was John Sibley's son-in-law, with whom he often corresponded. Johnson's son, Sibley's grandson, was hurt but survived.

85. "Indian Gaming" by an Old Army Officer, *Frank Leslie's Popular Monthly* 18 (July–December 1884), 248–50.

86. Purser and Williams, "Indian Ball Game," 344.

87. *Natchitoches Courier,* December 26, 1825, and December 5, 1826; Flint, *Recollections,* 265; Toumey, "Diary," 291, 301.

88. Sibley to Ann Eliza Sibley Johnston, January 6, 1831, in Miller, "Dr. John Sibley," 256; Toumey, "Diary," 300, 287.

89. "Showboat," in Bordman and Hischak, *Oxford Companion to American Theatre,* 568–69; Graham, *Showboats,* 21.

90. *Natchitoches Courier,* August 28, September 12, 1826; *True American* (New Orleans), January 12, 1839, morning ed.; July 31, 1838, morning ed., chroniclingamerica.loc.gov (accessed July 25, 2017); *Baton Rouge Gazette,* May 20, 1843 (accessed July 25, 2017); Huey, "An Abbreviated History of the Circus"; Toumey, "Diary," 296. The forty-two-foot ring was found to be the best size for riders to keep their balance while riding standing on the back of galloping horses (Jando, "Short History of the Circus").

91. Sibley to Johnston, December 29, 1828, in Miller, "Dr. John Sibley," 241.

92. Flint, *History and Geography of the Mississippi Valley* 1: 256.

93. Pearson and Wells, *Steamboats on Red River,* 19–21.

94. Tyson, *Red River,* 90; Foreman, "River Navigation," 50. A year later, the military returned and reestablished the post.

95. Foreman, "River Navigation," 47–58; Humphreys, "The 'Great Raft' of the Red River," 82. See Tyson, *Red River,* 90–102, for a discussion of the various congressional appropriations for this effort. The military built a permanent fort, Fort Towson, about six miles from the former location of Cantonment Towson. In May of 1831, Colonel Benjamin R. Milam left Natchitoches aboard the steamboat *Enterprise* (formerly known as the *Alps*), with two keelboats in tow. The steamboat and one of the keelboats were loaded with provisions for the U.S. garrison near Kiamichi Creek. Making its way through or around the raft, the *Enterprise* became the first steamboat to reach Fort Towson (Foreman, "River Navigation," 50); Wright, "Early Navigation and Commerce," 77–78.

96. Foreman, "River Navigation," 51, 53; Pearson and Wells, *Steamboats on Red River,* 19; Hyams, "History of Navigation on Red River," 27. For a full discussion of the life and accomplishments of Henry Shreve, see McCall, *Conquering the Rivers.*

97. Sibley to Josiah S. Johnston, September 24, 1827, quoting Colonel Milam in Miller, "Dr. John Sibley," 227. The Shawnee had left their lands in the Ohio and Cumberland valleys, the Delaware their ancestral homes in the Delaware River area, the Kickapoo the central Great Lakes region, and the Cherokee from what is today Western North Carolina and East Tennessee. The Cherokee chief claimed that the Mexican government had promised the tribe lands in Texas but was now denying it.

98. Claiborne to Jackson, New Orleans, October 28, 1814, Rowland, ed., *CLB* 6: 293–94.

99. Berlandier, *The Indians of Texas in 1830,* 107.

100. Carter, *Caddo Indians,* 253, 258–60; Lange, "The Caddo Treaty of July 1, 1835," 248–49; Sibley to Josiah S. Johnston, November 15, 1828, in Miller, "Dr. John Sibley," 238.

101. Sibley to Johnston, November 19, 1828, in Miller, "Dr. John Sibley," 239.

102. Sibley to Johnston, December 19, 1828, in Miller, "Dr. John Sibley," 242.

103. Carter, *Caddo Indians,* 264–65; Tanner, *The Territory of the Caddo Tribe of Oklahoma,* 98.

104. Carter, *Caddo Indians,* 262.

105. U.S. House Report, 1842, qtd. in Lange, "The Caddo Treaty," 251–52.

106. Carter, *Caddo Indians,* 265; Glover, "A History of the Caddo Indians," 917.

107. Carter, *Caddo Indians,* 267–69; Lange, "The Caddo Treaty," 260–62.

108. Carter, *Caddo Indians,* 271.

109. Glover, "A History of the Caddo Indians," 918.

110. Glover, "A History of the Caddo Indians," 918–19.

111. Glover, "A History of the Caddo Indians," 919.

112. Carter, *Caddo Indians,* 271–72; Lange, "The Caddo Treaty," 272, 302–3; Deposition of Larkin Edwards, December 16, 1840, House Report 1842, 36–37, qtd. in Lange, "Caddo Treaty," 300–302; Glover, "A History of the Caddo Indians," 918. The sad saga of the Caddo did not end with their treaty. See Carter, *Caddo Indians,* for a discussion of what happened to them after selling their lands in Louisiana.

113. Henry M. Shreve to President Jackson, April 29, 1836, in Lange, "Caddo Treaty," 284–85.

114. Henry M. Shreve to President Jackson, April 29, 1836, in Lange, "Caddo Treaty," 284–85.

115. Caddo chiefs to Senate of the United States, House Reports, 1842, 103–5 in Lange, "Caddo Treaty," 287.

116. Lange, "Caddo Treaty," 284–92. For a fuller discussion, see *United States v. Brooks* 52 U.S. 442 (1850), supreme.justia.com/cases/federal/us/51/442/ (accessed December 7, 2017). For more on Brooks's financial difficulties, see "Biographical Note," Jehiel Brooks, Brooks-Queen Family Collection, American Catholic History Research Center and University Archives, Washington, DC, collection no. ACUA 017.

117. U.S. Census, 1830; Sibley to Johnston, April 21, 1828, in Miller, "Dr. John Sibley," 231–32; Hong, "Evolution of the Red River Settlement Pattern," 76.

118. Russell, "Journal."

119. Toumey, "Diary," 288–89; Partain, *Tool Pushed by Providence,* 66.

120. Baptist, *The Half Has Never Been Told,* 270–72; Moore, *Agriculture in Antebellum Mississippi,* 71.

121. Baptist, *The Half Has Never Been Told,* 272–73; Moore, *Agriculture in Antebellum Mississippi,* 71.

Conclusion

1. Baudier, *Catholic Church in Louisiana,* 27.

2. Dollar, "Black, White, or Indifferent," 164.

3. Olmsted, *A Journey in the Seaboard Slave States,* 632.

4. Mills, *Biographical and Historical Memoirs of Northwest Louisiana,* 302.

5. Aaron Walker to H. R. Pease, September 5, 1865, Register of Weekly and Monthly Statistical Reports of Schools (Monthly School Reports, Records of the Superintendent of Education for the State of Louisiana, Bureau of Refugees, Freedmen, and Abandoned Lands, Record Group 105, roll 3, National Archives, Washington, DC, cited in Dollar, "Black, White, or Indifferent," 158). The emphasis is Walker's.

BIBLIOGRAPHY

Archives and Manuscript Collections

American Catholic History Research Center and University Archives.

Jehiel Brooks, Brooks-Queen Family Collections.

Bexar Archives Translations. University Publications of America, Bethesda, MD, microfilm reels 19, 20, 22. Typewritten copy, Cammie G. Henry Research Center, Northwestern State University, Natchitoches.

Cammie G. Henry Research Center, Northwestern State University, Natchitoches.

"Letter Book of the Natchitoches–Sulphur Fork Factory." Microfilm.

DeBlieux Collection.

Dellmon Collection.

Guardia, J. E., and Irma Sompayrac Willard. "A Guide to Historic Natchitoches." Historic Natchitoches Parish Scrapbook.

Historic New Orleans Collection.

Russell, Edward. "Journal." MSS 424, f. 2.

Louisiana State Land Office. wwwslodms.doa.la.gov.

Old Plat Maps.

Claim Papers.

U.S. Tract Book vol. 58.

Louisiana State University Archives.

Claiborne (William C. C.) Letters and Depositions (1799–1846), MSS 5018, Louisiana and Lower Mississippi Valley Collections.

Natchitoches Parish Courthouse, Clerk of Court.

Bound Conveyances.

Disposition of R. Vaughan, April 17, 1827. Sixth District Court, bundle 39, no. 649.

Government Records

American State Papers. memory.loc.gov.

American State Papers: Commerce and Navigation.
American State Papers: Foreign Relations.
American State Papers: Indian Affairs.
American State Papers: Military Affairs.
American State Papers: Miscellaneous.
American State Papers: Public Lands.

Government Publications

"Madison and the Problem of Mexican Independence: The Gutiérrez-Magee Raid of 1812, 1 September 1812 (Editorial Note)." *Founders Online.* founders.archives.gov/documents/Madison/03-05-02-0179 (accessed January 19, 2017). Original source: *The Papers of James Madison,* Presidential Series, vol. 5, July 10, 1812–February 7, 1813, ed. J. C. A. Stagg et al. Charlottesville: University of Virginia Press, 2004, 235–45.

Pearson, Charles E., and Tom Wells. *Steamboats on Red River: A History of Waterborne Commerce. . . .* Report submitted to U.S. Army Corps of Engineers, Vicksburg District, 1999.

Treaties

United States. Louisiana Purchase: Treaty between the United States of America and the French Republic. April 30, 1803. archives.gov/milestone-documents/louisiana-purchase-treaty (accessed November 18, 2023).

U.S. Bureau of Census

Microfilm. Washington, D.C.: National Archives and Records Administration; Cammie G. Henry Research Center, Northwestern State University of Louisiana.
The Third Census of the United States, 1810.
The Fourth Census of the United States, 1820.
The Fifth Census of the United States, 1830.

Maps

Broutin, J. F. *Carte Particuliere Des Natchitoches.* Map 3006, Map Collection, Cammie G. Henry Research Center, Northwestern State University of Louisiana.

Darby, William, *Map of Louisiana.* 1816. Map 2207, Map Collection, Cammie G. Henry Research Center, Northwestern State University of Louisiana.

Lafon, Barthelmy. *Carte Générale du Territoire D'Orleans comprenant aussi la Florida Occidentale et une Portion du Territoire Du Mississippi.* 1806. louisdl.louisianalibraries.org/cdm/searchtern/Lafon%20map%20o%20Louisiana (accessed August 31, 2014).

Leonard, B. Parish and Town Surveys, April 21, 1823. Map 931, Map Collection, Cammie G. Henry Research Center, Northwestern State University of Louisiana.

Old Plat Maps. www.slodms.doa.la.gov.

Newspapers and Magazines

Baton Rouge Gazette.

Frank Leslie's Popular Monthly.

El Mexicano.

Natchitoches Courier/Courrier des Natchitoches.

New Orleans Daily Crescent.

Niles' Register.

True American.

Books

Abernethy, Thomas Perkins. *The Burr Conspiracy.* New York: Oxford University Press, 1954.

Alliot, Paul. "Historical and Political Reflections on Louisiana." In *Louisiana Under the Rule of Spain, France, and the United States, 1785–1807: Social, Economic, and Political Conditions . . .*, vol. 1, trans. and ed. James Alexander Robertson, 125–27. Cleveland: Arthur H. Clark Company, 1911.

Atherton, Lewis E. *The Southern Country Store, 1800–1860.* Baton Rouge: Louisiana State University Press, 1949.

Austin Papers, vol. 2: *Annual Report of the American Historical Association for the Year 1922.* Washington, DC: Government Printing Office, 1928.

Baade, Hans W. "The Legal Heritage of the Louisiana Purchase." In *The Louisiana Purchase and Its Peoples: Perspectives from the New Orleans Conference,* ed. Paul E. Hoffman, 171–80. Lafayette: University of Louisiana at Lafayette, 2004.

Baldwin, Leland D. *The Keelboat Age on Western Waters.* Pittsburgh: University of Pittsburgh Press, 1941.

Baptist, Edward E. *The Half Has Never Been Told: Slavery and the Making of American Capitalism.* New York: Basic Books, 2014.

Bassett, John Spencer, ed. *Correspondence of Andrew Jackson.* Washington, DC: Carnegie Institution, 1927.

Bates, Alan L. *The Western Rivers Steamboat Cyclopoedium or, American Riverboat; Structure & Detail, Salted with Lore; with a Nod to the Modelmaker.* Leonia, NJ: Hustle Press, 1968.

Baudier, Roger. *The Catholic Church in Louisiana.* New Orleans, 1939.

———. *The Catholic Church in North Louisiana: A Historical Sketch of Pioneer Days and of the Diocese of Natchitoches. . . .* Compiled for the Diocese of Alexandria, 1953.

Beauchamp, M. K. *Instruments of Empire: Colonial Elites and U.S. Governance in Early National Louisiana, 1803–1815.* Baton Rouge: Louisiana State University Press, 2021.

Berlandier, Jean Louis. *The Indians of Texas in 1830.* Ed. John C. Ewers and trans. Patricia Reading Leclercq. Washington DC: Smithsonian Institution Press, 1969.

Bolton, Herbert Eugene. *Texas in the Middle Eighteenth Century: Studies in Spanish Colonial History and Administration.* Austin: University of Texas Press, 1970.

Bordman, Gerald Martin, and Thomas S. Hischak. *The Oxford Companion to American Theatre.* 3rd ed. New York: Oxford University Press, 2004.

Brasseaux, Carl A. "The Administration of Slave Regulations in French Louisiana." In *The Louisiana Purchase Bicentennial Series in Louisiana History,* vol. 1: *The French Experience in Louisiana,* ed. Glen R. Conrad, 209–25. Lafayette: University of Southwestern Louisiana, 1995.

Brooks, Philip Coolidge. *Diplomacy and the Borderlands: The Adams-Onís Treaty of 1819.* Berkeley: University of California Press, 1939.

Burton, H. Sophie, and F. Todd Smith. *Colonial Natchitoches: A Creole Community on the Louisiana-Texas Frontier.* College Station: Texas A&M University Press, 2008.

Byrd, Kathleen M. *Colonial Natchitoches: Outpost of Empires.* Bloomington, IN: Xlibris Corp., 2008.

Cantrell, Gregg. *Stephen F. Austin, Empresario of Texas.* New Haven, CT: Yale University Press, 1999.

Carter, Cecile Elkins. *Caddo Indians: Where We Come From.* Norman: University of Oklahoma Press, 1995.

Carter, Clarence Edwin, comp. and ed. *The Territorial Papers of the United States,* vol. 9: *The Territory of Orleans 1803–1812.* Washington, DC: Government Printing Office, 1940.

———. *The Territorial Papers of the United States,* vol. 15: *The Territory of Louisiana—Missouri: 1815–1821.* Washington DC: Government Printing Office, 1951.

———, *The Territorial Papers of the United States,* vol. 19: *The Territory of Arkansas: 1819–1825.* Washington, DC: Government Printing Office, 1953.

Cerami, Charles A. *Jefferson's Great Gamble: The Remarkable Story of Jefferson, Napoleon and the Men Behind the Louisiana Purchase.* Naperville, IL: Sourcebooks, 2003.

Chipman, Donald E., and Harriett Denise Joseph. *Notable Men and Women of Spanish Texas.* Austin: University of Texas Press, 1999.

———. *Spanish Texas 1519–1821.* Austin: University of Texas Press, 2010.

Coutts, Brian E. "Boom and Bust: The Rise and Fall of the Tobacco Industry in Spanish Louisiana, 1770–1790." In *The Louisiana Purchase Bicentennial Series in Louisiana History,* vol. 2: *The Spanish Presence in Louisiana 1763–1803,* ed. Gilbert C. Din, 229–65. Lafayette: University of Southwestern Louisiana, 1996.

Coxe, Tench. *A Statement of the Arts and Manufactures of the United States of America, for the Year 1810.* Philadelphia: A. Cornman, 1814. books.google.com (accessed November 13, 2023).

Darby, William. *The Emigrant's Guide to the Western and Southwestern States and Territories. . . .* New York: Kirk & Mercein, 1818.

———. *A Geographical Description of the State of Louisiana, The Southern Part of the State of Mississippi, and Territory of Alabama. . . .* New York: James Olmstead, 1817.

Dargo, George. *Jefferson's Louisiana: Politics and the Clash of Legal Traditions.* Cambridge, MA: Harvard University Press, 1975.

Davidson, Basil. *West Africa Before the Colonial Era: A History to 1850.* New York: Addison Wesley Longman, 1998.

Davis, Edwin Adams. *Louisiana: A Narrative History.* 3rd ed. Baton Rouge: Claitor's Publishing Division, 1976.

De Laussat, Pierre Clément. *Memoirs of My Life to My Son During the Years 1803 and After, Which I Spent in Public Service in Louisiana. . . .* Trans. Sister Agnes-Josephine Pastwa and ed. Robert D. Bush. Baton Rouge: Louisiana State University Press, 1978.

Din, Gilbert C., ed. *The Louisiana Purchase Bicentennial Series in Louisiana History,* vol. 2: *The Spanish Presence in Louisiana, 1763–1803.* Lafayette: University of Southwestern Louisiana, 1996.

Ellis, Joseph. "Jefferson and the Purpose." In *The Louisiana Purchase and Its People: Perspectives from the New Orleans Conference,* ed. Paul E. Hoffman. Lafayette: University of Louisiana at Lafayette, 2004.

Flint, Timothy. *The History and Geography of the Mississippi Valley. . . .* 3rd. ed. Boston: Carter, Hendee, and Co., 1833.

———. *Recollections of the Last Ten Years in the Valley of the Mississippi.* Carbondale: Southern Illinois University Press, 1968.

Flores, Dan L. *Jefferson & Southwestern Exploration: The Freeman & Custis Accounts of the Red River Expedition of 1806.* Norman: University of Oklahoma Press, 1984.

———. *Journal of an Indian Trader: Anthony Glass and the Texas Trading Frontier, 1790–1810.* College Station: Texas A&M University Press, 1985.

Garrett, Julia Kathryn. *Green Flag Over Texas.* New York: Cordova Press, Inc., 1939.

Gates, Paul W. *The Economic History of the United States,* vol. 3: *The Farmer's Age: Agriculture 1815–1860.* New York: Holt, Rinehart, and Winston, 1960.

———. *History of Public Land Law Development.* Washington, DC: Government Printing Office, 1968.

———. *Public Land Policies: Management and Disposal.* New York: Arno Press, 1979.

Gayarré, Charles. *History of Louisiana.* New Orleans: Pelican Publishing Co., 1965.

Gracy, David B., II. *Moses Austin: His Life.* San Antonio: Trinity University Press, 1987.

Graham, Philip. *Showboats: The History of an American Institution.* Austin: University of Texas Press, 1951.

Grant, U. S. *Personal Memoirs of U. S. Grant.* New York: Charles L. Webster Co., 1894.

Gray, Charles Martin. *The Old Soldier's Story: Autobiography of Charles Martin Gray, Co. A, 7th Regiment, U.S.I. . . .* Edgefield, SC: Edgefield Advertiser Print, 1868. Ed. and rpt. by Betsy R. Bloomer, 2005.

Hall, Gwendolyn Midlo. *Africans in Colonial Louisiana: The Development of Afro-Creole Culture in the Eighteenth Century.* Baton Rouge: Louisiana State University Press, 1992.

Hardin, J. Fair. *Northwestern Louisiana: A History of the Watershed of the Red River, 1714–1937.* Vols. 1 and 2. Shreveport: Historical Record Association, [1939].

Hatfield, Joseph. *William Claiborne: Jeffersonian Centurion in the American Southwest.* Lafayette: University of Southwestern Louisiana, 1976.

Hay, Thomas Robson, and M. R. Werner. *Admirable Trumpeter: A Biography of General James Wilkinson.* Garden City, NY: Doubleday, Doran and Co., 1941.

Henry, W. S. *Campaign Sketches of the War with Mexico.* New York: Harper and Brothers, 1847.

Horr, David Agee, ed. *Caddoan Indians II.* New York: Garland Publishing, 1974.

Humphreys, Hubert Davis. "The 'Great Raft' of the Red River." In *North Louisiana,* vol. 1: *To 1865: Essays on the Region and Its History,* ed. B. H. Gilley, 73–91. Ruston, LA: McGinty Trust Fund, 1984.

Hunter, Louis C. *Steamboats on the Western Rivers: An Economic and Technological History.* New York: Dover Publications, 1993.

Jacobs, James Ripley. *Tarnished Warrior, Major-General James Wilkinson.* New York: Macmillan Co., 1938.

Kapoun, Robert W., with Charles J. Lohrman. *Language of the Robe: American Indian Trade Blankets.* Salt Lake City: Gibbs Smith, 1992.

Kavangh, Thomas W. "Comanche." In *Handbook of North American Indians,* ed. William C. Sturtevant, vol. 13, pt. 2: *Plains,* ed. Raymond J. DeMallie, 886–906. Washington, DC: Smithsonian Institution, Government Printing Office, 2001.

Kinnaird, Lawrence, ed. *Spain in the Mississippi Valley, 1765–1794.* 4 vols. Washington, DC: American Historical Association, 1946.

Klier, Betje Black. *Pavie in the Borderlands: The Journey of Théodore Pavie to Louisiana and Texas, 1829–1830. . . .* Baton Rouge: Louisiana State University Press, 2000.

Kniffen, Fred B., Hiram F. Gregory, and George A. Stokes. *The Historic Indian Tribes of Louisiana: From 1542 to the Present.* Baton Rouge: Louisiana State University Press, 1987.

Labbe, Dolores Egger. *The Louisiana Purchase Bicentennial Series in Louisiana History,* vol. 3: *The Louisiana Purchase and its Aftermath 1800—1830.* Lafayette: Center for Louisiana Studies, University of Southwestern Louisiana, 1998.

Lange, Charles H. "The Caddo Treaty of July 1, 1835," In *Caddoan Indians II,* ed. Horr, 159–320.

Lankford, George E. "Chacato, Pensacola, Tohomé, Naniaba, and Mobila." In *Handbook of North American Indians,* ed. William C. Sturtevant, vol. 14: *Southeast,* ed. Raymond D. Fogelson, 664–68. Washington, DC: Smithsonian Institution, Government Printing Office, 2004:

Lepler, Jessica M. *The Many Panics of 1837: People, Politics, and the Creation of a Transatlantic Financial Crisis.* New York: Cambridge University Press, 2013.

Le Vere, David. *Caddo Chiefdoms: Caddo Economics and Politics, 700–1835.* Lincoln: University of Nebraska Press, 1998.

Linklater, Andro. *An Artist in Treason: The Extraordinary Double Life of General James Wilkinson.* New York: Walker Publishing Co., 2009.

Lipscomb, Andrew A., and Albert Ellery Bergh, eds. *The Writings of Thomas Jefferson.* 20 vols. Washington, DC: Thomas Jefferson Memorial Association, 1903.

Lloyd, James T. *Lloyd's Steamboat Directory, and Disasters on the Western Waters.* Cincinnati: James T Lloyd and Co., 1856.

Malone, Ann Patton. *Sweet Chariot: Slave Family and Household Structure in Nineteenth-Century Louisiana.* Chapel Hill: University of North Carolina Press, 1992.

Marshall, Thomas Maitland. *A History of the Western Boundary of the Louisiana Purchase, 1819–1841.* Berkeley: University of California Press, 1914.

Martin, François-Xavier. *The History of Louisiana, from the Earliest Period.* New Orleans: James A. Gresham, 1882.

McCall, Edith. *Conquering the Rivers: Henry Miller Shreve and the Navigation of America's Inland Waterways.* Baton Rouge: Louisiana State University Press, 1984.

McEwan, Bonnie G. "Apalachee and Neighboring Groups." In *Handbook of North American Indians,* ed. William C. Sturtevant, vol. 14: *Southeast,* ed. Raymond D. Fogelson, 669–76. Washington, DC: Smithsonian Institution, Government Printing Office, 2004.

Mills, Donna Rachal, ed. *Biographical and Historical Memoirs of Northwest Louisiana.* Tuscaloosa: Mills Historical Press, 1985.

Mills Elizabeth S. *Natchitoches Colonials: Censuses, Military Rolls, and Tax Lists, 1722–1803*. Chicago: Adams Press, 1981.

Mills, Elizabeth Shown. *Natchitoches Church Marriages, 1818–1850*. Bowie, MD: Heritage Books, 2004.

Mills, Gary B. *The Forgotten People: Cane River's Creoles of Color*. Rev. ed by Elizabeth Shown Mills. Baton Rouge: Louisiana State University Press, 2013.

Moore, John Hebron. *Agriculture in Antebellum Mississippi*. New York: Bookman Associates, 1958.

Neuman, Robert W. "Historical Locations of Certain Caddoan Tribes." In *Caddoan Indians II*, ed. Horr, 9–158.

———.*An Introduction to Louisiana Archaeology*. Baton Rouge: Louisiana State University Press, 1984.

Olmsted, Frederick Law. *A Journey in the Seaboard Slave States with Remarks on Their Economy*. New York: Dix & Edwards, 1856.

———. *A Journey through Texas or, a Saddle-trip on the Southwestern Frontier*. Austin: University of Texas Press, 1978.

Owsley, Frank L., Jr., and Gene A. Smith. *Filibusters and Expansionists: Jeffersonian Manifest Destiny, 1800–1821*. Tuscaloosa: University of Alabama Press, 1997.

Partain, Chad Anthony. *A Tool Pushed by Providence: Bishop Auguste Marie Martin and the Catholic Church in North Louisiana*. Austin, TX: Persidea Publishing, 2010.

Peake, Ora Brooks. *A History of the United States Indian Factory System 1795–1822*. Denver: Sage Books, 1954.

Pertulla, Timothy K. *"The Caddo Nation": Archaeological & Ethnohistoric Perspectives*. Austin: University of Texas Press, 1992.

Peterson, Merrill D. "Louisiana!" In *The Louisiana Purchase Bicentennial Series in Louisiana History*, vol. 3: *The Louisiana Purchase and Its Aftermath 1800–1830*, ed. Dolores Egger Labbe. Lafayette: University of Southwestern Louisiana, 1998.

———. *Thomas Jefferson and the New Nation: A Biography*. New York: Oxford University Press, 1970.

Pichardo, Josè Antonio. *Pichardo's Treatise on the Limits of Louisiana and Texas; An Argumentative Historical Treatise. . . .* Austin: University of Texas Press, 1931–46.

Pike, Zebulon Montgomery. *Exploratory Travels through the Western Territories of North America*. Denver: W. H. Lawrence & Co., 1889.

Portré-Bobinski, Germaine, and Clara Mildred Smith. *Natchitoches: The Up-to-Date Oldest Town in Louisiana*. New Orleans: Dameron-Pierson Co., 1939.

Pratt, Julius W. *Expansionists of 1812*. New York: Macmillan Co., 1925.

Prucha, Francis Paul. *American Indian Policy in the Formative Years: The Indian Trade and Intercourse Acts, 1790–1834*. Cambridge, MA: Harvard University Press, 1962.

———. *The Sword of the Republic: The United States Army on the Frontier, 1783–1846.* London: Macmillan Co., 1969.

Robin, C. C. *Voyage to Louisiana.* Ed. Stuart O. Landry Jr. New Orleans: Pelican Publishing Co., 1966.

Rowland, Dunbar, ed. *Official Letter Books of W. C. C. Claiborne, 1801–1816.* Jackson, MS: State Department of Archives and History, 1917.

Sherrod, Ricky L. *Plain Folk, Planters, and the Complexities of Southern Society: A Case Study. . . .* Nacogdoches, TX: Stephen F. Austin State University, 2014.

Shreve, Royal Ornan. *The Finished Scoundrel: General James Wilkinson, sometime Commander-in-Chief of the Army of the United States. . . .* Indianapolis: Bobbs-Merrill Co., 1933.

Sibley, John. *A Report from Natchitoches in 1807.* Ed. Annie Heloise Abel. New York: Museum of American Indian Foundation, 1922.

Smith, F. Todd. *The Caddo Indians: Tribes at the Convergence of Empires, 1542–1854.* Bryan: Texas A&M University Press, 1995.

———. *From Dominance to Disappearance: The Indians of Texas and the Near Southwest, 1786–1859.* Lincoln: University of Nebraska Press, 2005.

Smith, Ronald D. "Napoleon and Louisiana: Failure of the Proposed Expedition to Occupy and Defend Louisiana, 1801–1803." In *The Louisiana Purchase Bicentennial Series in Louisiana History,* vol. 3: *The Louisiana Purchase and its Aftermath 1800–1830,* ed. Dolores Egger Labbe, 52–66. Lafayette: University of Southwestern Louisiana, 1998.

Smith, W. Ryan, ed. *Military Heritage Archeological Resources Assessment and Survey of the Cane River National Heritage Area.* Natchitoches: Northwestern State University and Cane River National Heritage Area, 2010.

Stoddard, Amos. *Sketches, Historical and Descriptive, of Louisiana.* 1812. Rpt. Baton Rouge: Claitor's Publishing Division, 1974.

Swanton, John R. *The Indians of the Southeastern United States.* Washington, DC: U.S. Printing Office, 1946.

———. *Source Material on the History and Ethnology of the Caddo Indians.* Norman: University of Oklahoma Press, 1996.

Tanner, Helen Hornbeck. *The Territory of the Caddo Tribe of Oklahoma.* New York: Garland Publishing, 1974.

Taylor, Joe Gray. *Negro Slavery in Louisiana.* New York: Negro Universities Press, 1963.

Toumey, William S. "Diary of William S. Toumey." In *Northwestern Louisiana A History of the Watershed of the Red River, 1714–1937.* Vol. 1, ed. J. Fair Hardin, 283–306. Shreveport: Historical Record Association, [1939].

Tregle, Joseph G., Jr. *Louisiana in the Age of Jackson: A Clash of Cultures and Personalities.* Baton Rouge: Louisiana State University Press, 1999.

Tyson, Darl Newton. *The Red River in Southwestern History.* Norman: University of Oklahoma Press, 1981.

Usner, Daniel H., Jr. *American Indians in the Lower Mississippi Valley: Social and Economic Histories.* Lincoln: University of Nebraska Press, 1998.

Walker, Willard B. "The Creek Confederacy." In *Handbook of North American Indians,* ed. William C. Sturtevant, vol. 14: *Southeast,* ed. Raymond D. Fogelson, 373–92. Washington, DC: Smithsonian Institution, Government Printing Office, 2004.

Warren, Harris Gaylord. *The Sword Was Their Passport: A History of American Filibustering in the Mexican Revolution.* Port Washington, NY: Kennikat Press, 1972.

Webb, Clarence H., and Hiram F. Gregory. *The Caddo Indians of Louisiana.* Baton Rouge: Louisiana Department of Culture, Recreation, and Tourism, 1986.

Wesley, Edgar Bruce. *Guarding the Frontier: A Study of Frontier Defense from 1815 to 1825.* Westport, CT: Greenwood Press, 1970.

Wilkinson, James. *Memoirs of My Own Times.* Philadelphia: A. Small, 1816.

Yoakum, H. *History of Texas from Its First Settlement in 1786 to Its Annexation to the United States in 1846.* Vol. 1. New York: Redfield, 1856.

Articles

Atherton, Lewis E. "Itinerant Merchandising in the Ante-bellum South." *Bulletin of the Business Historical Society* 19 (1945): 35–59. jstor.org/stable/3110682?seq=1.

Austin, Stephen F. "Journal of Stephen F. Austin on his First Trip to Texas, 1821." *Quarterly of the Texas State Historical Association* 7, no. 4 (April 1904): 286–307.

Baker, Eugene C. "Austin, Stephen Fuller (1793–1836)." Texas State Historical Association, tshaonline.org/handbook/entries/austin-stephen-fuller (accessed November 18, 2023).

Bridges, Katherine, and J. Mitchell Reames. "The Bayou Pierre Settlement." *Louisiana Studies* 9 (Spring 1977): 127–41.

Coles, Harry L., Jr. "Applicability of the Public Land System to Louisiana." *Mississippi Valley Historical Review* 43 (June 1956): 39–58. www-jstororg.nsula.idm.oclc.org/stable/1895278 (accessed May 19, 2020).

———. "The Confirmation of Foreign Land Titles in Louisiana." *Louisiana Historical Quarterly* 38 (October 1955): 1–22.

Cox, Isaac Joslin. "The Louisiana-Texas Frontier during the Burr Conspiracy." *Mississippi Valley Historical Review* 10, no. 3 (December 1923): 274–84. www-jstororg.nsula.idm.oclc.org/stable/1891602 (accessed May 19, 2020).

———. "The Louisiana-Texas Frontier, Part II, The American Occupation of the Louisiana-Texas Frontier." *Southwestern Historical Quarterly* 17 (July 1913): 1–42.

Dethloff, Henry C. "Paddlewheels and Pioneers on Red River, 1815–1915, and the Reminiscences of Captain M. L. Scovell." *Louisiana Studies* 6, no. 2, (Spring 1967): 91–134.

Ewers, J. C. "The Influence of Epidemics on the Indian Populations and Cultures of Texas." *Plains Anthropologist* 18 (1973): 104–15.

Flores, Dan L. "The Ecology of the Red River in 1806: Peter Custis and Early Southwestern Natural History." *Southwestern Historical Quarterly* 88 (July 1984): 1–42.

———. "The Red River Branch of the Alabama-Coushatta Indians: An Ethnohistory." *Southern Studies* 16 (Spring 1977): 55–72.

Foreman, Grant. "River Navigation in the Early Southwest." *Mississippi Valley Historical Review* 15, no. 1 (1928): 34–55.

Garrett, Julia Kathryn, ed. "Letters and Documents, Doctor John Sibley and the Louisiana-Texas Frontier, 1803–1814." *Southwestern Historical Quarterly* 45–49 (1942–46): multiple pages in different volumes.

Gates, Paul W. "Private Land Claims in the South." *Journal of Southern History* 22 (May 1956): 183–204.

Glover, William B. "A History of the Caddo Indians." *Louisiana Historical Quarterly* 18 (January–October 1935): 872–946.

Gracy, David. "Austin, Moses (1761–1821)." Texas State Historical Association, tshaonline.org/handbook/entries/Austin-moses (accessed November 18, 2023).

"Gutiérrez de Lara, José Bernardo Maximiliano." Texas State Historical Association, tshaonline.org/handbook/entries/gutierrez-de-lara-jose-bernardo-maximiliano (accessed November 18, 2023).

Haggard, J. Villasana. "The House of Barr and Davenport." *Southwestern Historical Quarterly* 49 (July 1945): 65–88.

———. "The Neutral Ground between Louisiana and Texas 1806–1821." *Louisiana Historical Quarterly* 28 (October 1945): 1001–1128.

Hardin, J. Fair. "Fort Jesup—Fort Selden—Camp Sabine—Camp Salubrity: Four Forgotten Frontier Army Posts of Western Louisiana." *Louisiana Historical Quarterly* 16, no. 1 (January 1933): 5–26; no. 2 (April 1933): 277–92; no. 3 (July 1933): 441–53; no. 4 (October 1933): 670–80.

———. "An Outline of Shreveport and Caddo Parish History," *Louisiana Historical Quarterly* 18, no. 4 (October 1935): 845–63.

Huey, Rodney A. "An Abbreviated History of the Circus in America." Fédération Mondiale du Cirque, www.circusfederation.org (accessed July 27, 2017).

Jackson, Jack. "Nolan, Philip." Texas State Historical Association, tshaonline.org/handbook/entries/nolna-philip (accessed November 17, 2023).

Jando, Dominique. "Short History of the Circus." Circopedia, www.circopedia.org (accessed July 27, 2017).

Kinnaird, Lawrence, and Lucia B. Kinnaird. "Choctaws West of the Mississippi, 1766–1800." *Southwestern Historical Quarterly* 83 (April 1980): 349–70.

———. "The Red River Valley in 1796." *Louisiana History* 24, no. 2 (Spring 1983): 184–94.

Magnaghi, Russell M., ed. "The Red River Valley North of Natchitoches, 1817–1818: The Letters of John Fowler." *Louisiana Studies* 15 (Fall 1976): 287–94.

Malone, Dumas, ed. "John Sibley." *Dictionary of American Biography* 17: 147–48. New York: Charles Scribner's Sons, 1935.

Masson, Ann. "Barthélémy Lafon." *64 Parishes.* 64 parishes.org/entry/bathlmy-lafon.

M'Caleb, Walter Flavius. "The First Period of the Gutiérrez-Magee Expedition." *Quarterly of the Texas State Historical Association* 4, no. 3 (1901): 218–29.

McDonald, Archie P. "Edwards, Haden." Texas State Historical Association, tshaonline .org/handbook/entries/Edwards-Haden (accessed November 22, 2023).

Norman, N. Phillip. "The Red River of the South. . . ." *Louisiana Historical Quarterly* 25 (1942): 397–535.

Poret, Ory G. "History of Land Titles in the State of Louisiana." *Publications of the Louisiana Historical Quarterly, New Orleans, LA,* ser. 2, vol. 1 (1974): 25–42.

Purser, Joyce, and T. Harry Williams. "Indian Ball Game." *Louisiana History* 1, no. 4 (1960): 344.

Shepherd, William R., trans. "James Wilkinson to José de Iturrigaray, Natchez, Nov. 17, 1806." *American Historical Review* 9, no. 3 (April 1904): 533–37.

Sibley, John A. "An Account of the Red River." Sibley to Dearborn, April 10, 1805. *American State Papers, Indian Affairs* 1: 725–29. www.memory.loc.gov (accessed September 17, 2013).

———. "Historical Sketches of the several Indian tribes in Louisiana, south of the Arkansas river, and between the Mississippi and river Grande." *American State Papers, Indian Affairs* 1: 721–25. www.memory.loc.gov (accessed September 17, 2013).

Smith, F. Todd. "The Kadohadacho Indians and the Louisiana-Texas Frontier, 1803–1815." *Southwestern Historical Quarterly* 95 (October 1991): 177–204.

Somdal, Dewey A. "A Century of Steamboating on Red River to Shreveport and the Coming of the Railroad." In J. Fair Hardin, "An Outline of Shreveport and Caddo Parish History." *Louisiana Historical Quarterly* 18, no. 4 (October 1935): 845–63.

Van Osdell, Mary Ann. "A Bygone Era Resurrected through Wood." *Forests & People* 34, no. 1 (1984): 18–21.

West, Elizabeth H., ed. "Diary of Jose Bernardo Gutiérrez de Lara, 1811–1812, Part II." *American Historical Review* 34 (January 1929): 281–94.

Whittington, G. P. "Dr. John Sibley of Natchitoches, 1757–1837." *Louisiana Historical Quarterly* 10, no. 4 (October 1927): 467–513.

Wright, Mureil H., "Early Navigation and Commerce along the Arkansas and Red Rivers in Oklahoma." *Chronicles of Oklahoma* 8, no. 1 (March 1930): 65–88.

Theses and Dissertations

Brandt, P. S. "An Unpublished Letter of Doctor John Sibley of August 6, 1807, Annotated and Introduced with a Biographical Sketch." Paper in lieu of thesis, Northwestern State University of Louisiana, 1986.

Cook, Philip Charles. "Ante-bellum Bienville Parish." Master's thesis, Louisiana Polytechnic Institute, 1965.

Dollar, Susan E. "Black, White, or Indifferent: Race, Identity, and Americanization in Creole Louisiana." PhD diss., University of Arkansas, 2004.

Flores, Dan L. "The John Maley Journal: Travels and Adventures in the American Southwest, 1810–1813." Master's thesis, Northwestern State University of Louisiana, 1972.

Hall, John Whitling. "Louisiana Survey Systems: Their Antecedents, Distributions, and Characteristics." PhD diss., Louisiana State University, 1970.

Hong, Keumsoo. "The Evolution of the Red River Settlement Pattern, 1714–1860." PhD diss., Louisiana State University, 1999.

Hyams, Valery Gaiennie. "History of Navigation on Red River from 1815–1865." Master's thesis, Louisiana State University, 1939.

LeBreton, Marietta Marie. "A History of the Factory System Serving the Louisiana Indians, 1805–1825." Master's thesis, Louisiana State University, 1961.

———. "A History of the Territory of Orleans 1803–1812." PhD diss., Louisiana State University, 1969.

LaVere, David L. "Barr, Davenport, Murphy and Smith: Traders on the Louisiana-Texas Frontier." Master's thesis, Northwestern State University of Louisiana, 1989.

Lott, Wendy M., "Natchitoches and the Red River Steamboat Trade." Master's thesis, Northwestern State University of Louisiana, March 2000.

Lytle, Richard M. "The Public Life of Edward Dumaresque Turner: First American Commandant of Natchitoches." Master's thesis, Northwestern State University of Louisiana, 1998.

Mayer, John L. "Drake's Salt Dome: A Historical and Cultural Resources Management Study." Master's thesis, Northwestern State University of Louisiana, 2000.

Middleton, Harry F. "Outpost: A History of Fort Jesup, Louisiana, 1822–1846." Master's thesis, Louisiana State University, 1973.

Miller, Janet Karen Barefoot. "Dr. John Sibley (1757–1837): His Life and Letters." Master's thesis, Louisiana State University in Shreveport, 1999.

Miller, Marshall Stone, Jr. "The History of Fort Claiborne, Louisiana 1804–1822." Master's thesis, Louisiana State University, 1969.

Purser, Mary Joyce. "The Administration of Indian Affairs in Louisiana, 1803–1820." Master's thesis, Louisiana State University, 1961.

Seale, Richard. "From French Village to American Town: The Development of Natchitoches, Louisiana, 1788–1818." Master's thesis, Northwestern State University of Louisiana, 1991.

INDEX